VENICE &

NORTH EAST

ITALY

PASSPORT'S REGIONAL GUIDES OF ITALY

Florence & Tuscany
Naples & Campania
Umbria, the Marches & San Marino

Also available:
Passport's Regional Guides of France
Passport's Regional Guides of Portugal

VENICE &
NORTH EAST
ITALY

Paul Blanchard

PASSPORT BOOKS
a division of *NTC Publishing Group*

Published in 1997 by Passport Books, a
division of NTC Publishing Group, 4255
West Touhy Avenue, Lincolnwood
(Chicago), Illinois 60646–1975 U.S.A.

Originally published by A&C Black
(Publishers) Ltd, 35 Bedford Row, London
England

ISBN 0–8442–9960—X

Library of Congress Catalog, Card Number:
96–70352

Typeset in 9 on 11pt Optima.

To Isabella and Melissa

Acknowledgments

The author's deepest gratitude is owed to Jane Zaloga, who wrote the article on the
history and art of Northeastern Italy and helped compile the boxed texts; to the Italian
State Tourist Board, London; the Ufficio Parchi della Provincia Autonoma di Bolzano;
the Direzione del Parco di Paneveggio-Pale di San Martino; and to the Aziende per la
Promozione Turistica of Trieste, Udine, Venice, Treviso, Belluno, Padua, Vicenza,
Verona, Trento, Bolzano and Brescia, for their invaluable assistance; and to Norbert
Cristofolini and friends for their expert advice and guidance in the Dolomites.

CONTENTS

1. INTRODUCTION

Everybody in Italy is talking about the Miracle of the Northeast. This is the wealthiest region of the country and its fastest growing industrial district. But it is also the area where economic development has most successfully adapted itself to ideas of ecological and historical preservation. Thanks to a prevalence of small, flexible and clean industries, affluence has made a 'soft landing' in the area – whose stunning natural and artistic assets remain, relatively unspoilt, for all to see. As a result, the Northeast has become one of Europe's most successful 'post-industrial' experiments – a fascinating place to visit, but also a wonderful place to live.

For the foreigner, the star attraction is, of course, Venice, the city of water, which has charmed and offended visitors for centuries. 'An abhorrent, green, slippery city,' D.H. Lawrence called it; a 'gorgeous and wonderful reality ... beyond the fancy of the wildest dreamer,' in the words of Charles Dickens. But Venice is only a part of what this magnificent region has to offer. From the eastern provinces of Udine and Trieste – where James Joyce lived in self-imposed exile – to the western city of Verona, beyond whose walls the world ended (to paraphrase Shakespeare), northwards to the glorious rose-coloured peaks of the Dolomites – so dear to the composer Mahler – Northeastern Italy is a spectacle beyond words.

This guide offers a selection of only the best places: some 30 cities, towns, and alpine nature reserves, which together provide a fitting introduction to this rich and varied region. The first of these, and the one that is most thoroughly explored, is Venice, which is also taken as a starting point for excursions to the east, south, north and west. Cities are arranged in geographic 'constellations', leaving you the freedom to choose the route best suited to your personal tastes. Each constellation forms a chapter, at the end of which you'll find suggestions on how to get there and back, where to stay, where to eat, and what to do and when. A lot of care has gone into the preparation of these sections, in the conviction that pleasant accommodation, wholesome food and good wine can go a long way to determining the success or failure of a holiday.

You might find yourself leafing through these pages rather more than you expect: for although the general organisation of the guide is loose and open, the specific places are dealt with much more 'intensely', offering historic walking tours that take you round the major sights step by step (in the nature reserves of the Eastern Alps, overland hikes are proposed). In most cases these

1

walks are designed to last about two hours: after which, if you're human, you'll be more than ready for some form of refreshment – or in the case of larger towns like Padua or Verona (where you'll be ambling about for three to four hours), even for a cat-nap.

A word of warning: Italy possesses some two-thirds of the world's artistic heritage, and it's an old heritage, in constant need of conservation and restoration. If during your visit some of the works of art and architecture described in the guide are covered (in the case of buildings or public sculpture) or away for cleaning (paintings), don't let it spoil your day: just move on. Somehow the most memorable moments of a foreign journey are those one least expects.

2. HISTORY AND ART

by Jane Zaloga

From the awe-inspiring peaks of the Eastern Alps to the sun-drenched shores of the Adriatic Sea, Northeastern Italy amazes with its spectacular natural diversity. Reflecting such variation in the landscape, this very eclectic region presents an enchanting mélange of diverse artistic and architectural traditions as well. From the picturesque charm of Germanic Gothic villages, such as Bressanone, whose quaint, steeply-roofed cottages nestle snugly among the rugged mountains in the region known as Sud Tirol, to the vaguely exotic, Byzantine air of Venice, whose palaces and churches, sparkling like jewels in all of their mosaic and marble glory, reign over a myriad of shimmering canals that meander through the city on their way to the Adriatic, Northeastern Italy overflows with a feast of visual delights.

The artistic culture of this heterogeneous region is rather difficult to categorise. Geographically, the region is, in fact, comprised of three quite distinct provinces: the **Trentino-Alto Adige** to the mountainous north, bordering on the Austrian Alps and including the cities of Bolzano and Trento; **Friuli-Venezia Giulia** in the far northeast, extending to the border with Slovenia on the Adriatic Sea and including the cities of Udine and Trieste; and, finally, the **Veneto**, which spreads inland from Venice, encompassing the mainland (or *terra firma*) cities of Padua, Vicenza and Verona. Lying so close to the alpine border that separates the Italian peninsula from the rest of Europe, this disparate territory has been called the 'vestibule' of Italy, and indeed many cultures have entered this vestibule, invading and occupying the region over the course of the centuries. The art, architecture and urbanism of Northeastern Italy clearly reflect the passage of multiple peoples, in an idiosyncratic weaving together of diverse civilisations – Roman, Lombard, Byzantine, and Austrian to name a few – creating for each city in the region a virtually unique artistic tradition.

While art and architecture are frequently discussed in terms of broad stylistic periods – for example, Renaissance or Baroque – this approach is difficult to apply to Northeastern Italy. Because virtually each of the cities in this part of the peninsula was influenced in distinctive ways by diverse cultures (with their own interpretations of common artistic styles) at quite disparate times, an overall historical survey of the early arts of Northeastern Italy must be reinforced by a close look at each individual region.

Native, Invader and Neighbour

Originally inhabited by Celtic, Raetian, and Venetii peoples, Northeastern Italy was but one of the many regions which, to paraphrase Julius Caesar, the Romans 'came to, saw and conquered'. These invaders from the south brought with them the standard amenities of Roman cities: neatly gridded street systems, a variety of city gates, a smattering of triumphal arches, the theatre, the amphitheatre – in short, all those things that would make life pleasant and as much like home as possible for sophisticated Roman sensibilities. The gridded streets of many of the cities in Northeastern Italy, such as in the ancient centre of **Trent**, attest to Roman planning, as does the plethora of ancient ruins in the now almost deserted city of **Aquileia**, once the ancient capital of the bustling northeast region of the peninsula. However, as in many things, the Romans were shrewd colonialists and knew that one way to placate the conquered was to allow them to maintain some sense of their indigenous social and cultural structures. The standard Roman artistic and architectural forms, then, took on somewhat provincial interpretations so far away from the *caput mundi*. Wonderful examples of the local taste in architecture can be seen in the somewhat bizarre remains of the ancient monuments of **Verona** – especially the city gates known as the Porta dei Borsari and the Porta dei Leoni.

Towards the end of Roman domination on the peninsula, Christianity was legalised in the empire under the Edict of Constantine in 313. Several of the cities in Northeastern Italy were swept up in the new religion and had great basilicas constructed to house their growing congregations. If you visit the now almost forgotten city of Aquileia in present-day Friuli-Venezia Giulia, you can see the remains of its early Christian splendour in two important basilicas decorated with magnificent mosaics.

Early in the 5th century, a wave of new invaders – this time peoples from across the Alps who descended from the mountain passes – overran the sophisticated Romanised cities and left their own marks. These recurrent onslaughts, beginning with Alaric the Visigoth in 401, followed by Attila the Hun in 452, the Ostragoth Theodoric in 489, Gothic invaders in 493, and Lombards in 568, provoked a variety of responses in the widely divergent territory of Northeastern Italy. Some regions witnessed a blending of the established Italic culture and the provincial taste of the Northern invaders, who were clearly there to stay. An interesting example of this merging of cultures can be seen in the rich Lombard remains in **Cividale del Friuli**, which include the Baptistery of Callixtus, the Altar of Ratchis, and the Lombard Temple. Other cities, primarily those closest to the Alpine borders and thus directly exposed to the fiercest of invasions, saw their fabric devolve or disappear altogether, only to be reborn as fortified frontier towns in the medieval period or as fiefdoms of the bishop princes who received these territories from the Germanic Holy Roman Emperor. Thus many of these cities in the far northern Alpine areas tended to gravitate toward the Germanic world not only culturally but linguistically as well. Finally, the 'barbarian' onslaught caused still other inhabitants of Northeastern Italy, primarily those in the eastern territories, to flee in the face of these invasions, looking to the Adriatic Sea for safety. **Venice**, for example, was founded when Italic peoples from the Veneto mainland migrated to the lagoon islands on the Adriatic coast. Similarly, **Grado**, now known as a popular beach resort, was founded when the Patriarch of Aquileia fled to the sea for safety. Proximity to the Adriatic Sea, facing east, encouraged these areas to maintain ties to the rapidly changing empire, whose capital had been of late transferred to Constantinople (or Byzantium, as it was then called).

These connections with the North and with the East, with the Germanic culture and the Byzantine culture respectively, have reverberated in the art and architecture of Northeastern Italy. Each region, indeed each city within each of these three regions, has been affected in a unique way by the passage of time and by the mingling of native, invader and neighbour.

A Regional Perspective

Trentino-Alto Adige

Just south of the Austrian border, this province is comprised of two very culturally distinct regions: the mountain territory of Alto Adige in the north and the more varied Trentino in the south. Parts of this province, most exposed to the onslaught of invasions from the north, were absorbed into the feudal structure of the Holy Roman Empire and were later taken by Napoleon. In 1815 the province was annexed to the Austro-Hungarian Empire, which held it until the end of World War I, when Trentino-Alto Adige finally returned to Italy; however, this province's tenuous ties to the Italian peninsula are still evident in its administratively autonomous status.

In the art and architecture of this area, a distinctive provincial quality and a strong tradition of folk art prevail. In the early medieval period, wide-ranging influences gave birth to perhaps the most important frescoes in the region in the church of San Procolo in **Naturno** (8th–9th century), which are based on Irish miniatures. The stylised quality of Byzantine models as well as vivacious Northern chivalric types can be seen in frescoes in the town of **Ora**, in the church of San Daniele. Architecturally, the medieval period saw the expression of a local Romanesque followed by a provincial Gothic style that was based on Northern types – picturesquely evident in the streets of **Bressanone**, with their narrow, colourful houses featuring crenellated pediments, steeply sloping roofs, balconies and façade frescoes. Commanding castles and beautiful churches in the same style show this trans-Alpine influence as well – the cathedral of **Bolzano**, for example, was built on the great hall-church (*Hallenkirche*) plan in the Germanic tradition. In the Alto Adige and the northernmost regions of the Trentino, this provincial Gothic style persisted for quite some time. Again in Bolzano the elaborately lacy and elegant stonework of the pinnacle of the bell-tower of the cathedral, by the Swabian Hans Lutz, dates from the early 16th century, by which time Central Italy was in the midst of its High Renaissance style. In the southern regions of the Alto Adige and in the Trentino, on the other hand, the appeal of the Renaissance was apparent – especially in **Trent**, under the rule of the bishop prince Bernardo Clesio (1511–39), who enriched the city with his Renaissance taste, as seen in the harmonious church of Santa Maria Maggiore and the patrician palaces of the Piazza del Duomo.

Throughout the centuries, popular art maintained a hold in the minor centres, where humble functional churches, adorned with modest devotional images, proliferated. Later, the influence of the Austro-Hungarian Empire returned bold statements and grandiose gestures to the artistic repertoire of the region, as seen in the stately homes and promenades with which its cities were adorned.

Friuli-Venezia Giulia

Bordering on Eastern Europe, this far northeastern province tends to go rather underappreciated. Successively influenced by the Roman Empire, by invasions from the north, by Venice to its south, by the Austro-Hungarian Empire, and by its Balkan neighbours to the east, this region presents perhaps the most eclectic of artistic traditions. Its present form dates only from the post-World War II period and it, like the Trentino-Alto Adige, is an administratively autonomous province.

Always places of passage, the cities of Friuli-Venezia Giulia saw their fortunes rise and fall at various times, and their art and architecture reflect the periodic nature of their respective days in the sun. As we have already seen, **Aquileia** flourished as the Roman capital of the region and boasts a number of fine ruins, including parts of its ancient port, forum, and amphitheatre. Its early Christian remains are also among the most impressive in Italy. However, the Northern invasions spelled the beginning of the decline of Aquileia as the centre of power shifted to **Grado**, whose most splendid artistic achievements are still visible in its early Christian mosaic pavements. While Cividale was also a major city under the Romans, its prominence came about during Lombard domination in the 8th century, when it served as the capital of the Veneto Illyria region. A number of monuments survive from this period (see above), fusing Northern artistic tastes with Italic traditions. The gridded street system of the old quarter of **Trieste** attests to its ancient foundation; however, it has had a turbulent history, subject to various barbarian lords and then victim of a power struggle between the two great forces to the north and to the south – Austria and Venice. While there is some evidence of Venetian influence in Trieste – the 15th-century fortress of San Giusto, for example – this city has a much more Austrian appearance, having served as the chief port of the Austro-Hungarian Empire in the 18th century. The great Neo-Classical building style of Vienna emerges in Trieste, whose civic structures, featuring arcades and magnificent portals, give the city a distinctly Central European air. **Udine**, on the other hand, does not seem to have an ancient foundation, but instead developed around a feudal castle in the 10th century. Coveted by the Venetians, the city finally fell to its neighbour to the south in the 15th century and gradually took on a characteristically Venetian appearance with typical arcaded houses and mullioned windows. The famous Baroque Venetian painter Tiepolo produced some of his finest works in Udine.

The Veneto

Perhaps the best known of the three provinces of Northeastern Italy, the Veneto stretches from the northwestern shores of the Adriatic Sea inland through the *terra firma,* or mainland. Although several of the cities of the Veneto boast ancient origins, it is the foundation of Venice and its subsequent rise as a great mercantile and naval power that has left an indelible impression on the arts and architecture of the Veneto. With its extraordinary setting, perched at the edge of two contradictory worlds – the Western world of the Italian peninsula and the Eastern world of Byzantium – Venice was in a singular position to create a rarefied artistic tradition. In fusing the arts of these splendid traditions, Venice became one of the great centres of Italian art with characteristic schools of painting and architecture that would profoundly influence European culture.

Prior to their domination by Venice, cities on the *terra firma* assembled their own unique artistic cultures. These were typically based on local ancient remains and native traditions, frequently coloured by ideas from the North. Following the barbarian invasions, the Veneto experienced a great period of rebuilding: in **Verona**, a number of major churches, such as the church of San Fermo Maggiore (1065–1143), were rebuilt in a local Romanesque style with marvellous wooden ceilings; while in **Padua** we see an assimilation of Eastern and Western traditions in the 13th-century church of the Santo, where a typi-cally Western Romanesque/Gothic church was topped by a bevy of Byzantine domes.

Venice, in the mean time, having been founded from scratch, was in the process of creating her own artistic legacy. At San Marco, a very Byzantine Greek-cross church plan was crowned with a sequence of mosaic-encrusted domes, sparkling like the reflected sunlight that shimmers on the nearby lagoon. The palaces of Venice also developed a distinctive appearance. Their lustrous colours, ogival-arched windows, and mysteriously inviting central portal evoke the rather exotic air of Byzantium. This palace type appeared in many cities of the *terra firma* as well, including Vicenza and Verona.

The Renaissance in architecture arrived late in the Veneto. The Florentine,

Jacopo Sansovino, brought the monumentality of ancient Rome to Piazza San Marco and coloured it with a distinctly Venetian aura. Elsewhere, native sons Michele Sanmicheli and Andrea Palladio made good in their respective home cities of Verona and Vicenza, transforming both into elegant representations of the Renaissance city. Each architect proved himself in the cultural centre as well, designing churches and palaces for the Most Serene Republic, as Venice was known. Near the smaller towns and villages of the Veneto, such as **Treviso** and **Belluno**, these architects and others produced a series of imposing villas that exemplify the culture and commercial interests of 16th- and 17th-century Venetians and the gentry of the *terra firma.*

Meanwhile, in painting, works of local schools filled the churches of the Veneto until the arrival in 1305 of the Tuscan painter, Giotto, at the Arena Chapel in Padua. His work was to influence the Veneto traditions that followed, especially in Padua and Verona. Likewise, the visit of the Sicilian painter, Antonello da Messina, was to change Venetian art forever. His use of the oil technique, studied from the Flemish painters, inspired the great Venetian artists to take advantage of the shimmering colours, limpid light and soft, hazy atmosphere of Venice in a way not seen before.

Giovanni Bellini, perhaps the pre-eminent Venetian painter of the 15th century, bathed his works with an exquisite luminescence: all diffused light, delicate shadows, and sublime colours whose richness and depth seem to radiate from within. His followers, Giorgione and Titian and, later, Tintoretto, continued the Bellini legacy, reflecting the hazy, sensuous atmosphere of Venice in their own lyrical compositions. This artistic tradition swept throughout the Veneto as well, where Veronese decorated country villas with delightful scenes of the joys of bucolic life. This rare tradition of Venetian painting came to a close with the 17th–18th century *vedutisti* (view painters) such as Canaletto, whose painted views of Venice were brought home by travellers concluding their grand tour with a precious remembrance of the splendid and unparalleled city of Venice.

3. TOURING THE REGION

Before You Leave

Climate

Venice and Northeastern Italy enjoy a cool continental climate, somewhat tempered in the coastal areas by the presence of the Adriatic Sea. As a rule there are two rainy seasons (spring and autumn); hot, dry summers; and mild winters, with mean temperatures usually above or around 0° C (32°F). The Eastern Alps, of course, are much cooler, with very pleasant summers, but sub-zero temperatures and abundant snowfalls from November to March and sometimes early as October or as late as May. In general, however, the climate of the region is agreeable for much of the year, and a succession of more than two or three bad days is unusual.

The heat in July and August in the Po River Basin, the Val d'Adige, and on coasts sheltered from cooling breezes may be excessive. Throughout the year, the region is subject to winds and to abrupt changes of temperature. The *bora*, a cold, northerly wind often blows in winter in the area east of Venice; and the hot, dry North African *scirocco* is not uncommon in summer. The best time to visit the region is late spring (May–June) or early autumn (particularly September), when the temperature and rainfall are moderate and the droves of summer sun-seekers (Italian and foreign) that invade the coasts, especially between 15 July and 15 August, are still (or again) at home. Winter is particularly lovely in the Alps, and even Venice has a special charm: shrouded in fog or dusted with snow, it looks, feels and sounds like quite another city.

Formalities

Passports or ID cards are necessary for EU and American travellers entering Italy; American travellers must carry passports. No visa is required for a EU, US, or Canadian citizen holding a valid passport for a visit of less than 90 days. Citizens of other countries should check current visa requirements with the nearest Italian consulate before departure. Italian law requires travellers to carry some form of identification at all times. Also, all foreign visitors to Italy must register with the police within three days of arrival. If you are staying at a hotel, this formality is attended to by the management. If staying with friends or in a private home, you must register in person at the nearest police station. For information or help (including an interpreter), call the visitors' assistance numbers in Rome: 06 461950 or 06 486609.

Information

Brochures and other material can be obtained from:

UK
Italian State Tourist Board, 1 Princes Street., London W1R 8AY (tel. 0171 408 1254, fax 0171 493 6695).

USA
Italian Government Tourist Board, c/o Italian Trade Commission, 499 Park Avenue Avenue, New York, NY 10022 (tel. 212 843 6885, fax 212 843 6886); Italian Government Travel Office, 401 North Michigan Avenue, Suite 3030, Chicago 1, IL 60611 (tel. 312 6440996, fax 312 64430197); or Italian Government Travel Office, 12400 Wilshire Blvd, Suite 550, Los Angeles, CA 90025 (tel. 310 8200098, fax 310 8206357).

Canada
Italian Government Travel Office, 1 Place Ville Marie, Suite 1914, Montreal, Québec H3B 3M9 (tel. 514 866 7667, fax 514 866 0975).

The London office issues free an invaluable *Traveller's Handbook* (in the USA, *General Information for Travelers to Italy*), usually revised every year.

Disabled Travellers

All new public buildings are now obliged by law to provide easy access and specially designed facilities for the disabled. Unfortunately the conversion of historical buildings, including many museums and monuments, is made problematic by structural impediments such as narrow pavements (which make mobility difficult for everyone). In Venice, of course, the pervasiveness of stepped bridges makes it impossible to get around in a wheelchair – or even to push a baby in a pram. Hotels that are able to give hospitality to the disabled are indicated in the annual list of hotels published by the local tourist boards. Airports and train stations provide assistance, and certain trains are equipped to transport wheelchairs. Access is allowed to the centre of towns (normally closed to traffic) for cars with disabled drivers or passengers, and special parking places are reserved for them. For further information, contact the tourist board in the city of interest.

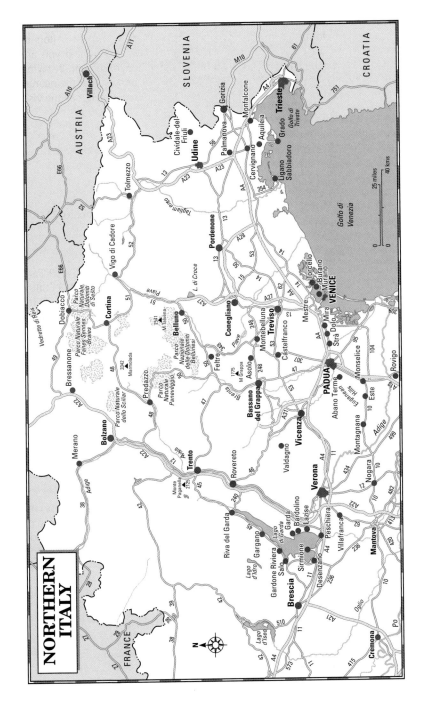

Getting There

By Air

Direct air services operate throughout the year between London and Venice, and from several British and North American cities to Milan and Rome, from which connections may be made with internal lines to Verona, Venice and Trieste. The carriers offering non-stop service between Britain and Italy are *British Airways* (tel. 0181 897 4000), *Alitalia* (tel. 0171 602 7111), and *Meridiana* (tel. 0171 839 2222). *Air France, Lufthansa,* and *Sabena* offer flights connecting through Paris, Frankfurt, and Brussels respectively. These may cost less than the direct flights.

Alitalia (tel. 1 800 223 5730) flies non-stop from New York (JFK or Newark) to Rome or Milan, from Boston and Chicago to Rome, and from Los Angeles to Rome or Milan; *American* from Chicago to Milan; *Canadian* from Toronto and Montreal to Rome; *Continental* (tel. 1 800 231 0856) from New York to Rome; *Delta* (1 800 241 4141) from New York to Milan and Rome; *TWA* (tel. 1 800 892 4141) from New York to Rome and Milan and from Los Angeles to Rome; and *United* (tel. 1 800 538 2929) from Washington DC to Rome. *British Airways, Air France, KLM,* and *Sabena* offer flights connecting through London, Paris, Amsterdam, and Brussels. These are often more economical than the direct flights.

Charter flights are also now run to most of the main cities in Italy; the fare often includes hotel accommodation. See your travel agent for details.

By Rail

The principal Italian cities are linked with Britain by a variety of rail routes, the most direct being from London via Paris and Turin, or via Paris and Milan. These services have sleeping cars (first class: single or double compartment; second class: three-berth compartments) and couchettes (seats converted into couches at night: first class: four; second class: six) and connect with trains directed to Venice and other cities in our area. Couchettes and sleeping compartments should be booked well in advance, although those that are not occupied at the time of departure can be hired directly from the conductor without paying a supplement. Reciprocal booking arrangements exist with Austria, Belgium, Denmark, France, Great Britain, Hungary, Luxembourg, the Netherlands, Portugal, Spain, and Switzerland.

Information and tickets on the *Italian State Railways* (but not seat reservations) can be obtained in Great Britain from Citalia, Marco Polo House, 3–5 Lansdowne Road, Croydon, Surrey CR9 1LL (tel. 0181 686 0677) and Wasteels Travel, 121 Wilton Road, London SW1V 1J2 (tel. 0171 834 7066).

In North America obtain information from CIT, 342 Madison Avenue, Suite 207, New York, NY 10173 (tel. 212 697 1482 for schedules), 212 697 2100 for rail pass information), 1 800 223 7987 to order tickets only, or 1 800 CIT TOUR for general information, fax 212 697 1394; Los Angeles Office, 6033 West Century Blvd, Los Angeles, CA 90045 (tel. 310 338 8616, fax 310

6704269); Montreal Office, 1450 City Councillors Street, Suite 750, Montreal H3A 2E6 (tel. 514 845 9101, fax 514 845 9137); Toronto Office, 111 Avenue Road, Suite 808, Toronto M5R 3JH (tel. 416 927 7712, fax 416 927 7206).

By Bus

A bus service operates, taking two days between London (Victoria Coach Station) and Rome (Piazza della Repubblica) via Dover, Paris, Mont Blanc, Aosta, Turin, Genoa, Milan, Bologna and Florence, daily from June to September, and once or twice a week for the rest of the year. Reductions are available for students. Information in London from the National Express office at Victoria Coach Station, from local National Express Agents, and in Italy from SITA offices.

By Car

The easiest approaches to Italy by road are the motorways through the Mont Blanc, St Bernard, Frejus, or Mont Cenis tunnels, or over the Brenner pass. British drivers taking their own cars by any of the routes across France, Belgium, Luxembourg, Switzerland, Germany,and Austria need the vehicle registration book, a valid national driving licence, an international insurance certificate (the 'green card', valid for 45 days), and a nationality plate (attached to the rear of the vehicle so as to be illuminated by the tail lamps). A Swiss Motorway Pass is needed for Switzerland, and can be obtained from the Royal Automobile Club (tel. 01345 333 1133), the Automobile Association (tel. 01256 20123), or at the Swiss border. If you don't own the vehicle you're driving you must possess the owner's permit for its use abroad. Foreign drivers hiring a car in Italy need only a valid national driver's licence.

By Sea

Adriatic Italy is connected by car ferry and hydrofoil to Greece (Patras, Igoumenitsa, Corfu), Albania (Durres, Vlore), and Croatia (Split). Information and reservations from Società Adriatica di Navigazione, Zattere 1141, Venice (tel. 041 781611, fax 041 781894; branch offices in Ancona, Bari, Brindisi, Corfu, Durres, Igoumenitsa, Patras, Split, Trieste).

On Arrival

Tourist Information

The Italian State Tourist Board (in Italian, ENIT, Ente Nazionale Italiano per il Turismo) has information offices at the border crossings with Austria (Valico autostradale Lupo di Brennero) and France (Casello Roverino di Ventimiglia), as well as at Milan Linate and Venice Marco Polo airports. Within Italy each *regione* has information services; where possible, these have been indicated in the text.

Money Matters

In Italy the monetary unit is the Italian *lira* (plural *lire*, abbreviated to L). Travellers' cheques and Eurocheques are the safest way of carrying money while travelling, and most credit cards are now generally accepted in hotels, shops and restaurants (and increasingly at petrol stations). The commission on cashing travellers' cheques can be quite high. For banking hours, see under 'Helpful Hints' below. Money can be changed at banks, post offices, travel agencies, and some hotels, restaurants and shops, though the rate of exchange can vary considerably from place to place. Exchange offices are usually open seven days a week at airports and most main railway stations. A limited amount of lire can be obtained from conductors on international trains and at certain stations. For small amounts of money, the difference between hotel and bank rates may be negligible, as banks tend to take a fixed commission on transactions.

If you're a non-EU resident, remember that you can claim **sales tax rebates** on purchases made in Italy provided the total expenditure is more than L300,000. Ask the vendor for a receipt describing the goods acquired and send it back to him when you get home (but no later than 90 days after the date of the receipt). The receipt must be checked and stamped by Italian Customs upon leaving Italy. On receipt of the bill, the vendor will forward the sales tax rebate (the present tax rate is 19 per cent on most goods) to your home address.

Accommodation

Hotels

In this guide a selection of hotels has been given at the end of each chapter. The hotels listed, regardless of their cost, have been chosen on the basis of their personality or character: all have something special about them (beautiful surroundings, distinctive atmosphere), and even the humblest are quite comfortable. The local tourist offices will help you find accommodation on the spot; nevertheless you should try to book well in advance, especially if you're planning to travel between May and October. Hotels equipped to offer hospitality to the disabled are indicated in the tourist boards' hotel lists.

Campsites

Camping is well organised throughout Italy. Full details of the sites in Italy are published annually by the Touring Club Italiano, Corso Italia 10, 20122 Milano (tel. 02 85261, fax 02 852 6362) in *Campeggi e Villaggi Turistici in Italia.* The national headquarters of the Federazione Italiana del Campeggio, at 11 Via Vittorio Emanuele, 50041 Calenzano (Firenze), tel. 055 882 391, fax 055 882 5918, also publishes an annual guide (*Guida Camping d'Italia*) and maintains an information office and booking service.

Alternative Accommodation

A new type of hotel, called a **residence,** has recently been introduced into Italy. Often in a building of historic interest, such as a castle or monastery, this sort of establishment tends to have only a few rooms and can be a delightful place to stay. Residences are listed separately in the tourist boards' hotel lists, with their prices.

Comfortable accommodation at very reasonable prices is offered by **religious organisations** in some cities; a complete listing is available from local tourist boards or from the *Arcivescovado* of the city concerned.

Agriturismo, which provides accommodation in farmhouses in the countryside, is highly recommended for travellers with their own transport and for families. Terms vary greatly, from bed-and-breakfast to self-contained flats, and some farms require a stay of a minimun number of days. Cultural or recreational activities are sometimes also provided. For information contact the *Associazione Nazionale per l'Agriturismo, l'Ambiente e il Territorio,* Corso Vittorio Emanuele 101, 00186 Roma (tel. 06 685 2342, fax 06 685 2342).

The *Associazione Italiani Alberghi per la Gioventù* (Italian Youth Hostels Association), Via Cavour 44, 00184 Rome (tel. 06 487 1152) runs 52 **hostels,** which are listed in their free annual guide. A membership card of the AIG or the International Youth Hostel Federation is required for access to Italian Youth Hostels. Details from the *Youth Hostels Association,* Trevelyan House, 8 St Stephen's Hill, St Albans, Herts AL1 2DY, and from the National Offices of American Youth Hostels Inc., Washington DC 20013-7613 (tel. 202 7836161).

Getting Around

By Rail

The Italian State Railways (*FS – Ferrovie dello Stato*) now run eight categories of trains. (1) *EC* (*Eurocity*), international express trains running between the main Italian and European cities; (2) *EN* (*Euronotte*), overnight international express trains with sleeping car or couchette service; (3) *P* (*Pendolini*), high-speed trains running between major Italian cities; (4) *IC* (*Intercity*), express trains running between major Italian cities; (5) *E* (*Espressi*), long-distance trains not as fast as the Intercity trains; (6) *D* (*Diretti*), intermediate-distance trains making more stops than the Espressi – also called *IR* (*Interregionali*), the new name for Diretti; (7) *R* (*Regionali*), local trains stopping at all stations; and (8) *M* (*Metropolitani*), surface or underground commuter trains. Service in all categories is improving rapidly as the State Railways proceed in their ambitious modernisation program.

Seats can be booked in advance, as early as two months and as late as three hours before departure, from the main cities at the station booking office (open daily 7.00–22.00), or at travel agencies representing the Italian State Railways. Seats on a Pendolino can be reserved up to 30 minutes before departure at the Pendolino booking counter in the station. The timetable of the train services changes in late September and late May every year. Excellent timetables are published twice a year by the Italian State Railways (*In Treno;* one volume for the whole of Italy; trains with facilities for the disabled are marked) and by several private publishers. These can be purchased at news-stands and train stations.

Tickets must be bought at the station (or from travel agents representing the Italian State Railways) before starting a journey, otherwise a fairly large supplement has to be paid to the ticket-collector on the train. Time should be allowed for buying a ticket, as there are often long queues at the station ticket counters. Some trains charge a special supplement; and on others seats must be booked in advance. It is therefore always necessary to specify which train you are intending to take as well as the destination when buying tickets. And don't forget: you must stamp the date of your journey on the ticket in the meters located on or near the station platforms *before you get on the train.* If you buy a return ticket, you must stamp your ticket before beginning the outbound *and* the return journey. In the main stations the better known credit cards are now generally accepted (although a special ticket window must be used when buying a ticket with a credit card). There are limitations on travelling short distances on some trains.

Fares in Italy are still much lower than in the UK or the USA. Children under four travel free, and between four and twelve pay half price. There are also reductions for families and for groups of as few as three persons. For travellers over the age of 60 (with Senior Citizen Railcards), the *Rail Europ Senior* card offers a 30 per cent reduction on Italian rail fares. The *Inter-rail* card (valid one month), which can be purchased in Britain or North America by young people up to the age of 26, is valid in Italy. In Italy the *Carta d'Argento* and the *Carta Verde* (both valid one year) allow a 20 per cent reduction on rail fares, respectively, for those over 60 and between the ages of 12 and 26. A *Biglietto chilometrico* (Cumulative Ticket) is valid for 3000 kilometres over a two-month period and can be used by up to five people at the same time. The *Euro Domino* and *Euro Domino Junior* cards, available to those resident outside Italy, gives freedom of the Italian railways for three, five, or ten days. These cards can be purchased in Britain or at main stations in Italy. The *Carta Blu* is available for the disabled. Other forms of discounted travel are *Rail Inclusive Tours*, which offer transport, accommodation, excursions, etc., in a single package; the *Tessera di Autorizzazione* (Special Concession Card), which provides a 20 per cent discount and exemption from special supplements for frequent travel in first class, second class, or both.

Restaurant cars are attached to most international and internal long-distance trains. Some trains now also have self-service restaurants. Also, snacks, hot coffee and drinks are sold throughout the journey from a trolley wheeled down the train. At every large station snacks are on sale from trolleys on the platform and you can buy them from the train window. These include carrier-bags with sandwiches, drink and fruit (*cestini da viaggio*), or individual sandwiches (*panini*).

Additional services available at main stations include assistance for the disabled; special car-hire offers; automatic ticketing; porterage; and left luggage offices (open 24 hours at the main stations; often closed at night at smaller stations). Porters are entitled to a fixed amount, shown on notice boards at all stations, for each piece of baggage.

By Bus

Local and long-distance buses between the main towns in Northeastern Italy are frequent, though as increasing numbers of residents become independently mobile, service is diminishing. Except in areas of particular interest to non-residents (such as the Dolomites), most buses now carry schoolchildren from the villages to the towns in the early morning, and from the towns to the villages in the afternoon. Buses still serve most towns not reached by rail at least once a day; generally speaking, they leave major cities from a depot at or near the train station. Accurate area timetables can be obtained from the local tourist boards.

City buses are an excellent means of getting about in most towns – including Venice, where water buses called *vaporetti* ply the city's canals. Almost everywhere tickets must be purchased before boarding (at tobacconists, bars, news-stands, information offices, etc.) and stamped on board.

By Car

Regardless of whether you are driving your own car or a hired vehicle, Italian law requires that you carry a valid driving licence accompanied by an Italian translation or by a declaration issued by the *Automobile Club d'Italia* (*ACI*) at its frontier or provincial offices. It is now compulsory to wear seat belts in the front seat of cars in Italy, and crash helmets are compulsory when driving or riding a motorcycle. Traffic is generally faster (and more aggressive) than in Britain or America. In cities and towns, the speed limit is 50km/h (31mph); on main roads, 90km/h (56mph); on superhighways, 130 km/h (80mph). Pedestrians have the right of way at zebra crossings. Unless otherwise indicated, cars entering a road or roundabout from the right are given precedence. Italian drivers frequently change lanes without warning; they tend to ignore pedestrian crossings; and they view red lights with a certain cynicism. Everywhere the drivers of motorcycles, mopeds, and Vespas weave in and out of traffic, snapping up the right of way. The concept of the safe following distance is unknown, and if you leave a gap between your car and the vehicle in front of you, it will be filled immediately.

Roads in Italy

Italy probably has the finest motorways in Europe. They are called *autostrade,* and they are indicated by green signs or, near the entrance ramps, by large overhead light boards. Tolls are charged according to the rating of the vehicle and the distance covered. All *autostrade* have service areas open 24 hours, and most have SOS points every 2km. At the entrance to motorways, the two directions are indicated by the name of the most important town (and not by the nearest town), which can be momentarily confusing. Similar to *autostrade,* but not provided with service stations, SOS points or emergency lanes, are the dual-carriageway fast roads called *superstrade* (also indicated by green signs).

You'll also find an excellent network of secondary highways (*strade statali* or *provinciali,* indicated by blue signs), which are usually well engineered and provide fine views of the countryside. Local traffic, however, can be extremely heavy, especially around major cities. Throughout Italy buildings of historic interest are often indicated by yellow signs (although there are long-term plans to change the colour to brown), townships (*comuni*) and their component villages (*frazioni*), by white signs. The territory of a *comune* is often much larger than the town of the same name that is its administrative centre – another source of confusion.

Fuel And Service

Petrol stations are open 24 hours on motorways, elsewhere 7.00–12.00, 15.00–20.00; winter 7.30–12.30, 14.30–19.30. Twenty-four-hour self-service stations can also be found in or near the larger towns. Pumps are operated by L10,000 or L50,000 banknotes. All varieties of petrol (including diesel and unleaded) are now readily available in Italy, although they cost more than in the UK, and considerably more than in America. Most stations offer basic maintenance service (motor oil, brake fluid, etc.).

Parking

Many cities in Northeastern Italy have taken the wise step of closing their historic centres to traffic (except for residents), which makes them much more pleasant to visit on foot. Access is allowed to hotels and for the disabled. It is advisable to leave your car in a supervised car park, although with a bit of effort it is almost always possible to find a place to park free of charge, away from the town centre. Always lock your car when parked, and never leave anything of value inside it.

Car Hire

You can arrange to hire a car before departure through the airlines (at specially advantageous rates in conjunction with their flights) or in Italy through any of the principal car-hire firms (the best known include *Maggiore*, *Avis*, and *Hertz*), which offer daily, weekly, 5-day and weekend rates. Special leasing rates are available for periods of 30 days and over. The State Railways also offer special rail-car combinations.

Maps

The *Touring Club Italiano (TCI)* publishes several sets of excellent maps, including *Carta Stradale d'Europa: Italia* on a scale of 1:1,000,000; the *Atlante Stradale Touring* (1:800,000); and the *Carta Stradale d'Italia* (1:200,000). The latter is divided into 15 sheets covering the regions of Italy. These are also published as an atlas (with a comprehensive index) called the *Atlante Stradale d'Italia,* in three volumes. The one entitled Nord covers our area. These maps can be purchased from the TCI offices and at many book-sellers; in London they are obtainable at Stanfords, 12–14 Long Acre, WC2 9LP. The *Istituto Geografico Militare,* via Cesare Battisti 10, Florence, publishes a map of Italy on a scale of 1:100,000 in 277 sheets, and a field survey, partly 1:50,000, partly 1:25,000, invaluable for the detailed exploration of the country, especially its more mountainous regions; the coverage is, however, still far from complete at the larger scales, and some of the maps are out of date. For the computer literate, *Route 66 Geographic Information Systems BV* of Veenendaal, The Netherlands, distributes software that calculates and displays routes from any origin to any destination in Italy.

By Air

Frequent internal flights are operated between most main towns. Reductions are granted for weekend travel.

Cycling and Walking

Cycling and walking holidays have become more popular in Italy in recent years and more information is now available locally. The local offices of the *Club Alpino Italiano* (*CAI*) and the World Wide Fund for Nature provide all the information necessary. Maps are published by the *Istituto Geografico Militare* (see above) and by CAI at a scale of 1:50,000.

Taxis

Taxis are hired from ranks or by telephone; there are no cruising cabs. Fares vary from city to city but are generally cheaper than London taxis, though considerably more expensive than New York taxis. No tip is expected, but 1000 lire or so can be given. A supplement for night service, and for luggage, is charged. There is a heavy surcharge when the destination is outside the town limits (ask roughly how much the fare is likely to be).

Helpful Hints

Opening Times

The opening times of museums, sites and monuments have been given at the end of each chapter, but they often change without warning. The tourist boards in major cities keep updated timetables of most **museums** in their area of competence. Entrance fees to Italian museums vary (from free to L10,000) by age and nationality; British citizens under 18 and over 60 are entitled to free admission to national museums and monuments thanks to reciprocal arrangements in Britain. During the *Settimana per i Beni Culturali e Ambientali* (Cultural and Environmental Heritage Week), usually early in December, entrance to national museums is free for all.

Churches in Italy open quite early in the morning (often for 6.00 Mass). They normally close for a couple of hours during the middle of the day, although cathedrals and some of the large churches may be open without a break during daylight hours. The sacristan will show closed chapels, crypts, etc., and a small tip should be given. Some churches now ask that sightseers do not enter during a service, but normally visitors may do so, provided they are silent and do not approach the altar in use. At all times they are expected to cover their legs and arms, and generally dress with decorum. In Holy Week most of the pictures are covered and are on no account shown.

Shops generally open Monday–Saturday 8.30/9.00–13.00 and 15.30/16.00–19.30/20.00. Shops selling clothes, etc., are usually closed on Monday morning, and food shops on Wednesday afternoon, except from mid-June to mid-September, when all shops instead close on Saturday afternoon. In resorts, during July and August, many shops remain open from early morning until late at night. **Banks** are open Monday through Friday, 8.30–13.30, 14.30–15.45. They are closed on Saturday and holidays, and close early (about 11.00) on days preceding national holidays.

Public Holidays

The Italian National Holidays, when offices, shops, and schools are closed, are 1 January, 25 April (Liberation Day), Easter Sunday and Easter Monday, 1 May (Labour Day), 15 August (Assumption), 1 November (All Saints' Day), 8 December (Immaculate Conception), Christmas Day and 26 December (St Stephen). Each town keeps its patron saint's day as a holiday.

Health

British citizens, as members of the EU, have the right to claim health services in Italy if they have the E111 form (available from post offices). There are also a number of private holiday health insurance policies. Italy has no medical programme covering US citizens, who are advised to take out an insurance policy before travelling. First aid services (*pronto soccorso*) are available at all hospitals, train stations and airports. Chemist shops (*farmacie*) are usually open Monday–Friday 9.00–13.00, 16.00–19.30 or 20.00. A few are open also on Saturdays, Sundays, and holidays (listed on the door of every chemist). In all towns there is also at least one chemist shop open at night (also shown on the door of every chemist). For emergencies, dial 113 (State Police) or 112 (Carabinieri).

Embassies and Consulates

Help is given to British, US and Canadian travellers who are in difficulty by the British, US and Canadian consulates in Italy, and by the British, US, and Canadian Embassies in Rome. They will replace lost or stolen passports, and will give advice in emergencies. The British Consulate in Venice is located at Dorsoduro 1051 (Accademia; tel. 041 522 7207); the nearest US Consulate is in Milan, at 2/10 Via Principe Amedeo (tel. 02 290 351); the Canadian Embassy in Rome, at Via G.B. de Rossi 27 (tel. 06 445 981, fax 06 445 98750).

Crime

Pickpocketing is a widespread problem in towns all over Italy: it is always advisable not to carry valuables in handbags, and to be particularly careful on public transport. Never wear conspicuous jewellery, including necklaces and watches; women, when walking, should keep their handbags on the side of their bodies nearest the wall (never on the street side). Crime should be reported at once to the police, or the local Carabinieri office (found in every town and small village). A detailed statement has to be given in order to get an official document confirming loss or damage (essential for insurance claims). Interpreters are provided. For all emergencies, dial 113.

Telephone and Postal Services

Stamps are sold at tobacconists and post offices. Correspondence can be addressed c/o the post office by adding *fermo posta* to the name of the locality. There are numerous **public telephones** all over Italy, and card-operated phones are becoming increasingly common in major cities and resort areas. Local calls cost L200. Cards offering L5000 of L10,000 in prepaid calls are available at post offices, tobacconists, and certain news-stands. They are particularly convenient for phoning abroad. Long-distance calls in Italy are made by dialling the city code (for instance, 041 for Venice), then the tel. number; international and intercontinental calls, by dialling 00 plus the country code, then the city code (for numbers in Britain, without the initial zero), and the tel. number (for instance, the central London number 855 2000 would be 0044 171 855 2000). You can reach an AT&T operator at 172 1011, MCI at 172 1022, or Sprint at 172 1877.

Suggestions on Tipping

A service charge of 15 to 18 per cent is added to **hotel** bills. The service charge is already included when all-inclusive prices are quoted, but it is customary to leave an additional tip in any case. As a guideline, and depending on the category of your hotel, the following tips are suggested: chambermaid, L1000/day; concierge, L3000/day (additional tip for extra services); bellhop or porter, L1500/bag; doorman (for calling a cab), L1000; room-service waiter, L1000 and up (depending on amount of bill); valet service, at least L1000.; hotel bar, 15 per cent.

A service charge of approximately 15 per cent is added to all **restaurant** bills. It is customary, however, to leave a small tip (5 to 10 per cent) for good service. In cafés and bars, leave 15 per cent if you were served at a table and if a bill does not already include service; and L100–500 while standing at a counter or bar drinking coffee, cocktails, etc.

At **opera, concerts** and the **theatre**, tip ushers L1000 and up, depending on the price of your seat.

Language

Even a few words of Italian are a great advantage outside of Venice, where English is not so widely spoken as in the city. Local dialects vary greatly and are usually unintelligible to the foreigner; but even where dialect is universally used nearly everybody can speak and understand standard Italian.

Words should be pronounced well forward in the mouth, and no nasal intonation exists in Italian. Double consonants call for special care as each must be sounded. Consonants are pronounced roughly as in English with the following exceptions; *c* and *cc* before e and i have the sound of *ch* in chess; *sc* before e and i is pronounced like *sh* in ship; *ch* before e and i has the sound of *k*; *g* and *gg* before e and i are always soft, like *j* in jelly; *gh* is always hard, like *g* in get; *gl* is nearly always like *lli* in million (there are a few exceptions, e.g. *negligere*, where it is pronounced as in English); *gn* is like *ny* in lanyard; *gu* and *qu* are always like *gw* and *kw*. *S* is hard like *s* in six except when it occurs between two vowels, when it is soft, like the English *z* or the *s* in rose; *ss* is always hard. *Z* and *zz* are usually pronounced like *ts*, but occasionally have the sound of *dz* before a long vowel. Vowels are pronounced openly and are given their full value; there are no true diphthongs in Italian, and every vowel should be articulated separately. The stress normally falls on the last syllable but one; in modern practice an accent sign is written regularly only when the stress is on the last syllable, e.g. *città*, or to differentiate between two words similarly spelt with different meaning: e.g. *e* (and); *è* (is).

Manners and Customs

Throughout Italy it is customary to open conversation in shops, etc., with the courtesy of *buon giorno* ('good day') or *buona sera* ('good afternoon/evening'). The expression *prego* ('don't mention it') is everywhere the obligatory and automatic response to *grazie* ('thank you'). The phrases *per piacere* or *per favore* ('please'), *permesso* ('excuse me'), used when pushing past someone (essential on public vehicles), *scusi* ('sorry'; also, 'I beg your pardon', when something is not heard), should not be forgotten. You'll be wished *Buon appetito!* before beginning a meal, to which you should reply *Grazie, altrettanto.* This pleasant custom may be extended to fellow passengers taking a picnic meal on a train. Shaking hands is an essential part of greeting and leave-taking. In shops and offices a certain amount of self-assertion is taken for granted, since queues are not the general rule and it is incumbent on the enquirer or customer to get himself a hearing.

There are few restrictions on photography in Italy, but permission is necessary to photograph the interiors of churches and museums and may sometimes be withheld. Care should also be taken before photographing individuals, notably members of the armed forces and the police. Photography is forbidden on train stations and airports as well as in frontier zones and near military installations.

The metric system of weights and measures is used in Italy: the *metro* is the unit of length, the *grammo* of weight, the *ara* of land-measurement, the *litro* of capacity. Greek-derived prefixes (deca-, etto-, chilo-) are used with those names to express multiples; Latin prefixes (deci-, centi-, milli-) to express fractions (*kilometro* – 1000 metri, *millimetro* – 1000th part of a metro). For approximate calculations the *metro* may be taken as 39 inches and the *chilometro* as 0.6 mile, the *litro* as 1.75 pint, an *etto* as 3.5oz, and the *chilo* as 2.2lb.

4. FOOD AND WINE

Italian food is usually good and inexpensive. Generally speaking, the least pretentious **ristorante** or **trattoria** (there is very little difference between the two) provides the best value. In this guide you'll find a selection of restaurants at the end of each chapter. The places listed have been chosen on the basis of the quality and distinction of their menu, and even the simplest are quite good.

A full **Italian meal** usually consists of an appetiser, a first course of soup or pasta, an entrée of meat or fish accompanied by a vegetable, then salad, fruit and/or dessert. Odd as it may seem, this combination is not fattening, as the various food groups are all present in carefully established proportion. If you want to be on the safe side, though, try having pasta and a salad at lunch (you'll burn off the calories in the afternoon), and your meat and vegetables in the evening. Or just go with a **pizza,** which is made to order in a *pizzeria* but can be bought on the run in cafés, bakeries and any number of other places. Excellent refreshments, including sandwiches and salads, can also be found in **cafés,** many of which have outside tables. As a rule, if you eat at the bar you must pay the cashier first, then present your receipt to the barman in order to get served. If you sit at a table the charge is usually higher, and you will be given waiter service (so you should not pay first).

Remember always that **pasta** is *the* essential ingredient of Italian cuisine – and the one where the Italian culinary fantasy is at its best. An ordinary Italian supermarket usually stocks about 50 different shapes, but some experts estimate that there are more that 600 shapes in all. *Pasta corta* ('short pasta') is much more varied than *pasta lunga* ('long pasta'). The latter may be tubular (like macaroni), or threadlike (spaghetti, vermicelli, *capellini*); smooth (*fettucce, tagliatelle, linguine*), ruffled (*lasagne ricce*), or twisted (*fusilli*). *Pasta corta* comes in the shape of shells (*conchiglie*), stars (*stelle*), butterflies (*farfalle*), etc., and may be smooth (*penne*) or fluted (*rigatoni*). The differences of shape translate into differences of flavour, even when the pasta is made from the same dough, or by the same manufacturer. The reason for this is that the relation between the surface area and the weight of the pasta varies from one shape to another, causing the sauce to adhere in different ways and to different degrees. But even when pasta is served without a sauce, experts claim to perceive considerable differences in flavour due to the fact that different shapes cook in different ways. In Northeastern Italy most regional dishes call for *pasta all'ovo,* which is made with egg batter, rather than *pasta-sciutta,* a simple flour and water paste.

Bear in mind also that Italy is considered to have the best **coffee** in Europe. *Caffè* (or *espresso*, black coffee) can be ordered *alto* or *lungo* (diluted), *corretto* (with a liqueur), or *macchiato* (with hot milk). A *cappuccino* is an espresso with more hot milk than a *caffè macchiato* and is generally considered a breakfast drink. A glass of hot milk with a dash of coffee in it, called *latte macchiato*, is another early-morning favourite. In summer, many customers take *caffè freddo* (iced coffee). **Ice cream** (*gelato*) is another widely famed Italian speciality. It is always best in a *gelateria*, where it is made on the spot.

Spotlight on Pizza

There is an infinite variety of pizza recipes, all based on bread dough. The secret of a successful pizza is a blazing hot oven. Only violent heat, in fact, is capable of cooking the pizza in such a way that it is soft, yet crunchy at the same time; if the oven is not hot enough the dough becomes tough as shoe-leather. A wood-fired oven is best, although it is possible to produce an acceptable pizza in an electric or gas oven.

Regional Cuisine

The cuisine of Northeastern Italy reveals all the treasures of its marvellous landscape – a landscape of blue seas and and fertile plains, hills festooned with sun-kissed vineyards, and highland plains abounding with aromatic herbs and juicy berries. From village to village, province to province, these diverse topographical conditions, coupled with different historical and cultural traditions, have given rise to an almost countless number of local specialities.

Friuli-Venezia Giulia

Situated in the extreme northeast of Italy, Friuli-Venezia Giulia extends from the Alps to the Adriatic between the Veneto, Carinthia, and Slovenia. Subjected to wave after wave of foreign invasion, it has known centuries of war, poverty and devastation during which nutrition was reduced to the bare essentials: little meat (generally pork), and porridges made of millet, buckwheat and corn with milk, cheese, vegetables and wine were the traditional fare here. The dishes for which the region is best known today developed during the 19th century and have their roots in the Bohemian, Austrian, Hungarian, Jewish, Slavic, Greek and Turkish traditions.

Triestine cuisine features a variety of sweet-and-sour specialities, such as *pistum* (bread balls with aromatic herbs and raisins, served in broth), *lasagne* *al papavero* (lasagne dressed with sugar, butter and poppy seeds), *gnocchi di prugne* (potato gnocchi stuffed with a dried prune), and *lepre alla boema* (stuffed hare in a sauce of white vinegar and sugar). Old favourites include *iota* (bean soup, common throughout the region), *brovada* (white turnips fermented in the dregs of pressed grapes and served with polenta meal; or else beans, potatoes, sauerkraut, and rind of lard), and the traditional *gulasch*. There is an excellent choice of fish, including *sardoni in savor* (marinated sardines), and *granseola alla triestina* (the spiky, scarlet spider-crabs of the Adriatic, dressed with oil and lemon and served in their own shell). Other distinctive dishes are *zuf* (corn porridge) and *cevapcici* (grilled meatballs). Among the regional sweets are *gubana* (sweet bread roll stuffed with dried fruits) and *presnitz* (almond puff pastry).

Rice is a major ingredient of the cuisine of **Udine** and its environs, *ris e lujanis* (rice and beans) and *risotto e asparagi* (with asparagus) being two of the more common specialities. Bean soup with barley and vegetables – *la jota* – is a popular everyday dish. Square-shaped homemade pasta (*blecs*) is served with various meat or game sauces. Also typical are *bisna* (cornmeal polenta with sauerkraut), *cialzons* (ravioli filled with cheese, meat, eggs, and aromatic herbs, or else calves' brains, chicken, and herbs), *brovada* (white turnips fermented in grape dregs, cut in strips) with *cotechino* (stuffed pig's trotter), and *salame alla friulana* (cut in slices, sautéed and served with polenta). The most typical entrées are *bolliti* (boiled meats) served with marinated vegetables; stews with rich sauces accompanied by abundant polenta; and last but not least, goulasch and tripe. In the right season you will find any number of game dishes, particularly birds on the spit or in a sauce with polenta. Omelettes are made with wild herbs (*primaverile*); wild or cultivated vegetables such as hops (*urtizon*), poppies (*confernon*), butcher's broom (*riscli*), valerian (*ardielut*) and red chicory (*radicchio*). Winter lettuces are sautéed with lard or bacon and vinegar. The lightly salted *prosciutto di San Daniele* is considered the best in Italy. The typical sweet is *gubana*; other sweets are made with ricotta cheese, aromatic herbs, and fruit.

The Veneto

In **Venice** rice is served in a variety of ways, especially with seafood and vegetables. Classic specialites are *risi e bisi* (risotto with peas) and *risotto nero* (coloured and flavoured with the ink of cuttlefish). Thick soups are also popular. The best of these is *pasta e fasioi* (pasta and beans), which is eaten lukewarm, having been left to 'set' for an hour or so before being served – generally in deep plates or, better yet, clay bowls. The classical *pasta e fasioi* once called for *bigoli*, a local variant of spaghetti. *Bigoli* are homemade, in a special press, and their composition, with just water and buckwheat or wholewheat flour, is such that the pasta is dark. But *bigoli* are rare today and have been replaced with other types of pasta that range from *subiotino* to *ditalini* to *lingue di passero* to *lasagna* to *tagliatelle* – always with flour and water, but without eggs.

A Short History of Pasta

Whereas the invention of egg pasta is generally credited to the Chinese, the origin of *pastasciutta* may well be Italian. The Etruscan Tomb of the Reliefs at Cerveteri, near Rome, has stucco decorations representing pasta-making tools: a board and a rolling pin for rolling out the dough, knives, even a toothed cutting-wheel for making decorative borders. References to lasagne may be found in Cicero and other Roman writers; the name itself is probably derived from the Latin *lagana* or *lasana,* a cooking pot. By the end of the Middle Ages pasta was known throughout Italy. The 14th-century *Codice dell'anonimo toscano,* preserved in the library of Bologna University, contains several serving suggestions; and the poet Boccaccio, in his masterpiece, the *Decameron,* describes an imaginary land of grated parmesan cheese inhabited by people whose only pastime is the making of *maccheroni e raviuoli.* Of course, tomato sauce was unheard of until the discovery of America; Boccaccio's contemporaries cooked their macaroni and ravioli in chicken broth and dressed them with fresh butter.

Fish and seafood form the basis of Venice's best entrées. Local specialities include *granseola* (lagoon crabs), *sarde in saor* (marinated sardines) and *seppioline nere* (cuttlefish cooked in their own ink). An outstanding seafood dish is the *brodeto di pesce* or *boreto di Grado* – strictly served *in bianco* (without tomatoes), which testifies to its origins in an age before the discovery of America. Cornmeal polenta is another staple, often served with the famous *fegato alla veneziana* (calves' liver and onions). *Tiramisù* (see page 28 is the favourite dessert, though you'll also find rich cakes and pastries of Austrian inspiration.

Paduan cuisine is basically Venetian with local variations, as in the case of *risi e bisi,* to which the Paduans add *oca in onto* (pieces of goose preserved in their own fat). Distinctive dishes are rice and tagliatelli *in brodo d'anatra* (duck broth), and *risotto con rovinasassi* (chicken giblets). Sweets include *pinza* (a cake made with cornmeal and white flour), *fugassa, smegiazza* (both with crumbled polenta, toasted bread, milk, and molasses), and *sugoli* (grape-juice preserve).

As in Udine, rice is a basic ingredient of the cuisine of **Vicenza.** It was once grown extensively on the low, wet plains at the foot of the Alps. Here, along with the usual *risi e bisi* you'll find a wide range of risotti – with squash, asparagus, hops and quail, flanked by *bigoli* in duck sauce. Nevertheless the best known of local specialities is *baccalà alla vicentina* (salt cod stewed with milk and onions) and grilled polenta, followed closely by *bovoloni, bovoletti* or *bogoni* (snails in butter, garlic, and parsley), *piccioni torresani allo spiedo* (pigeon on the spit) and *cappone alla canavera* (capon cooked inside an ox bladder). Among the better local sweets are *amaretti* (almond macaroons).

Many **Veronese** specialities are common also in other cities of the Veneto. Distinctive dishes are *zuppa scaligera,* a rich version of the more popular *sopa coada* (see Treviso, below), made with chicken and white wine as well as pigeon. Another Veronese speciality is gnocchi in butter or tomato sauce, or topped with the famous *pastizzada de caval* (horse meat stewed with aromatic herbs). Other distinctive dishes are *paparele (pappardelle)* with pea sauce, *bigoli con sardine,* fish from Lake Garda, including a rare variety of carp, and *bolliti misti* with *pearà* (a sauce of breadcrumbs, butter, ox marrow, parmesan cheese, salt and pepper). Among Veronese sweets, the most delectable are certainly the great fluffy cake *pandoro* and the less well-known variations of this recipe, the Christmas *natalino* and Easter *brasadella.*

The leading role in **Trevisan** cuisine is played by *radicchio trevigiano* (the long, narrow heads of Treviso's red-leaved chicory), which is eaten in salads, grilled, fried or in risottto. Other specialities are *risotto al tajo* (made with shrimp and eel), *risotto alla sbiraglia* (with chicken and chicken stock), *zuppa di trippe* (tripe soup), *oca arrosto col sedano* (roast goose with celery), *anguille e gamberi di San Polo* (a stew of shrimp and eel); *sopa coada* (boned pigeon baked with bread) and the sausage called *salsiccia trevisana* or *luganega,* cooked whole with rice in consommé *(risi e luganega)* or grilled. Trevisans claim to have invented the rich dessert *tiramisù,* a combination of creamy mascarpone cheese, sponge fingers, eggs, brandy, coffee and cocoa.

In the hills and woodlands to the north, around **Belluno, Feltre** and **Asolo,** local dishes present a singular combination of Alpine and Venetian influences. Characteristic pastas include *gnocchi alla cadorina, casunzei* (ravioli with pumpkin or spinach, ham and cinnamon), *lasagne da formel* (dressed with a sauce of nuts, raisins, dried figs and poppy seeds), and *riso alla lamonese* (with lamon beans); favourite entrées feature game stewed in a rich sauce *(salmì).*

Trentino-Alto Adige

The regional specialities of the Trentino-Alto Adige combine the rustic character of Alpine cuisine with the naturalness and digestibility of Italian cooking, taking the best from both traditions.

The cuisine of **Trent** is a medley of Venetian, Lombard, and Tyrolean influences. The basic ingredients here are polenta and cheese. The most typical Trentine polenta is made from potatoes; dressed with cream, it is found in traditional dishes such as *smacafam* (baked with lard and sausage). Many dishes are hand-me-downs from the Austro-Hungarian tradition; examples include *canederli,* the Trentine version of *Knödel* (large stuffed dumplings), *gulasch,* smoked meat with sauerkraut, and *zelten alla trentina* (bread dough baked with eggs and dried fruit). Other distinctive dishes are *strangolapreti* (vegetable gnocchi), *anguilla alla trentina* (eel seasoned with cinnamon) and *pollo ripieno alla trentina* (chicken boiled and stuffed with walnuts, pine nuts,

An Alpine Picnic

A basic ingredient of any picnic is bread – which people in Italy's Eastern Alps make *con i fiocchi* ('with ribbons and bows'), as the saying goes. Wheat (*frumento*), rye (*segale*), barley (*orzo*) and oats (*avena*) have been used in local recipes for ages, partly because they were among the few products of the field that could easily be cultivated on the steep slopes of the Alps. The region's breads are high in nutritional value because they are made with healthy wholegrain flours and without preservatives.

In this neck of the woods bread is often eaten with *speck,* a delicacy born of the necessity to preserve freshly slaughtered pork. Farmers realised that by hanging a ham in the chimney of their hearths and then exposing it to the cool, dry air of the forests, they could preserve it for a long time. Over the years both the conservation and the flavour of the meat were improved by salting it before smoking it; and as knowledge of herbs and spices increased, the curing mixture was enriched with new aromas and the smoking was refined by the addition of juniper branches.

And of course, one can't talk about Alpine cuisine without mentioning cheese. The Trentino-Alto Adige, with its abundant valleys, rivers, streams and lakes, has hundreds of microclimates that, together with the particular composition of the soil, influence both the variety and flavourof the alpine flora, giving the grass of the pastures (during the summer grazing period) and the hay of the valley floors (during the winter) particular characteristics that make their way into the region's cheeses, with flavours and aromas typical of each 'form'. In bygone days, before the advent of cheese-making on an 'industrial' scale, every malga had its own cheese, its special style deriving from the characteristics of the feed and the skill of the farmer – a secret skill that was often handed down from father to son. Now there are cheese 'factories' that process the milk of an entire valley. This has led to the disappearance of many small producers. If you look hard enough, however, you can still find great local cheeses. Try *spressa,* a low-fat, flavourful cheese typical of the Val Rendena; or the famous *puzzone di Moena,* from the Val di Fassa, whose curious name ('stinker') doesn't do justice to its flavour and aroma. On the other side of the Passo Rolle, at Primiero, is the homeland of fresh *tosella,* eaten with polenta accompanied by the wild yellow mushrooms known as *finferli.*

Finally, the forests of the Trentino-Alto Adige produce red and black whortleberries, wild strawberries, raspberries, gooseberries, redcurrants and rose hips – all important elements of the very special tradition of this area. These fruits initially provided subsistence-level

> food and drink, their use improving over time when it was noticed that they could be preserved longer in sweets. A slice of cheese cake or buckwheat cake with wild fruit topping is a very satisfying experience indeed – almost a meal in itself.

raisins, and marrow). Sweets include *fiadoni alla trentina* (pastries stuffed with a mixture of almonds, honey, and rum).

In Bolzano, Bressanone and the Dolomites a marked Germanic bias prevails. Distinctive dishes include *Hirnprofesen* (calves' brains on toast), *Knödel* (or *canederli*), *Gertensuppe* (barley soup with chopped *speck* – smoked ham), *Frittatensuppe* (soup with strips of omelette), *Milzschittensuppe* (soup accompanied by toast with spleen spread), *Rindgulasch* (beef goulash), *Schmorbraten* (stew), *Gröstl* (boiled diced beef and boiled potatoes, sautéed), various sausages (*Würstel*) and *speck*. The incomparable sweets of the region include strudel, *Zelten* (Christmas cake of rye bread dough with figs, dates, raisins, pine nuts and walnuts), and *Kastanientorte* (chestnut cake served with cream).

Wines

Most Italian wines take their names from the geographical area in which they are produced, the blend of grapes of which they are made, and the estate on which the grapes were grown. The best come in numbered bottles and are marked **DOC** (*di origine controllata*), which freely translated into English means 'no fooling around'. The vinification of DOC wines is carefully monitored from beginning to end by an independent authority, and only the best barrels from vintners located in a particular geographic area are admitted to this exclusive club (the others are packaged and sold under the generic name, *vino da tavola*, 'table wine').

Wine-making is still very much an art in Italy, and each region has its own characteristic varieties, of which inhabitants are duly proud. To avoid the horrible *faux-pas* of ordering Chianti with your fish (this would probably get you thrown out of Harry's Bar – it cost a Spectre agent his life in a James Bond novel), you might want to take a brief look at the breakdown of regional wines offered below.

Friuli-Venezia Giulia

The best wines of the **Trieste** area include the three DOC wines that carry the name of the Carso, the plateau behind the city: they are the white *Malvasia del Carso* and the reds, *Rosso del Carso* and *Terrano del Carso*. The DOC wines of **Udine** come from three distinct growing districts, indicated on the labels respectively as *Grave del Friuli*, *Aquileia e Latisana,* and *Colli Orientali*

A Gourmet Primer

Here, for quick reference, is a translation of some common menu listings.

antipasti (hors d'œuvre): *prosciutto e melone,* ham (raw) and melon; *carciofi o finocchio in pinzimonio,* raw artichokes or fennel with an olive-oil dip; *antipasto misto,* mixed cold hors d'œuvre; *antipasto di mare,* seafood hors d'œuvre; *crostini,* toast with fresh liver or vegetable pâté.

primi piatti (first course): *brodo,* clear soup; *gnocchi,* a nugget-like pasta made from potato, flour and eggs; *ravioli,* egg pasta, filled with spinach and ricotta cheese or minced veal; *spaghetti al pomodoro,* spaghetti with tomato sauce; *spaghetti al sugo* or *al ragù,* spaghetti with meat sauce; *spaghetti alle vongole,* spaghetti with clams; *tortellini,* small coils of pasta filled with a rich meat stuffing; *zuppa,* thick soup.

secondi piatti (entrées): *agnello,* lamb; *coniglio,* rabbit; *fagiano,* pheasant; *lepre,* hare; *maiale,* pork; *manzo,* beef; *piccione,* pigeon; *pollo,* chicken; *vitello,* veal; *acciughe,* anchovies; *calamari,* squid; *cozze,* mussels; *dentice,* dentex; *gamberi,* prawns; *orata,* bream; *sarde,* sardines; *tonno,* tuna; *trota,* trout; *arrosto,* roast; *bollito,* boiled; *fritto,* fried; *alla griglia,* grilled.

contorni (vegetables): *asparagi,* asparagus; *fagioli,* beans; *funghi,* mushrooms; *insalata,* salad; *melanzane,* aubergines; *patate,* potatoes; *peperoni,* red peppers; *pomodori,* tomatoes; *spinaci,* spinach; *zucchine,* courgettes.

dolci (sweets): *crostata,* fruit flan; *pasta,* pastry; *torta,* tart; *zabaione,* whipped eggs with Marsala wine.

frutta (fruit): *albicocche,* apricots; *anguria* or *cocomero,* water melon; *arance,* oranges; *ciliege,* cherries; *fichi,* figs; *fragole,* strawberries; *fragoline di bosco,* wild strawberries; *mele,* apples; *melone,* melon; *pere,* pears; *pesche,* peaches; *uva,* grapes; *macedonia di frutta,* fruit salad; *con panna,* with cream; *con limone,* with lemon.

del Friuli. Common to these denominations are *Cabernet* and *Merlot* reds, a pleasant rosé (*rosato*), and the *Pinot Bianco, Pinot Grigio, Chardonnay, Verduzzo Friulano, Sauvignon, Traminer Aromatico,* and *Tocai Friulano* whites. The Grave del Friuli area also produces the *Cabernet Franc, Cabernet Sauvignon, Pinot Nero, Refosco dal peduncolo rosso* reds, and the white *Riesling Renano;* the Aquileia e Latisana area makes the *Cabernet Franc, Cabernet Sauvignon, Refosco di Aquileia* and *Refosco dal peduncolo rosso di*

Latisana reds; and the Colli Orientali del Friuli produces the *Riesling Renano, Ribolla gialla, Picolit, Ramandolo, Tocai Friulano, Sauvignon* and *Malvasia Istriana* whites and the *Refosco, Schioppettino* and *Pinot Nero* reds.

The Veneto

The shores of Lake *Garda,* the *Soave* district, the *Valpolicella* region and the *Valdadige* produce **Veronese** DOC wines. From Garda come the red *Bardolino, Bardolino Chiaretto* and *Bardolino Classico,* and the *Bianco di Custoza* and *Lugana* whites. Soave makes an excellent dry white wine, while the Valpolicella region makes *Valpolicella* and *Valpantena* reds. Bardolino, Soave and Valpolicella *classico* are made from grapes grown in the oldest vineyards. The denomination *Valdadige* applies to just a small part of Verona province; for details see the Trentino-Alto Adige, below.

The DOC wines of **Vicenza** come from *Gambellara,* from the *Colli Bèrici* and from the *Breganzese.* Gambellara is always white, whereas the Colli Bèrici wines include *Cabernet, Merlot,* and *Tocai Rosso* reds as well as *Garganega, Pinot Bianco, Sauvignon* and *Tocai Bianco* whites. The Breganzese area produces *Breganze Bianco* and *Breganze Rosso, Cabernet* and *Pinot Nero* reds as well as *Pinot Bianco, Pinot Grigio* and *Vespaiolo* whites.

Three different regional denominations precede the names of **Trevisan** DOC wines: *Conegliano Valdobbiadene, Montello e Colli Asolani* and *Piave.* The first is limited to *Prosecco* white, which can also be called *Prosecco di Valdobbiadene* and *Prosecco di Conegliano;* the long name *Conegliano Valdobbiadene Prosecco Superiore di Cartizze* is reserved for the product of a very small area in the commune of Valdobbiadene. *Montello e Colli Asolani* makes *Cabernet* and *Merlot* reds as well as *Prosecco* white. The Piave growing area, shared with the province of Venice, produces *Cabernet, Merlot, Pinot Nero* and *Raboso* reds, in addition to *Pinot Bianco, Pinot Grigio, Tocai* and *Verduzzo* whites.

The Euganean Hills are where Paduan wines are made. The best are the *Colli Euganei Bianco* and *Rosso,* the *Cabernet* and *Merlot* reds and the *Moscato, Pinot Bianco* and *Tocai Italico* whites.

Trentino-Alto Adige

The indication *Trentino* precedes the name in almost all the DOC wines from the vineyards in this province; in addition to Trentino Bianco and Trentino Rosso there are the reds, *Cabernet, Cabernet Franc, Cabernet Sauvignon, Lagrein Rubino* (there is also a *Lagrein Rosato*), *Marzemino, Merlot, Pinot Nero;* the whites *Chardonnay* (also *spumante*), *Müller-Thurgau, Nosiola, Pinot Bianco* (also *spumante*), *Pinot Grigio* (also *spumante*), *Riesling Italico,Riesling Renano* and *Traminer Aromatico;* and finally, three dessert wines, *Moscato Giallo* (also *liquoroso*), *Moscato Rosa* (also *liquoroso*) and *Vin Santo.* The other wines of the province are *Casteller* red, *Sorni* white and red and *Teroldego Rotaliano* (rosé and red). The denomination *Valdadige* (white, red, rosé, Pinot Grigio and Schiava) refers to a territory that also includes parts of the provinces of Bolzano and Verona.

Because the Alto Adige is bilingual, the wine labels are also in Italian and German. The DOC wines, whose area of production embraces the entire province of Bolzano-Alto Adige, carry the designation Alto Adige after the name (in German, the term *Südtiroler* precedes the name) These wines are the reds: *Cabernet, Lagrein Scuro* (*Lagrein Dunkel*), *Lagrein Rosato* (*Kretzer*), *Malvasia* (*Malvasier*), *Merlot, Pinot Nero* (*Blauburgundeer,* also *spumante* made as a white), *Schiava* (*Vernatsch*); and the whites: *Chardonnay, Pinot Bianco* (*Weissburgunder,* also *spumante*), *Pinot Grigio* (*Rulander,* also *spumante*), *Riesling Italico* (*Welschriesling*), *Riesling Renaro* (*Rheinriesling*), *Riesling Sylvaner* (*Müller-Thurgau*), *Sauvignon, Sylvaner* and *Traminer Aromatico* (*Gewürztraminer*). To these must be added *Moscato Giallo* (*Goldenmuskateller*), *Moscato Rosa* (*Rosenmuskateller*) and *Spumante dell'Alto Adige* (*Südtiroler Sekt*). The Müller-Thurgau, Pinot Grigio, Sylvaner, Traminer Aromatico and Veltliner whites produced in the Valle dell'Isarco bear the denomination *Valle Isarco* (or *Bressanone,* in German *Eisacktaler*). From hills around Bolzano come the two reds *Colli di Bolzano* (*Bozner Leiten*) and *Santa Maddalena*. The red *Lago di Caldaro* (*Kalterersee*) comes from the vineyards on the lake of the same name. *Terlano* (*Terlaner*) is a white wine produced east of Bolzano. The denomination *Valdadige* or *Etschtaler,* finally, denotes that territory which extends also into the provinces of Trent and Verona.

When ordering, remember that many DOC wines come in versions labelled *spumante, liquoroso, recioto* and *amarone*. Spumante is the Italian equivalent of champagne and uses some of the same methods to obtain its foamy (*spumante*) effervescence. It is much bubblier than sparkling whites such as *Prosecco,* which is popular both before meals and as a light dinner wine. *Liquoroso* means 'liqueur-like' and usually refers to dessert wines. The term *recioto* is applied to wines made from grapes that have been dried like raisins; *amarone* is the dry, mellow version of *recioto*.

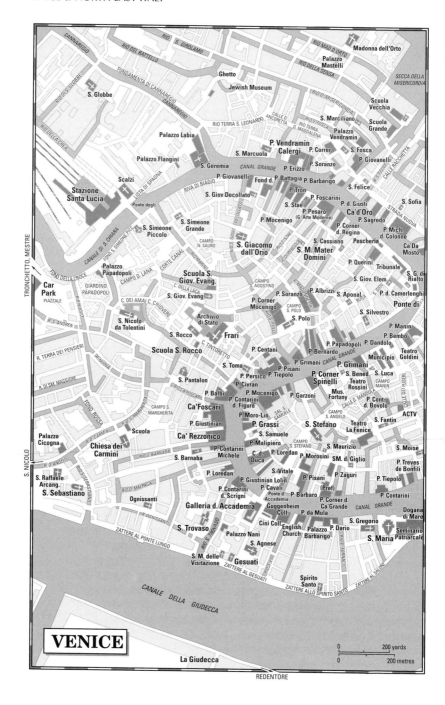

VENICE

La Giudecca

REDENTORE

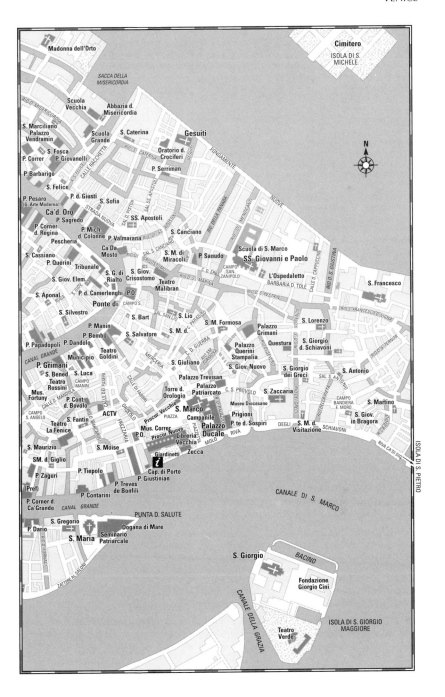

5. VENICE

The 19th-century English essayist and critic John Ruskin once wrote: 'Well might it seem that such a city had owed its existence rather to the rod of the enchanter, than the fear of the fugitive; that the water which encircled her had been chosen for the mirror of her state, rather than the shelter of her nakedness; and that all which in nature was wild or merciless – time and Decay, as well as the waves and tempests, had been won to adorn her instead of to destroy, and might still spare, for ages to come, that beauty which seemed to have fixed for its throne the sands of the hour-glass as well as those of the sea' (*The Stones of Venice*, 1851–53). More than a century later another writer, Maurice Rowdon, voiced the same implicit lament: 'Venice was created by logic as little as it excited logic in its admirers; if anything it made them impatient with everything they had known before; they began to think it absurd to build cities on land' (*The Fall of Venice*, 1970). And yet there is a very clear logic underlying the creation of this city on stilts, surrounded and crisscrossed by the rather unclear and sometimes unruly waters of its lagoon. It is the logic of survival.

Venice, in Italian *Venezia*, was founded in the wetlands between the mouths of the Piave and the Brenta rivers by fugitives from the barbarian invasions inland, around AD450, and its population grew as a result of the Lombard invasion of 568–69. In the 9th century the centre was the *Civitas Rivoalti* – the modern zone of the Rialto, San Marco and Castello. The city was first governed by *tribuni* named by the Byzantine exarch of Ravenna, and subsequently by a duke (*doge* in Venetian) who, by playing the interests of the Eastern Empire against those of the Germanic Holy Roman Empire to the north, attained first a relative independence, and then complete sovereignty, in the 11th century. As the power of its maritime republic increased, the city grew in size, gradually extending over more than 100 islands. Later, after winning a war with Genoa for the control of the Eastern Mediterranean, it extended its dominions on the mainland.

The Turkish expansion and the development of the European powers, however, caused a gradual waning of its political and economic importance – an effect that was compounded by the discovery of the New World and the establishment of alternative trade routes. Conquered by Napoleon in 1797 and annexed to Austria, it was joined to Italy in 1866.

Today Venice is threatened by another kind of peril: the degradation caused by the gradual sinking of the lagoon floor, which, together with the continuous flight of its population and the pollution caused by the industries of the mainland (the now derelict port of Marghera is a sore exception to the eco-friendly model of industrial development mentioned in the introduction) is posing serious problems of conservation. What the future holds is anyone's guess.

Venice is divided in two by the Grand Canal and irregularly linked by quays (called *fondamenta*), narrow streets (*calli* or *salizzade*) and small squares (*campi*), laid out parallel to the canals or intersecting one another in a closely woven network. It is unique in Europe in that its historic centre practically coincides with the entire extension of the city. The principal neighbourhoods, or *sestieri,* are San Marco, Dorsoduro, Santa Croce, San Polo, Canareggio and Castello. These, together with the 'near' islands of San Giorgio and the Giudecca, and the 'distant' islands of Murano, Burano and Torcello, provide the general framework of the visits described below.

The Grand Canal

The Grand Canal is the main thoroughfare of Venice and possibly its most famous sight. In terms of beauty and sheer dramatic impact, it rivals the boulevards of the great European capitals, most of which, it should be remembered, were constructed much later and with a clear master-plan in mind. What distinguishes the Grand Canal – besides, of course, the fact that it is paved with water – is that its appearance was constructed over half a millennium, slowly, spontaneously, as the consequence of that blessing and bane of all mercantile cultures, competition. Strictly speaking, the Grand Canal has more in common with midtown Manhattan than with the Champs-Élysées – for it was the Venetian spirit of individualism which led each patrician family to build a mansion larger and more magnificent than its neighbour, or to lavish more money on the parish church.

It is important to remember that at the time these buildings were built, direct contact was the only means of commercial communication. Foreign clients would be entertained and business would be conducted in the sumptuous rooms behind these grand façades, and on Sunday clients would be ushered off to Mass in churches that were as magnificent as human imagination allowed. Gradually, form took precedence over orthodox religious content in the art and architecture of Venice, as in those of the other Italian city-states, setting European civilisation on the road that would eventually lead to the secular culture of the modern age.

The Grand Canal weaves through the city from northwest to southeast, forming a reversed 'S' some 4km long, 6m deep and 40–130m wide. The best way to see its extraordinary architectural parade – indeed, the only way to see it in its entirety – is from the water. Whether you choose a gondola, water taxi or *vaporetto* (the slow No. 1 from Piazzale Roma or the train station is ideal), make sure you have a good view to both sides.

Ponte Scalzi to Ponte di Rialto

From **Santa Lucia Station**, built in 1954 to replace the city's original 19th-century terminal, the boat enters the Grand Canal leaving on the right the church of San Simeone Piccolo, with its tall green dome and Corinthian portico. The church of the **Scalzi**, adjoining the station quay, is a Baroque edifice designed by Baldassarre Longhena for a Carmelite community in the mid-17th century. The modern bridge here is one of the three that span the Grand Canal.

The first building of note that comes into sight is the 18th-century church of **San Geremia**, on the left bank opposite the Riva di Biasio landing stage. Its façade faces the Canale di Cannaregio, the largest in the city after the Grand Canal. An inscription on the wall announces that the church contains the body of St Lucy, martyred in Syracuse in AD304. Her body was stolen from Constantinople in 1204, when the Venetians sacked the imperial capital during the Fourth Crusade. On the right bank, opposite the San Marcuola landing stage, is one of the better-known buildings of the Veneto-Byzantine type, the **Fondaco dei Turchi**, unfortunately somewhat carelessly restored in 1858–69. A Turkish warehouse from 1621 to 1838 and now the Natural History Museum, it is recognisable by the tall towers on either side of its colonnade. Among the several sarcophagi beneath its portico is one which once held the remains of Doge Marin Falier, beheaded for treason in 1355. Across the Rio del Megio is the plain crenellated façade of the 15th-century Granaries of the Republic, flanked by the Palazzo Belloni Battagia, a 17th-century palace by Baldassarre Longhena with an elaborate watergate and fine first-floor loggia. The magnificent house on the left bank here is the Palazzo Vendramin Calergi, begun by Mauro Codussi and completed by Pietro Lombardo and his assistants (1509). Now the winter home of Venice's *Casinò*, its Renaissance façade, with a delicately carved cornice and frieze, is faced with white Istrian limestone. The German composer Richard Wagner died here in 1883.

At the next landing are the church of **San Stae**, with a Baroque façade by Domenico Rossi (1709) and (left of the façade) the charming little Scuola dei Battiloro e Tiraoro, once the seat of the confraternity of goldsmiths. The next important building on this side of the canal is the exuberant **Ca' Pesaro**, a Baroque masterpiece begun by Baldassarre Longhena in 1628 and completed by Giacomo Gaspari in 1710. The palace houses the city's Galleria d'Arte Moderna and Museo Orientale. On the left bank, overlooking the broad Rio di Noale, is Palazzo Gussoni, a handsome 16th-century mansion attributed to the Veronese architect Michele Sanmicheli and once decorated with frescoes by Tintoretto. These were erased long ago by sun, wind and rain. **Ca' Corner della Regina**, a classical edifice by Domenico Rossi (1724) on the right bank, belonged to the family of Caterina Cornaro, Queen of Cyprus, who was born on this site in 1454. It now holds the archives of the Venice Biennale.

At the next landing stage is the superb **Ca' d'Oro**, possibly the most beautiful Gothic mansion in Venice. In the 15th century, when it was built, the

Impressions of Venice

Venice has left a lasting impression on innumerable travellers down through the centuries. Here are a few of their remarks.

'*Pria Veneziani, poi Christiani* '('A Venetian first, and then a Christian'), says an old proverb. Another saying goes: '*Venetia, Venetia, chi non te vede non te Pregia, / M chi t'ha* troppo veduto *te Dispreggia*', which the 17th-century traveller James Howel set in English as: 'Venice, Venice, None Thee unseen can prize / Who hath seen too *much will* Thee *despise.*'

Whatever else it was, Venice was a place of freedom for visitors from the Puritan North: 'It is so much the established fashion for every body to live their own way, that nothing is more ridiculous than censuring the actions of another,' wrote Lady Mary Wortley Montagu (Letter to Lady Pomfret, 6 Nov 1739). But it was not for everyone: 'Of all the towns in Italy, I am the least satisfied with Venice; Objects which are only singular without being pleasing, produce a momentary surprise which soon gives way to satiety and disgust. Old and in general ill built houses, ruined pictures, and stinking ditches dignified with the pompous denomination of Canals; a fine bridge, spoilt by two Rows of houses upon it, and a large square decorated with the worst Architecture I ever yet saw, such are the colours I should employ in my portrait of Venice; a portrait certainly true in general, tho' perhaps you should attribute the very great darkness of the shades to my being out of humour with the place.' (Edward Gibbon, Letter to Dorothea Gibbon, 22 Apr 1765.)

It was nevertheless endowed with a certain fascination: 'In the evening there generally is, on St Mark's Place, such a mixed multitude of Jews, Turks, and Christians; lawyers, knaves, and pickpockets; mountebanks, old women, and physicians; women of quality, with masks; strumpets barefaced; and, in short, such a jumble of senators, citizens, gondoliers, and people of every character and condition, that your ideas are broken, bruised, and dislocated in the crowd, in such a manner, that you can think, or reflect, on nothing; yet this being a state of mind which many people are fond of, the place never fails to be well attended, and, in fine weather, numbers pass a great part of the night there. When the piazza is illuminated, and the shops, in the adjacent streets, are lighted up, the whole has a brilliant effect; and ... it is the custom for the ladies, as well as the gentlemen, to frequent the cassinos and coffee-houses around.' (John Moore, *A View of Society and Manners in Italy,* 1781.)

The build-up can be somewhat excessive at times, and end in disillusionment: 'Expected to see a gay clean-looking town, with quays on either side of the canals, but was extremely disappointed; the houses are in the water, and look dirty and uncomfortable on the outside; the innumerable quantity of gondolas, too, that look like swimming coffins, added to the dismal scene, and, I confess, Venice on my arrival struck me with horror rather than pleasure.' (Elizabeth Lady Craven, *A Journey thrugh the Crimea to Constantinople,* 1789.) And yet ever seductive: 'Tis certain my beloved town of Venice ever recalls a series of eastern ideas and adventures. I cannot help thinking St. Mark's a mosque, and the neighbouring palace some vast seraglio, full of arabesque saloons, embroidred sofas, and voluptuous Circassians.' (William Beckford, *Dreams Waking Thoughts and Incidents,* 1783.)

There is something unreal about it: 'As a city, even when seen, it still appears rather a phantom than a fact.' (Lady Morgan, *Italy,* 1820.) And something contradictory: 'Dangerous and sweet-tongued Venice.' (Samuel Rogers, *Italy,* 1822–34.) If for no other reason, because it is unique: 'A city built in the air would be something still more wonderful; but any other must yield the palm to this for singularity and imposing effect.' (William Hazlitt, *Notes of a Journey through France and Italy,* 1826)..Which is not to say, attractive: 'A city for beavers.' (Ralph Waldo Emerson, *Journal,* June 1833.)

Perhaps, hallucinogenic: 'Nothing in the world that you have ever heard of Venice, is equal to the magnificent and stupendous reality. The wildest visions of the Arabian Nights are nothing to the piazza of St Mark, and the first impression of the inside of the church. The gorgeous and wonderful reality of Venice is beyond the fancy of the wildest dreamer. Opium couldn't build such a place, and enchantment couldn't shadow it forth in a vision.... It has never been rated high enough. It is a thing you would shed tears to see.' (Charles Dickens, Letter, 1844, in Forster, *Life of Dickens,* 1872–73.) And definitely disorienting: 'I have been between heaven and earth since our arrival at Venice. The heaven of it is ineffable. Never had I touched the skirts of so celestial a place. The beauty of the architecture, the silver trails of water up between all that gorgeous colour and carving, the enchanting silence, the moonlight, the music, the gondolas – I mix it all up together, and maintain that nothing is like it, nothing equal to it, not a second Venice in the world. Do you know when I came first I felt as if I could never go away. But now comes the earth side. Robert, after sharing the ecstasy, grows uncomfortable, and nervous, and unable to eat or sleep.... Alas for these mortal Venices – so exquisite and so bilious.' (Elizabeth Barrett Browning, Letter to Miss Mitford, 4 Jun 1851.) Or bewitching: 'Well might it seem that such a city had owed its existence rather to the rod of the enchanter, than the fear of the fugitive; that the water which encircled her had been chosen for the mirror of her state, rather than the shelter of her nakedness; and that all which in nature was wild or merciless – time and Decay, as well as the waves and tempests, had been won to adorn her instead of to destroy, and might still spare, for ages to come, that beauty which seemed to have fixed for its throne the sands of the hour-glass as well as those of the sea.' (John Ruskin, *The Stones of Venice*, 1851-3.)

An entertainment for the disillusioned: 'What a funny old city this Queen of the Adriatic is! Narrow streets, vast, gloomy marble palaces, black with the corroding damp of centuries and all partly submerged; no dry land visible anywhere, and no side-walks worth mentioning; if you want to go to church, to the theatre, or to a restaurant, you must call a gondola. It must be a paradise for cripples, for verily a man has no use for legs here.' (Mark Twain, *The Innocents Abroad*, 1869.) Or a numinous force for the enthusiast: 'It is a great pleasure to write the word; but I am not sure there is not a certain impudence in pretending to add anything to it. Venice has been painted and described many thousands of times, and of all the cities in the world it is the easiest to visit without going there.' (Henry James, 'Venice', 1882, in *Portraits of Places*, 1883.)

A city not of stone or cement, but of pure, unmitigated sensual pleasure: 'If we were asked what is the leading colour at Venice we should say pink, and yet, after all, we cannot remember that this elegant tint occurs very often. It is a faint, shimmering, airy, watery pink; the bright sealight seems to flush with it, and the pale whitish-green of lagoon and canal to drink it in. There is, indeed in Venice a great deal of very evident brickwork, which is never fresh or loud in colour, but always burnt out, as it were, always exquisitely mild. There are certain little mental pictures that rise before the sentimental tourist at the simple mention, written or spoken, of the places he has loved. When I hear, when I see, the magical name I have written above these pages, it is not of the great Square that I think, with its strange basilica, and its high arcades, nor of the wide mouth of the Grand Canal, with the stately steps and the well-poised dome of the Salute; it is not of the low lagoon, nor the sweet Piazzetta, nor the dark chambers of St Mark's. I simply see a narrow canal in the heart of the city – a patch of green water and a surface of pink wall. The gondola moves slowly; it gives a great, smooth swerve, passes under a bridge, and the gondolier's cry, carried over the quiet water, makes a kind of splash in the stillness. A girl is passing over the little bridge, which has an arch like a camel's back, with an old shawl on her head, which makes her look charming; you see her against the sky as you float beneath. The pink of the old wall seems to fill the whole place; it sinks even into the opaque water. Beneath the wall is a garden, out of which the long arm of a white June rose – the roses of Venice are splendid – has flung itself by way of spontaneous ornament. On the other side of this small water-way is a great shabby façade of Gothic windows and balconies

– balconies on which dirty clothes are hung and under which a cavernous-looking doorway opens from under a low flight of slimy water-steps. It is very hot and still, the canal has a queer smell, and the whole place is enchanting.' (Ibid.)

Almost as though it were a sort of illness: 'The charm of Venice grows on me strangely; at first I had no real personal impression: and then one rainy day, when the wind, with the sound of bells in it, blew up the Grand Canal, and everything was half blotted in a veil of rain, I suddenly felt all the melancholy charm – the charm of silence and beauty and decay. The strangest thing is to go at night, as we often do in our little boat, up the Grand Canal, & then turn in anywhere, and lose ourselves in the blackness and silence. The great palaces are so high that these little canals seem almost like subterranean rivers, save for the strip of sky and the vague stars above. Sometimes we come suddenly, round a corner, on a square with yellow lights & footsteps & music. Then we glide away into the darkness till at last we come out by the Grand Canal again.' (Logan Pearsall Smith, Letter to his mother, 15 Nov 1895, in John Russell, *Portrait of Logan Pearsall Smith,* 1950.)

Or a chimaera: 'It has become a phrase, almost as meaningless as Arcadia. And indeed it is difficult to think of Venice as being quite a real place, its streets of water as being exactly real streets, its gondolas as being no more than the equivalent of hansoms, its union of those elsewhere opposed sentiments of the sea, the canal, the island, walled and towered land, as being quite in the natural order of things. I had had my dreams of Venice, but nothing I had dreamed was quite as impossible as what I found... The Doge's palace looked exactly like beautifully painted canvas, as if it were stretched on frames, and ready to be shunted into the wings for a fresh "set" to come forward. Yes, it is difficult to believe in Venice, most of all when one is in Venice.' (Arthur Symons, *Cities,* 1903.) Almost too good to be true: 'I was surprised to find what pleasure it gave me to be in Venice again. It was like coming home, when sounds and smells which one had forgotten stole upon one's senses; and certainly there is no place like it in the world: everything there is better in reality than in memory. I first saw it on a romantic evening after sunset in 1900, and I left it on a sunshiny morning, and I shall not go there again.' (A.E. Housman, Letter to his sister, Mrs E.W. Symons, 23 Jun 1926.)

A place far from paradise: 'The whole of Venice ... was one vast explosion of cut-throat competition in luxury and swagger; that was why Ruskin had gone about it cursing and lamenting, and inventing strange theories to excuse himself for yielding to its charm.' (Desmond MacCarthy, *Experience,* 1935.) And yet able to leave a lasting impression on even the most prosaic: 'Wonderful city, streets full of water, please advise.' (Robert Benchley, Cable, attributed, c 1947.)

A place of which authors never tire of writing: 'A wholly materialist city is nothing but a dream incarnate. Venice is the world's unconscious.' (Mary McCarthy, *Venice Observed*, 1961.) 'Venice is like eating an entire box of chocolate liqueurs at one go.' (Truman Capote, *Observer*, 'Sayings of the Week', 26 Nov 1961.) 'Venice was created by logic as little as it excited logic in its admirers; if anything it made them impatient with everything they had known before; they began to think it absurd to build cities on land.' (Maurice Rowdon, *The Fall of Venice*, 1970.) 'Venice, like a drawing room in a gas station, is approached through a vast apron of infertile industrial flatlands, crisscrossed with black sewer troughs and stinking of oil, the gigantic sinks and stoves of refineries and factories, all intimidating the delicate dwarfed city beyond.... The lagoon with its luminous patches of oil slick, as if hopelessly retouched by Canaletto, has a yard-wide tidewrack of rubble, plastic bottles, broken toilet seats, raw sewage, and that bone white factory froth the wind beats into drifts of foam. The edges of the city have succumbed to industry's erosion, and what shows are the cracked back windows and derelict posterns of waterlogged villas, a few brittle Venetian steeples, and farther in, but low and almost visibly sinking, walls of spaghetti-colored stucco and red roofs over which flocks of soaring swallows are teaching pigeons to fly.' (Paul Theroux, *The Great Railway Bazaar*, 1975.)

carved details of the façade were gilt and much of the remaining surface was painted deep red or bright blue. The palace now houses the Galleria Giorgio Franchetti, with a fine collection of Venetian painting and sculpture. Three more important houses follow: the **Palazzo Michiel dalle Colonne**, rebuilt in the late 17th century, with a ground-floor colonnade and elegant loggias; Palazzo Mangilli-Valmarana, designed by Antonio Visentini for the English consul Joseph Smith (1682–1779), patron of Canaletto; and the Veneto-Byzantine Ca' da Mosto (birthplace of the explorer Alvise Da Mosto, 1432–88), one of the older houses on the Grand Canal and another fine example of the Veneto-Byzantine style.

On the right bank, on a projecting quay, is the **Pescheria**, a Gothic-revival edifice built in 1907 on the site of the 14th-century fish market. Here begin the Rialto markets, which include the arcaded Fabbriche Nuove, built in 1554–56 by the Florentine architect and sculptor Jacopo Sansovino, the Fabbriche Vecchie, built by Scarpagnino in 1522, and the Erberia, an open-air fruit and vegetable market. This is followed closely by the **Palazzo dei Camerlenghi**, an elegant Renaissance building of 1528 with two storeys of arcades, now leaning conspicuously to one side (like many Venetian buildings) due to the gradual subsidence of the piles on which it is built. On the left as the boat turns to approach the Ponte di Rialto is the **Fondaco dei Tedeschi**, once the most important of the trading centres established by the

Venetians for foreign merchants. In *The Merchant of Venice* Shakespeare alludes to the business relations between Venice and the various German states in a remark made by Shylock concerning a diamond purchased in Frankfurt; the Fondaco dei Tedeschi was where these Northern European traders were obliged to live and conduct their affairs. The building was reconstructed by Scarpagnino to plans by Girolamo Tedesco, in 1505–08, after a fire, and the exterior was adorned with frescoes by Giorgione and Titian (these paintings, too, have disappeared, but detached fragments are displayed in the Ca' d'Oro). It now houses the main post office.

The sudden appearance of the **Ponte di Rialto** invariably draws an expression of surprise and wonder from first-time visitors to Venice. What is without a doubt the most photographed bridge in the world was built in 1588–92 by Antonio da Ponte, whose design was chosen by the Venetian Senate over those of several more famous architects, including Michelangelo, Palladio and Sansovino. Its single arch, 28 metres across and 7.5 metres high, carries three parallel walkways divided by two rows of shops. The reliefs of St Mark and St Theodore are by Tiziano Aspetti; the Annunciation on the downstream side is by Agostino Rubini.

Ponte di Rialto to Ponte dell'Accademia

Near the Rialto landing stage the Renaissance Palazzo Dolfin Manin, designed by Jacopo Sansovino (1536–75), is now the Banca d'Italia. During office hours you can see its beautiful atrium and courtyard. **Palazzo Loredan** and **Ca' Farsetti**, both Veneto-Byzantine buildings of the 12th and 13th centuries, together constitute the town hall. They have nearly identical loggias and arcades. Palazzo Loredan is the more ornate of the two, with statues beneath Gothic canopies and the arms of the famous Corner family. Elena Corner Piscopia (1646–84), who lived here, was the first woman to receive a university degree (in philosophy, from Padua University). The Renaissance **Palazzo Grimani**, on the left bank adjoining the Rio di San Luca, was designed by Sanmicheli shortly before his death in 1559 and built by Giangiacomo dei Grigi. Behind its stately three-storey Renaissance façade, with broad arches on pilaster strips and columns, is the modern Court of Appeal.

On the right bank here are Palazzo Papadopoli, a sumptuous 16th-century house with two broad loggias; Palazzo Bernardo, a refined 15th-century Gothic palace with delicate tracery on its front; and Palazzo Grimani-Marcello, an early 16th-century building in the Renaissance style called Lombardesque, after the prominent sculptor and architect Pietro Lombardo and his family, who worked extensively in and around Venice. On the opposite bank is **Palazzo Corner Spinelli**, another fine Renaissance building designed by Mauro Codussi (1490–1510), with a rusticated ground floor and large mullioned windows above. Across the Grand Canal from the Sant'Angelo landing stage are Palazzo Pisani-Moretta, an early 15th-century Gothic palace with two fine loggias; Palazzo Giustinian-Persico, a 16th-

Grand Canal in a gondola

century Renaissance building; and, adjoining the San Tomà stop, Palazzo Marcello dei Leoni, named after the two Romanesque lions beside the door. The four Palazzi Mocenigo, on the left bank, appear as one building with a long, symmetrical façade. Here Byron wrote the beginning of *Don Juan* and entertained Irish poet Thomas Moore.

On the right bank, as the canal swings sharply to the left, are Palazzo Balbi, a large building of classical aspect attributed to Alessandro Vittoria, and the late Gothic **Ca' Foscari** (1452), commissioned by Doge Francesco Foscari, displaying handsome columns, fine tracery and a frieze of putti bearing the Foscari arms. It is now part of the university. There follow the Palazzi Giustinian, elegant Gothic buildings of the late 15th century where Wagner composed the second act of his opera, *Tristan and Isolde* (1858–59); and the magnificent Baroque **Ca' Rezzonico**, designed by Longhena (1649) and completed by Massari (c 1750), now home to the city's collection of 18th-century art. On the left bank, the large, white **Palazzo Grassi** was begun in 1748 by Giorgio Massari. It is now a venue for exhibitions. The *campo* and landing stage here receive their names from San Samuele, an 11th-century church rebuilt in 1685.

Further on, on the right bank, rises the 15th-century Palazzo Loredan dell'Ambasciatore, a late Gothic building with shield-bearing youths in niches on the façade. Just beyond the Rio San Trovaso stands Palazzo Contarini degli Scrigni, made up of two buildings – one late Gothic, the other designed by Vincenzo Scamozzi in 1609. On the left bank is Palazzo Giustinian Lolin, a Baroque palace by Baldassarre Longhena (c 1630) with two levels of tall loggias. The Galleria dell'Accademia, in the former convent of Santa Maria della Carità, comes into sight on the right bank.

Ponte dell'Accademia to San Marco

You are now approaching the last of the canal's three bridges, the wooden **Ponte dell'Accademia**, a 1986 replica of a 1930s reconstruction, in wood, of a 19th-century iron bridge. On the left bank amid gardens, just beyond the bridge, is Palazzo Cavalli Franchetti, a 15th-century palace renovated and enlarged in the late 19th century. Across the narrow Rio dell'Orso are the two Palazzi Barbaro, of which the one on the left is 15th-century Gothic and the other from the 17th century. The older one was bought in the 19th century by the Curtis family of Boston, whose guests included writers Robert Browning and Henry James (who wrote *The Aspern Papers* during his stay and described the palace in *The Wings of the Dove*), and painters John Singer Sargent, James Whistler and Claude Monet. On the right bank is Palazzo Contarini Dal Zaffo, a fine example of the Lombardesque architectural style; and on the narrow Campo San Vio, Palazzo Da Mula, a late Gothic building of the 15th century with three orders of quatrefoil loggias. Past the latter, again on the right, is the **Palazzo Venier dei Leoni**, begun in 1749 but abandoned after just one storey had been built (there is a tale that the powerful Corner family, fearing that their palace across the Grand Canal would be overshadowed by what promised to be a more magnificent building, drove the owners to bankruptcy). Here Peggy Guggenheim lived from 1949 until her death in 1979; now owned by the Solomon R. Guggenheim Foundation, which also administers the Guggenheim Museum in New York, the building displays her collection of modern art. Also on this side is the leaning Palazzo Dario, built in 1487 (possibly to a design by Pietro Lombardo) and recognisable by its multicoloured marble façade and its many chimneys.

Pre-eminent on the left bank of the canal is **Palazzo Corner della Ca' Grande**, a magnificent building by Jacopo Sansovino (c 1545), with three-storey High Renaissance façade, now the Prefecture. Beyond the landing stage of Santa Maria del Giglio, squeezed tightly by its neighbours, is the 15th-century Palazzo Contarini-Fasan, with just three windows on the piano nobile and two on the floor above; here legend places the home of Desdemona, heroine of the Shakespeare's *Othello*. On the right bank, before the canal broadens into the expanse facing San Marco, is Longhena's magnificent basilica of **Santa Maria della Salute**.

As the boat makes its final crossing of the Grand Canal before stopping at San Marco, you pass (left) the classical façade of the 17th-century Palazzo Treves de' Bonfili; and another Ca' Giustinian, a late Gothic building (1474) with three orders of windows and loggias. It is occupied by the offices of the tourist bureau and the Venice Biennale. The right bank ends at the **Dogana da Mar**, or customs house, a Doric edifice by Giuseppe Benoni (1676–82) dramatically marking the entrance to the San Marco basin and terminating – appropriately – in a golden globe and a revolving weathervane of Fortune.

San Marco

Our first Venetian walk takes us through the heart of 'downtown' Venice. It begins with a visit to the great public buildings around Piazza San Marco, then loops around to the west and north, touching upon the churches of Santa Maria del Giglio and Santo Stefano, the fascinating house-museum of the Art Nouveau painter and designer Mariano Fortuny and the curious spiral Scala del Bovolo, to the foot of the Rialto Bridge. From here you return to San Marco along the medieval high street known as the Mercerie, past the churches of San Salvador and San Zulian. There is a lot to see, and if you decide to tour the interior of the Palazzo Ducale (optional), you'll be on your feet for almost three hours. The walk actually makes a very pleasant morning, especially if you break for coffee, pastry or ice-cream at one of the spots suggested below.

Venice gravitates around the incomparable scenario of **Piazza San Marco**, for more than a thousand years the emblem of the city and the centre of its public life. The product of a long process of adaptation to the functional and symbolic needs of the Venetian Republic, today it appears as an immense open space flanked by porticoed buildings developing around St Mark's

Venice and the Poets

Venice has left a lasting impression on innumerable travellers down through the centuries. Here are a few of their more poetic remarks.

Once did she hold the gorgeous East in fee;
And was the safeguard of the West: the worth
Of Venice did not fall below her birth,
Venice, the eldest Child of Liberty.
She was a maiden City, bright and free;
No guile seduced, no force could violate;
And, when she took unto herself a mate,
She must espouse the everlasting Sea.
And what if she had seen those glories fade,
Those titles vanish, and that strength decay;
Yet shall some tribute of regret be paid
When her long life hath reach'd its final day:
Men are we, and must grieve when even the Shade
Of that which once was great is pass'd away.
William Wordsworth, *On the Extinction of the Venetian Republic*, 1802

Venice ... is my head, or rather my *heart*-quarters.
Lord Byron, Letter to Thomas Moore, 11 Apr 1817

She looks a sea Cybele, fresh from ocean,
Rising with her tiara of proud towers
At airy distance, with majestic motion,
A ruler of the waters and their powers:
And such she was ...

States fall, arts fade – but Nature doth not die,
Nor yet forget how Venice once was dear,
The pleasant place of all festivity,
The revel of the earth, the masque of Italy!
Lord Byron, *Childe Harold''s Pilgrimage,* Canto the Fourth, 1816

Underneath day's azure eyes
Ocean's nursling, Venice lies
A peopled labyrinth of walls,
Amphitrite's destined halls,
Which her hoary sire now paves
With his blue and beaming waves ...
Sun-girt city, though hast been
ocean's child, and then his queen

Now is come a darker day
And thou soon must be his prey,
If the power that raised thee here
Hallow so thy watery bier.

...

Those who alone thy towers behold
Quivering through aerial gold,
As I now behold them here,
Would imagine not they were
Sepulchres, where human forms,
Like pollution-nourished worms
To the corpse of greatness cling,
Murdered, and now mouldering.
Percy Bysshe Shelley, *Lines Written among the Euganian Hills,*
Oct 1818

Mourn not for Venice; though her fall
Be awful, as if Ocean's wave
Swept o'er her, she deserves it all,
And Justice triumphs o'er her grave.
Thus perish ev'ry King and State,
That run the guildy race she ran,
Strong but in ill, and only great
By outrage against God and man!
Thomas Moore, *Rhymes of the Road,* 1819

Basilica with its tall, free-standing campanile. At all hours one of the world's more spectacular squares (Napoleon called it the finest drawing room in Europe), Piazza San Marco is most beautiful in the subdued light of early morning and late evening when the mosaics of the church come alive and the buildings take on a warm, golden glow. This is also the best time to avoid the crowds, which in high season can make serious sightseeing impossible.

Basilica of San Marco

The focal point of the square and the fulcrum of religious life in the city is the **Basilica of San Marco**, built in the 9th century to enshrine the relics of the Evangelist Mark, stolen from Alexandria, Egypt, in 828. Originally the chapel of the doges (and only since 1897 the cathedral of Venice), it has substantially maintained its early form and appearance despite alterations of the 11th, 14th and 16th centuries. Ruskin described it as 'a multitude of pillars and white domes, clustered into a long low pyramid of coloured light; a treasure heap'; his American contemporary Mark Twain called it 'a vast warty bug taking a meditative walk'. Whatever the case may be, San Marco is unique.

Its architecture is inspired by the church of the Twelve Apostles in Constantinople (no longer extant) and resembles the slightly later church of St Front at Perigueux in France. Built in the form of a Greek cross, with a large central dome over the crossing and smaller domes over the aisles and transepts, it is adorned with marbles and mosaics combining Romanesque, Byzantine and Gothic influences. The façade has two superimposed orders of five arches, of which the one in the middle is the widest, and five doorways separated by groups of columns with capitals of Middle Eastern inspiration (these date from the 12th and 13th centuries). The arches springing from the balcony have imaginative Gothic aedicules, pinnacles, tracery and sculpture, added in the 14th and 15th centuries; the tabernacles at the ends contain an *Annunciation* (on one side, the Archangel Gabriel, on the other, the Virgin Mary) attributed to the Florentine sculptor Jacopo della Quercia. On the balcony itself are copies of the four bronze horses brought in 1204 from Constantinople and now in the cathedral museum for safe-keeping (see below).

The **narthex**, or vestibule leading into the nave of the church, is an ecclesiastical adaptation of the Roman triumphal arch, using columns rather than statues and mosaics rather than reliefs to animate its front. The north door incorporates the *Arrival of the Body of St Mark in Venice* (1260–70), the oldest mosaic on the façade, containing the earliest known image of the church. The other lunette mosaics date from the 17th to the 19th centuries. The central doorway is carved with 13th-century reliefs which, read from the inside outwards, represent allegories of the months, personifications of virtues, and Christ and the prophets. Within, the narthex has a marble mosaic pavement of the 11th and 12th centuries, and its walls, vaults and domes are covered with extraordinary gold-ground mosaics, of Veneto-Byzantine workmanship. These tell Old Testament stories. Particularly interesting are the 13th-century *Stories of Genesis* in the dome above the bronze Porta di San Clemente (11th century, from Constantinople) and the 11th- and 12th-century figures of the Evangelists, in the bay in front of the main door. In the south flank of the church are the door of the baptistery, preceded by two finely carved freestanding columns, possibly of 5th- or 6th-century Syrian workmanship, and in a corner, two 4th-century porphyry reliefs known as the Tetrarchs, believed to represent Diocletian and three other Roman emperors. They may be Egyptian works of the 4th century.

The dazzling **interior** is an epitome of Byzantine decorative craftsmanship. The 12th-century floor has a richly decorative design of marble, porphyry and other stones, which is fully uncovered only in late July and early August: the ripple effect is due to the settling of the building over the centuries. Each arm of the cross has three aisles separated by colonnades, above which runs the *matroneum* – a gallery for women in the Greek Orthodox rite, here an ingenious device for masking the buttresses that support the five great domes. The sanctuary is raised above the crypt and set off from the rest of the church by an elaborate screen. An immense Byzantine chandelier hangs at the centre of the nave.

Visitors are directed through the church in a circuit that begins on the

Venetian Painting

Of all the arts of Venice, the art of painting sparkles as the crown jewel in this city illuminated by the subtle shimmer of reflected light and colour through moist and misty air. By the mid-15th century, the Bellini family (Jacopo and his sons, Gentile and Giovanni) were capturing the luminescence of the atmosphere of Venice in their beautifully rendered altarpieces. Giovanni's *Madonna and Child with Saints* in the church of San Zaccaria is a masterpiece of the brilliant colouration and subtle light effects that have come to characterise Venetian painting. The Bellini inspired a number of other painters, most notably Giorgione, whose enigmatic *Tempest* (now in the Accademia) continues to haunt the viewer with the mysterious atmosphere of an approaching storm; Titian, whose works in the church of the Frari are radiant examples of lustrous Venetian colourism; and Paolo Veronese, who mixed illusionistic perspectives with sacred and profane themes. Tintoretto left hundreds of paintings in the churches of Venice, working very quickly and impressionistically, sharply focusing his dramatic light effects. The era of the great Venetian painters closes in the age of the Grand Tour, when the *vedutisti,* such as Canaletto, painted lyrical images of the city which capture most poetically the unique atmosphere of Venice.

south side and ends on the north. Before moving too far away from the entrance, step out of the flow and look up. The upper walls and ceiling vaults are completely covered with mosaics. Most are by Byzantine and Venetian artists of the 12th and 13th centuries, though some – recognisable by their greater naturalism – were done over in the 16th and 17th centuries to designs by Titian, Tintoretto, Veronese and other Venetian painters. The mosaics celebrate the triumph of Christ and His Church. As is customary in Byzantine iconography, *Christ Pantokrator* ('The All-Powerful') is enthroned in the apse; he sits above four protectors of Venice, SS Nicholas, Peter, Mark and Hermagorus. The cupola above the high altar is devoted to the Prophets, who heralded the coming of Christ. The central cupola shows the *Ascension* over figures of virtues; the arch between this and the west dome, scenes from the *Passion of Christ.* The dome above the nave, where the congregation gathered, represents *Pentecost.* On the west wall, Christ seated between the Virgin and St Mark looks towards the high altar. Higher up are scenes from the *Apocalypse,* and the barrel vault over the narthex bears a representation of the *Last Judgement* (from a design by Tintoretto). Minor mosaics are arranged around these. The cupolas in the transepts represent *Action and Meditation in the Service of the Church:* the south cupola has figures of SS Nicholas, Clement, Blaise, Leonard and, in the squinches, Erasmus, Euphemia, Dorothy and Tecla, all of them martyrs; the north cupola has scenes from the *Life of St John the Evangelist* supported by the *Doctors of the Western Church* in the squinches. All around are scenes from the *Life of Christ*.

From the south aisle of the nave you enter the **baptistery** (1343–54), built by closing off a portion of the narthex. Here are a baptismal font designed by Jacopo Sansovino (1545) and the tombs of several doges – including that of Andrea Dandolo, the friend of Petrarch, who commissioned the 14th-century mosaics of the *Life of St John the Baptist* and the *Early Life of Christ*. The baptistery altar incorporates a granite slab on which Christ is said to have rested; it was brought from Tyre in the 13th century. Pius X, honoured by a statue above the altar, was Patriarch of Venice before becoming pope in 1903. Reached by a door at the west end of the baptistery is the burial chapel of Cardinal Giovanni Battista Zen (died 1501), with a bronze statue of the Madonna (called the *Madonna of the Shoe*) by Antonio Lombardo, a fine doorway to the narthex and late 13th-century vault mosaics, all of which merit a glance.

The **Treasury of San Marco**, one of the richer ensembles of religious art in Italy, is reached from the end of the south transept. Here you can see a very interesting display of liturgical objects by Eastern craftsmen (including, chalices, icons, reliquaries, prayer books and altar frontals mainly from the 12th and 13th centuries), many of which were brought back in 1204 from Constantinople. All reveal the medieval preoccupation with symbolism, and many show the distinctively Byzantine concern for richness, colour and texture. Highlights include an Islamic rock-crystal ewer carved with reliefs of two seated lions; a black glass bowl decorated in enamel with nude figures and classical busts, a work of the 11th-century Byzantine 'Renaissance'; and the so-called crown of Leo VI, decorated with enamel medallions of saints and an emperor, made in Constantinople between 886 and 912. When viewing these pieces it is important to remember that in Byzantium, as in China, there was no division between the major and minor arts.

The highest civil and religious ceremonies of the republic took place in the **sanctuary**, which is raised over the crypt and enclosed by a marble iconostasis crowned by a silver and bronze crucifix by Jacopo di Marco Bennato and statues of the Virgin, St Mark and the Apostles by Pier Paolo and Jacobello Dalle Masegne (1394). Two ambones constructed in the 14th century out of earlier materials adjoin the ends of the screen: from the one on the left the Epistle and the Gospel were read; from that on the right the newly elected doges showed themselves to the people. The high altar, which rises over the body of St Mark, is supported by four historiated (New Testament scenes) alabaster columns with 12th-century capitals and surmounted by a ciborium decorated with six 13th-century statues. Behind it is the famous **Pala d'Oro**, a remarkable gold altarpiece encrusted with enamels and gems, made by Byzantine and Venetian goldsmiths between the 10th and 14th centuries. Among the precious stones that adorn the work are emeralds, rubies, amethysts, sapphires, topaz and pearls. In the apse are an altar with six tall columns, a gilt tabernacle by Jacopo Sansovino, and statues by Lorenzo

Bregno; and the bronze door of the sacristy, Sansovino's last work (1546–69). Beneath the sanctuary are the beautiful crypt and the little 15th-century church of San Teodoro, with an *Adoration of the Child*, painted by Tiepolo in 1732.

The 12th-century Byzantine icon of the **Madonna Nicopeia** ('Bringer of Victory'), set in a magnificent enamel frame, gives its name to the chapel at the beginning of the north transept. This is the most venerated image in the cathedral, considered the Protectress of Venice. It bears the epithet *nicopeia* because it was carried into battle by the Byzantine emperors before being 'captured' in Constantinople in 1204. Placed in the basilica in 1234, it has never been removed, except in 1968 when a radical cleaning removed many of the additions that had been made over the centuries and revealed the glittering, enamel-like colours of the original, restoring life to a primitive image that exudes all the mysterious fascination of the Orient but is, at the same time, intensely human.

There are two chapels at the end of this transept. The larger is dedicated to St Isidore, who evangelised the island of Chios and was martyred there in 250. His remains were brought from Chios to Venice in 1125 but hidden until the mid-14th century, when Doge Andrea Dandolo had this chapel prepared to enshrine them. The mosaics on the walls and vault tell the story of the saint, whose statue is in a niche behind the altar. The smaller chapel is dedicated to the Madonna dei Mascoli, and once belonged to a confraternity of laymen (*mascoli* is 'males' in Venetian dialect). It has a *Virgin and Child between SS Mark and James* over the altar and mosaics of the *Life of the Virgin* on the vault. The latter were carried out under the direction of Michele Giambono using cartoons attributed to Andrea del Castagno, Jacopo Bellini and Andrea Mantegna – all pioneers of Renaissance art in Venice.

A winding staircase reached from the narthex leads up to the **Museo Marciano**, arranged on the upper floor of the cathedral. It includes illuminated manuscripts, fragments of mosaics from the basilica, paintings, tapestries and antique Persian silk-pile carpets. Here, too, are the splendid Hellenistic Greek bronze *Horses* brought to Venice from Constantinople in 1204 and beautifully restored in 1978–81 to reveal their original gilding. The horses were looted a second time by Napoleon, who swept them off (with, among other Italian artworks, 506 paintings) to Paris for display on the Arc du Carousel. Other exhibits include the cover for the *Pala d'Oro*, painted in 1345 by Paolo Veneziano, and vestments adorned with delicate Venetian lace. The fine view of the piazza from the loggia alone justifies a visit to the museum.

Piazza San Marco

Look right as you come out of the basilica and you'll see the **Torre dell'Orologio**, a delightful construction built by Mauro Codussi in 1496-99. The *orologio* in question is a very handsome astronomical clock on top of which two bronze Moors (1497) strike the hours on a great bell. The event is worth waiting for, but to see it you must step back at least to the centre of the square.

Beyond the Torre dell'Orologio extends the former residence and offices of the Procurators of St Mark known as the **Procuratie Vecchie**, with a double portico built in the 12th century and remodelled in the 16th under the direction of Jacopo Sansovino, who added the third floor after 1532. On the opposite side of the square stretches its near twin, the **Procuratie Nuove**, begun in 1582 by the Vicentine architect Vincenzo Scamozzi to a plan by Sansovino and completed in 1640 by Baldassarre Longhena. Napoleon made this building his royal palace and demolished the church of San Geminiano, which had stood at the western end of the piazza, to build the neoclassical **Ala Napoleonica** (or *Procuratie Nuovissime*) in 1809.

Beneath the porticoes of the Procuratie Nuove, about half way along, is the 18th-century **Caffè Florian**, the most famous café in the city, with a richly decorated interior and an orchestra outside on summer evenings. During the Austrian occupation this was the watering-place of Italian patriots, and its orchestra often engaged in battles to the last note with that of the philo-Austrian **Caffè Quadri**, on the other side of the square. Both are good (though pricey) places to take a break.

The area between the basilica and the waterfront is known as **Piazzetta San Marco**. At the far end, against the magnificent backdrop of the Isle of San Giorgio, are two Syrian granite columns erected in 1180 and topped by Venice's two historic patrons: St Theodore, patron of the original republic,

---

About Mosaics

An heir to Byzantium, Venice long held onto the traditions of the East in her rich mosaic art. At San Marco, mosaics glitter in the low light of the basilica, revealing abstract, almost icon-like figures. The earliest mosaics at San Marco, dating from the 11th to the 14th centuries, cling most strongly to their Byzantine cousins in style. In these early mosaics (seen in the apse, the domes and the narthex of the church), individual cubes of coloured glass, stone, and enamels, called *tesserae,* were set into a plaster bed at different depths and at different angles. This irregular setting catches as much light as possible, intensifying the brilliant, sparkling glow of the mosaic. Early mosaic technique also had a limited range of *tessera* colours, which encouraged a rather non-naturalistic pictorial style with attention focused on line and simplified colour definition. By the mid-15th century, however, Venice saw the arrival of Florentine painters who designed mosaics with *tesserae* laid as smoothly as possible, minimising surface irregularity and eliminating the fantastic light effects of earlier mosaics. These artists also developed a range of tile colours that could produce delicate gradations of tonal values. With these innovations, mosaics lost the stylisation of earlier works and gained a painterly naturalism in the depiction of form, becoming, in essence, 'paintings in stone'.

who perches with his crocodile, and the saint who displaced him, Mark, portrayed in his traditional mode as a winged lion. In the area between the columns public executions took place.

Opposite the southwest corner of the basilica, at the corner of the Procuratie Nuove, rises the **Campanile**, erected in the 12th century, altered in 1511 and completely rebuilt after collapsing (fortunately without causing casualties) on the morning of 14 July 1902. At the bottom is the elegant marble **Loggetta** (1537–49), with an ornate façade adorned by three arches with sculptures and, inside, a terracotta *Madonna and Child,* all by Jacopo Sansovino. Initially a meeting place of the Venetian patricians, the Loggetta later housed the honour guard when the Great Council was in session. A lift ascends to the top, nearly 100m above the square.

Extending from the basilica to the water is the **Palazzo Ducale**, the residence of the doge and the seat of the highest magistrature of the Venetian Republic. Although it has stood on this site since the 9th century, its present appearance is the product of a late Gothic reconstruction (c 1340–1420), the general design of which is attributed to the sculptor and architect Filippo Calendario. With its vast walls of white Istrian limestone and pink Verona marble, fine portico, delicate loggia, magnificent balconies (by Pier Paolo and Jacobello dalle Masegne) and crenellated roof, it is by far the highest expression of Venetian Gothic architecture. Well-preserved medieval carvings (as well as some good 19th-century copies) adorn the 36 capitals of the lower colonnade, representing the months, animals and foliage. Of special note are the marble reliefs of moral exemplars high up on the corners: on the northwest (nearest the basilica), the *Judgement of Solomon* with the archangel Gabriel; on the southwest (facing the lagoon), *Adam and Eve* with the archangel Michael; and on the southeast, the *Drunkenness of Noah* with the archangel Raphael – all of uncertain 14th-century attribution.

The palace is joined to San Marco by the **Porta della Carta** (1438), which forms the main entrance to the courtyard. The 'Paper Door' is possibly so called because placards displayed here once decreed the Republic's ordinances. This splendid gateway, a masterpiece of Venetian Gothic architecture and sculpture, was executed in 1438–42 by Giovanni and Bartolomeo Bon and their assistants. Its sculptural programme is a celebration of Justice (personified in the figure enthroned at the top) as the highest principle of government, accompanied by Temperance, Fortitude, Prudence and Charity. Doge Francesco Foscarini, who commissioned the work, is shown kneeling before the lion of St Mark in the lower part. His statue is an 1885 reproduction of the original, smashed in 1797.

The Porta della Carta takes you into the magnificent courtyard, probably the best part of the palace interior and the only part that can be viewed without charge. Here the unitary architectural image of the exterior gives way to a medley of styles united only by a desire for impressive magnificence. The Renaissance classicism of Antonio Rizzo's east façade (1485), decorated by Pietro, Antonio and Tullio Lombardo, predominates over the Gothic west and south sides. The **Scala dei Giganti**, a monumental staircase overlooked by colossal statues of Mars and Neptune – by Sansovino, who finished them in the mid-16th century – leads up to the first-floor loggia. At its top doges were crowned after a religious service in San Marco; and from this landing they subsequently received important visitors.

You should think twice before passing the ticket office and entering the palace: the building caught fire in 1577, destroying a remarkable collection of Renaissance painting by Giovanni Bellini, Titian, Gentile da Fabriano and Pisanello, for which the Tintoretto and Veronese school pieces that now adorn the interior are very weak replacements. If the palace is crowded and there is a wait to get in, you are better off spending your time elsewhere.

If you do go in, a staircase beneath the southeast side of the portico takes you up to the Gothic loggia, from which the Scala d'Oro – designed by Sansovino in 1554 and bearing gilt stuccoes by Alessandro Vittoria in the ceiling – ascends to a succession of 16th-century rooms, many of which have carved, gilt ceilings and fine Renaissance chimney pieces. The best are the **Sala degli Scarlatti**, decorated by Pietro Lombardo, with a marble bas-relief and blue and gold ceiling; the **Cappella Privata del Doge**, which has a St Christopher frescoed on the outside by Titian; the **Sala delle Quattro Porte**, named after the monumental doors decorated with statues and columns and containing Titian's *Doge Antonio Grimani Kneeling before Faith;* the **Sala dell'Anticollegio**, with Tintoretto's *Vulcan's Forge, Mercury and the Graces, Bacchus and Ariadne,* and *Minerva and Mars,* and a *Rape of Europa* by Veronese; the **Sala del Collegio**, designed by Andrea Palladio, with canvases on the walls by Tintoretto (each showing a doge among the saints) and Veronese (*Sebastiano Venier Thanking God for the Victory of Lepanto*) and a carved ceiling with more opulent paintings by Veronese; the **Sala del Consiglio dei Dieci**, with paintings by Veronese in the carved and gilt ceiling; the **Sala dell'Armamento**, with what is left of the magnificent fresco of *Paradise* by Guariento (1365–67, ruined in the fire of 1577) and, in the adjoining loggia, the statues of Adam and Eve carved by Antonio Rizzo in 1468 for the Arco Foscari in the courtyard; and the **Sala del Maggior Consiglio**, or Great Council Chamber, a vast (53 x 24m) hall whose decoration, like that of the adjacent Sala dello Scrutinio, was executed after the fire. On the walls is the huge *Paradise* painted by Tintoretto and assistants in place of Guariento's (reputedly the largest oil painting in the world). The frieze is decorated with portraits of doges (that of Marin Falier, beheaded in 1355 for treason, has been replaced by a black curtain) and the ceiling holds Veronese's great *Apotheosis of Venice,* surrounded by paintings by Tintoretto and Palma Giovane. The palace is connected to the 17th-century prison by the famous **Ponte dei Sospiri** (Bridge of Sighs, 1602), over which the condemned were led, often never to emerge alive. The best exterior view of the bridge is from the beautiful 15th-century Ponte della Paglia, on the quayside.

The piazzetta is bordered on the west by the **Libreria Sansoviniana**, a masterpiece of 16th-century Venetian architecture begun by Sansovino and completed after the architect's death by Scamozzi. The solemnly classical building, with its portico and loggia, Ionic columns and rooftop balustrade,

Detail of Adam and Eve, Palazzo Ducale

was built to house the Biblioteca Marciana, the Library of St Mark established by Cardinal Bessarione in 1468, but is now used as a venue for exhibitions. A monumental staircase ascends to the vestibule, with a ceiling frescoed by Titian (*Wisdom*), and to the magnificent main hall, with paintings of philosophers by Veronese, Tintoretto and Andrea Schiavone. The adjoining rooms of the Procuratie Nuove house the **Museo Archeologico**, which you *can* (and should) visit. It has an important collection of Greek and Roman sculpture, including a series of Greek female statues dating from the 5th and 4th centuries BC (*Demeter, Hera, Athena*); three *Wounded Gauls* (3rd century BC), the *Grimani Altar*, of Hellenistic workmanship; busts of Trajan and Vitellius; and the Hellenistic *Zulian Cammeo*. There are also marbles, inscriptions and a collection of Roman coins.

Next door to the Libreria is the **Palazzo della Zecca**, or Mint, likewise designed by Jacopo Sansovino and built between 1537 and 1566. It is the modern home of the Biblioteca Marciana, possessing numerous rare books and manuscripts, notably the splendid *Breviario Grimani,* a masterpiece of 15th-century illumination.

A monumental staircase beneath the arches of the Ala Napoleonica leads up to the **Museo Correr**, with collections illustrating Venetian art and history from the 13th to the 16th century. Highlights include works by Jacopo Bellini (*Crucifixion*) and his sons Gentile (*Portrait of Doge Mocenigo*) and Giovanni (*Crucifixion, Transfiguration and Pietà*); Vittore Carpaccio (*Two Venetian Ladies*), Antonello da Messina (*Pietà*), Lorenzo Lotto (*Portrait*), Lucas Cranach and Hugo Van der Goes. The same building houses a small museum of the Risorgimento with documents and memorabilia ranging from the late 18th century to the incorporation of the city into the Kingdom of Italy (1866).

Sestiere of San Marco

To explore the *sestiere* of San Marco, pass beneath the arch of the Ala Napoleonica and take the broad Salizzada San Moisè, which takes you past the church of the same name, a soot-blackened operatic, self-indulgent and spectacular building interesting above all for its façade, a stage-set where you must search determinedly for any trace of the religious. From here the broad Calle Larga XXII Marzo leads westward, running parallel to the Grand Canal amid luxury hotels and expensive shops. A few steps along, Calle del Sartor da Veste diverges right to Campo San Fantin, a picturesque old square surrounded by elegant white façades; the well-heads date from the 15th century. Here stands the **Teatro La Fenice**, an 18th-century building destroyed by fire in 1837 and again in 1996, and presently under reconstruction. Across from the theatre is the Renaissance church of **San Fantin**, begun by Scarpagnino. The beautiful apse was added by Jacopo Sansovino, who was probably also responsible for the marble cantoria inside. On the left is the former Scuola di San Fantin, seat since 1812 of a literary-scientific academy founded by Napoleon.

Return to Calle Larga and follow it to its end. Left, right and over the bridge

A Masterpiece at the Correr

One of the most significant works in the Correr is Giovanni Bellini's *Pietà*, ascribed to the period between 1445 and 1455. Unknown to critics until a few decades ago, this painting is important because it was done at the beginning of the artist's career, possibly during his sojourn in Padua, where the Florentine sculptor Donatello was working at the same time. In fact, whereas the cityscape in the background suggests the archaeological accuracy of Mantegna (who, incidentally, was Bellini's brother-in-law), the angels holding up the dead Christ recall the bronze angels that Donatello made for the famous altar in the basilica of Sant'Antonio in Padua. In addition to this evidence of early influences one can see traces of that use of colour which was to become the hallmark of Bellini's work – for instance, in the way the artist uses thin layers of paint to create atmospheric effects both in the distant landscape and in the foreground figures of Christ and the angels. This specific characteristic of Bellini's artistic language, indicative of a new interest in naturalism, is one of the first signs of the arrival of the Renaissance in Venetian painting.

is **Santa Maria del Giglio** (or Santa Maria Zobenigo, 1683), another example of Baroque decorative exuberance with a façade by Giuseppe Sardi. Here, too, the secular character of the design overwhelms any latent religious content: the financial patron (General Antonio Barbaro) stands above the door (in a position usually reserved for the patron saint), between figures of *Honour* and *Virtue*, while four relatives peer down on passers-by; detailed low reliefs of the fortresses the family commanded appear at the bottom of the façade. The interior has several fine paintings: on the south, in the Cappella Molin, a *Madonna and Child with the Young St John*, by Pieter Paul Rubens; on the third south altar, a *Visitation* by Palma Giovane; behind the high altar, an *Addolorata* by Sebastiano Ricci and *Four Evangelists* by Jacopo Tintoretto, who also did the painting of *Christ and Saints* over the third north altar.

The street ends in Campo Santo Stefano (or Campo Morosini), at an important crossroads. The statue in the middle represents Niccolò Tommaseo, a 19th-century patriot. **Santo Stefano** (right) is a church of the 14th and 15th centuries, with a 15th-century façade displaying mullioned windows and a white marble Gothic doorway somewhat darkened by soot. The vast interior has three aisles and a polygonal apse, a fine ship's-keel roof and tomb monuments of various epochs. The best of these are the tombs of Giacomo Surian, on the west wall and of the jurist G.B. Ferretti in the chapel on the north of the sanctuary. Both were made in the Renaissance; the Ferretti tomb has been attributed to Michele Sanmicheli. The church's most valuable artworks, however, are in the sacristy; here you can see a crucifix by Paolo Veneziano (c 1348), a polyptych by Bartolomeo Vivarini, a *Holy Family* by Palma

Scala del Bovolo

Vecchio, and three large canvases (*Last Supper, Washing of the Feet* and *Agony in the Garden*) by Tintoretto. A door in the left aisle leads to the interesting 16th-century cloister, with an Ionic colonnade attributed to Scarpagnino. At the beginning of the same aisle is the entrance to the Cappella del Battista, with a *Baptism of Christ* by Pomponio Amalteo over the altar and the funerary stele of a member of the Falier faily, by Antonio Canova, on the wall.

Caffè Paolin, across the street from the church, is known for its ice-cream; if you prefer pastries, backtrack to the Calle del Spezier (by which you entered the square) and walk just a few paces to **Marchini**, on the left before the bridge.

Go right as you leave Santo Stefano. Walk around the side of the church and over the bridge to Campo Sant'Angelo (where the composer Domenico Cimarosa lived: his house is marked by a plaque). Cross the square and descend the steps in the left-hand corner to Calle dei Avocati, take your first right and cross another little bridge. On your right will be **Palazzo Fortuny**, a 15th-century palace whose Gothic façade overlooks the little Campo San Beneto. Here is the house-museum of the Spanish painter and designer Mariano Fortuny y Madrazo (1871–1949), whose fashions and textiles were the rage of *fin-de-siècle* Europe. Fortuny himself furnished and decorated the rooms, which now contain a number of his designs, together with curios and memorabilia.

With your back to the little church of San Beneto, walk to the end of Salizzada de la Chiesa and take Calle de la Mandorla left. You'll come out in Campo Manin. A narrow alley on the right here (marked) winds its way eventually to the **Scala del Bovolo**, in the garden court of Palazzo Contarini. This

Rialto Bridge at sunset

splendid late 15th-century spiralling stair (*bovolo* in Venetian) allowed external access to the upper floors of the palace. Although you can buy a ticket and climb to the top, there's not much reason to do so: the best viewpoint is from the pavement just outside the garden.

Back in Campo Manin, walk diagonally across the square and bear left to reach the Grand Canal; the **Ponte di Rialto** appears quite suddenly on your right, at the end of a pleasant quay. This and the quay on the opposite bank – both of which are lined with small restaurants and cafés – are among the few places in Venice where you can actually walk along the canal. On the corner of Calle del Carbon is a commemorative plaque to Elena Lucrezia Cornaro Piscopia, born in this house in 1646. The plaque recalls that she was graduated from Padua University on 25 June 1678 – making her the first woman in history to receive a degree. A little further on is Sansovino's Palazzo Dolfin Manin (now the Banca d'Italia).

Just a few steps south of the Rialto Bridge, Campo San Bartolomio stands at the crossroads of streets coming from Piazza San Marco and the train station. The monument at the centre commemorates Venetian playwright Carlo Goldoni (1707–93). South of the square begins the lively succession of shopping streets known as the **Mercerie**. From its corner the white Baroque façade of the 16th-century church of **San Salvador** overlooks the *campo* to which it gives its name. Inside are sculptures by Sansovino and two late paintings by Titian: the *Annunciation* over an altar in the south aisle, and the *Transfiguration,* over the high altar. South of the church is the former convent, with two 16th-century cloisters.

On the Merceria dell'Orologio are the campo and church of **San Zulian**, a very old foundation rebuilt in its present form by Jacopo Sansovino in 1553–55. Some believe Sansovino also made the bronze statue of the financial patron, the physician Tommaso Rangone, above the doorway. Inside are works by Paolo Veronese (*Pietà*, first south altar) and Palma Giovane (*Glory of St Julian,* on the wooden ceiling; *Assumption,* second south altar; *Resurrection,* in the arch of the chapel north of the sanctuary). From here it is a very short walk down the Mercerie and through the Torre dell'Orologio to Piazza San Marco.

Dorsoduro

For those with a genuine interest in the subject, but no specialist training as art historians, the best approach to Venetian painting is a visit to the city's main museum, followed by a look at a few of the works that are still to be found *in situ* in Venice's churches, palaces and *scuole*. The starting point of this walk is, naturally enough, the Galleria dell'Accademia – after which you may or may not want to take a quick spin through the lavish period rooms of Ca' Rezzonico, Venice's 18th-century palace-museum. A stop at the Scuola Grande dei Carmini, magnificently decorated by Tiepolo, is a must for those with even the remotest interest in Venetian art; and San Sebastiano (where Veronese painted) and the nearby quay of the Zattere (a favourite place of the Venetian view painters) also repay a visit. The walk ends with masterpieces of international painting and sculpture of the 20th century in a setting of rare peace and beauty – the home of that very special friend and patron of artists, Peggy Guggenheim – from which the return is easily made to the Galleria dell'Accademia. Total walking time is roughly two hours. As the queue at the Accademia can be quite long during high season (only a few visitors are admitted at a time), plan to arrive at least 20 minutes before opening time. If you are not a morning person, the last hour before closing is also a good time.

Accademia to Ca' Rezzonico

The sound of voices over water and the rumble of the *vaporetto* become noticeably clearer as you make your way from Campo Santo Stefano to the great wooden arch of the **Ponte dell'Accademia**, first built by the Austrians in order to move troops quickly from one part of the city to another. The view of the Grand Canal from the top is inspiring, to say the least: on one side is the Bacino di San Marco, with the church of Santa Maria della Salute and the Punta della Dogana on the right; on the other, the great, wide bend called Volta del Canal.

Just beyond the bridge is the **Galleria dell'Accademia**, one of the great museums of Europe. The entrance is through the neoclassical doorway of the former Scuola della Carità, which dates from 1765. The collection here ranges over five centuries of Venetian painting. There are 14th-century works

---

Pietro Longhi at Ca' Rezzonico

One of the most subtle and fascinating of Pietro Longhi's works at Ca' Rezzonico – which are all of more or less the same small size – is **The Moor and the Letter**. In this depiction of a Moorish slave delivering a secret letter to a young Venetian patrician, the workroom in which the lady sits with her maids is depicted in far too intimistic a way to be 'merely' realistic. And, perhaps, the Zuccarelli painting recognisable on the wall of the room – a sensual vision of Arcadia – is too clear an allusion to a moment of pleasure enjoyed by the unknown writer of the letter. Longhi's works sometimes suggest that the artist was a bit of a *frondeur* – especially when he charges his paintings with repressed eroticism (visits paid by important personages, little *tête-à-tête* suppers with English lords, procuresses offering saucy girls). It is even said that the Inquisition was keeping its eye on him. Even without giving credence to these unsubstantiated rumours, there is no doubt that Longhi belonged to that intellectual bourgeoisie which was becoming increasingly critical of the *veneta nobiltà*.

varying between Byzantine-style paintings and the Gothic works of Paolo Veneziano, 15th-century painting represented by the early Renaissance works of the Bellini family and Carpaccio, and 16th-century works ranging from the powerful paintings of Giorgione and Titian to the late mannerism of Bassano, Tintoretto and Veronese. The theatrical 17th century is represented by the works of foreign artists visiting the city and by the Baroque works of Maffei; while the 18th-century collection ranges from the great Rococo decorators Ricci, Pellegrini, Tiepolo and Antonio Guardi, to the more naturalistic works of Longhi, Canaletto and Francesco Guardi. The collection is arranged chronologically, and the works are well labelled.

Hop on a *vaporetto* to reach **Ca' Rezzonico**, one stop up the Grand Canal on the left; or, if you like, risk getting lost in the maze of *calli* and bridges (actually quite pleasant) north and west of the Accademia. This powerful Baroque palazzo on the Grand Canal, begun in 1649 by Baldassarre Longhena and completed after 1750 by Giorgio Massari, is a refined example of an 18th-century patrician home. It hosts the **Museo del Settecento Veneziano**, which, in sumptuous rooms (some with ceilings frescoed by Tiepolo and his pupils) creates a vivid image of Venetian life and culture in the 18th century, drawing on tapestries, furniture, lacquerwork, costumes and paintings. Among the latter are a fine series of small canvases with scenes of family life and rustic idylls by Pietro Longhi (1702–85), who occupies a very special place among the 'realist' painters of the second half of the 18th century. His work marks the introduction into Venetian art of the 'conversation piece' painting – a European genre that was being popularised in France by Watteau and in England by Hogarth. The Ca' Rezzonico also has a room hung with the pastel portraits of Rosalba Carriera (1675–1757), one of Europe's first internationally acclaimed women artists. Admired and courted by many of the ruling families of Europe, she used an eminently naturalistic artistic language which made her talents respected by all. She was a significent influence on the great French pastel artists Quentin de la Tour and Chardin.

Philanthropists, Carmelites and Veronese's Church

Down the little canal from Ca' Rezzonico (fruit and vegetables are sold from boats here on weekday mornings) and to the right is Campo Santa Margherita, a charming working-class square and marketplace, surrounded by old houses. At the west end of the square, flanked by its church, stands the 17th-century **Scuola Grande dei Carmini**. This was one of Venice's six *scuole grandi,* or philanthropic confraternities (the others are the Scuola Grande dei Greci, della Misericordia, di San Giovanni Evangelista, di San Marco and di San Rocco), which engaged in charitable activities throughout the republic. *Scuole* were formed by laymen involved in the same trade, who often shared a common national ancestry and were committed to a particular religious cult. These confraternities are of particular artistic interest, since their participants' annual membership fees decorated the headquarters, often supporting the more prominent Venetian artists of the day. This building's design is attributed to Baldassarre Longhena. The rooms of the interior are decorated with stuccoes, wooden benches and 17th- and 18th-century paintings. In the great upper hall, or Salone, is a fine ceiling with nine paintings by Giovanni Battista Tiepolo (1739–44) centring around a depiction of the Virgin presenting St Simon Stock with the scapular of the Carmelite Order, a work of the artist's later years. The Sala dell'Archivio has a beautiful carved wooden ceiling with paintings by Balestra, and the passage contains a *Judith and Holofernes* by Piazzetta.

The conventual church of **Santa Maria del Carmine** (or I Carmini), built in 1348, preserves a 14th-century doorway and porch on the north flank. The Renaissance façade with its arched gable was added in the early 16th century. The interior, with three aisles on monolithic columns (faced with carmine-red damask at Christmas and Easter) and a Gothic polygonal apse, has a magnificent 17th/18th-century wooden decoration in the nave incorporating statues of Prophets and Saints between the arches and a continuous frieze of paintings above. These illustrate the history of the Carmelite Order and are by minor artists. Over the second south altar is an *Adoration of the Shepherds* by Cima da Conegliano; the chapel on the south of the sanctuary holds a bronze relief of the *Deposition* by Francesco di Giorgio Martini and a charming little *Sacra Famiglia* by Veronese with a particularly playful young St John. Lorenzo Lotto's moody painting of *St Nicholas in Glory* hangs over the second north altar. Adjoining the church is the entrance to the former monastery (now a school), with a fine 16th-century cloister.

Upon leaving the church turn left, then left again along canals to reach **San Sebastiano**, rebuilt in the early 16th century (1504–48) in elegant Renaissance forms. It is famous for the impressive decorative scheme created between 1555 and 1565 by Paolo Veronese, who was buried here in 1588. The splendid complex of canvas and frescoes covers the ceiling, the walls of the nave and sanctuary, the sacristy and the nuns' choir. Particularly noteworthy are the three canvases of the nave ceiling (*Stories of Esther*); the organ shutters (*Purification of the Virgin* outside and *Pool of Bethesda* inside; the large canvases with *Stories of St Sebastian* in the sanctuary; the *Virgin in Glory with SS Sebastian, Peter, Catherine and Francis,* over the high altar; and the ceiling compartments of the sacristy (*Coronation of the Virgin, Evangelists*), the artist's first work in Venice. Among the other works of art preserved in the church are a beautiful marble group of the *Madonna and Child with the Young Saint John* by Tullio Lombardo, over the second south altar; the *Tomb of Livio Podocattaro* by Sansovino after the third south chapel; and a *St Nicholas* by Titian over the altar of the vestibule. The former convent, rebuilt in 1851, now hosts a part of the university.

Along the Zattere to the Salute

Le Zattere is the name of the pleasant quay along the wide Canale della Giudecca, which separates the city from the long Isle of the Giudecca.

Zattere in Venetian means 'lighters', and the *fondamenta* is named after the large, flat-bottomed barges that used to unload wood here. Almost 2km long, it is divided into four parts, which take their name from their most distinctive element: Zattere al Ponte Lungo, ai Gesuati, allo Spirito Santo and ai Saloni. As you cross the first little canal (Rio de San Trovaso), look left and you'll see one of Venice's last remaining *squeri*, the boatyards where gondolas are made and repaired. Further on, roughly half-way along the quay, stands the 18th-century church of the **Gesuati**, which holds works by Tiepolo (over the first south altar and ceiling fresco), Piazzetta (third south altar) and Tintoretto (third north altar).

The Punta della Dogana, the promontory separating the Grand Canal from the Canale della Giudecca, projects into the Bacino di San Marco towards the Isle of San Giorgio. It receives its name from the long, low building known as the **Dogana da Mar**, the Maritime Customs House, built over an earlier edifice by Giuseppe Benoni in 1676–82. The spectacular construction, designed to resemble an arcaded ship's prow, terminates in a triangular piazza offering unforgettable views over the city and the lagoon. From here you can imagine what it must have been like to arrive in Venice by sea – and it should not be forgotten that the principal approach to the city *was* by sea, and not, as today, over land. Sailing ships moored at the Molo di San Marco, at the foot of the Palazzo Ducale, where foreign visitors were immediately confronted by the highest symbols of political and religious power. Above the Doric façade of the Dogana di Mare rises Bernardo Falcone's sculptural composition of atlantes carrying a golden globe, topped by a weathervane in the shape of that most fickle of influences, Fortune.

Just around the point, on the Grand Canal, is **Santa Maria della Salute**, a masterpiece of Venetian Baroque architecture. It was built to a design of Baldassarre Longhena to commemorate the end of a terrible plague that swept the city in 1630. The church is designed in the shape of a crown, possibly in reference to the invocations to the Queen of Heaven in the Venetian litany that was recited in times of plague, or to the mention in Revelation of 'a woman clothed with the sun, and the moon under her feet, and upon her head a crown of twelve stars'. A statue of the Virgin with these attributes stands atop the cupola. At a lower level, on huge scrolls, are statues of the Apostles – the 12 stars in Longhena's 'crown'.

The interior of the church is a spacious octagon with an ambulatory, a lofty dome and a second, smaller dome over the sanctuary. An inscription in the centre of the pavement – *unde origo inde salus* ('whence the origin, thence the salvation and health') – alludes to the legend that Venice was founded under the protection of the Virgin. Around the church are a number of important artworks: the high altar, designed by Longhena with sculptures by Josse Le Court, holds a venerated Byzantine icon; on the left is the Sagrestia Grande (Great Sacristy), over the altar of which is a *St Mark Enthroned between SS Cosmas, Damian, Roch and Sebastian,* an early work of Titian painted to commemorate the plague of 1510. Titian also painted the three fine paintings on the ceiling (*Sacrifice of Abraham, David and Goliath, Cain and Abel*) originally for the church of Santo Spirito. On the wall to the south of the altar is the *Marriage at Cana,* a large painting by Tintoretto.

At the foot of the church extends the Campo della Salute, one of the few Venetian squares facing the Grand Canal. It offers a fine view over the Bacino di San Marco. West of the church, high above the steps, is the Seminario Patriarcale, a severe building by Baldassarre Longhena (1671) organised around a cloister and a monumental staircase. Here is the small **Pinacoteca Manfrediniana**, with paintings by 15th- to 18th-century artists, notably Giorgione, Cima da Conegliano, Filippino Lippi and Domenico Beccafumi; and sculpture, including two Renaissance reliefs by Tullio Lombardo and a terracotta bust by Antonio Canova.

You leave Campo della Salute by the apse of the little Gothic church of San Gregorio (now a conservation laboratory), then follow the signs through the narrow *calli* to the ivy-clad entrance of the **Peggy Guggenheim Collection**. This fascinating group of works by European and American avant-garde arists is arranged in the 18th-century Palazzo Venier dei Leoni, on the Grand Canal, where the spirited American heiress and patron of the arts lived from 1949 until her death in 1979. Artists represented in the collection include Piet Mondrian, Paul Klee, Giacomo Balla, Gino Severini, Max Ernst, Joan Miró, Giorgio De Chirico, Pablo Picasso and Jackson Pollock. There is also a cool, shady garden and a sun-baked terrace on the canal where weary feet may be rested. To the surprise of many, the Guggenheim Collection is the second most visited museum after the Accademia Gallery, so in high season come a few minutes before opening time or just before closing for quieter viewing. When you leave the Guggenheim walk west (right), and you'll soon come out at the Accademia.

San Polo and Santa Croce

This walk begins on the right bank of the Grand Canal, in the midst of the busy Rialto markets. From here you wind through the *sestiere* of San Polo to Ca' Pesaro, home of Venice's Oriental Museum and Gallery of Modern Art, then loop around to take in the extremely pleasant back-streets of Santa Croce, between the church and campo of San Giacomo dell'Orio and the great Franciscan church of Santa Maria dei Frari. This, together with the nearby church of San Rocco and the Scuola di San Rocco, magnificently decorated by Tintoretto, form the most important building complex in the city after San Marco and the Palazzo Ducale. From here the return to Rialto is made via the unusual church of San Polo, with its large, wooded square. Walking time is about one and a half hours

Campo San Giacomo di Rialto, formerly the centre of the city's financial life and now the centre of a colourful fruit and vegetable market, lies at the foot of the Rialto Bridge on the side farthest from San Marco. Flanked by the porti-

Rialto Market

coes of the Fabbriche Vecchie, it is overlooked by the 15th-century façade of San Giacomo di Rialto (San Giacometto), built in the 12th century and rebuilt in 1531 and 1601. From the campo Ruga degli Orefici ('Goldsmiths' Row') leads into Ruga degli Speziali ('Apothecaries'). Meandering along in a more or less northwesterly direction you eventually come to the 17th-century church of San Cassiano, on the north side of its campo. An old foundation several times altered, it has a 13th-century brick campanile and some paintings by Tintoretto.

From here you must carefully follow the signs for the Ferrovia and the Galleria d'Arte Moderna to reach **Ca' Pesaro**, one of the most magnificent Venetian palaces on the Grand Canal. Entrance to the palazzo is by a modest door on the garden side; the vast courtyard has a large well attributed to Jacopo Sansovino.

On the first floor is the **Galleria d'Arte Moderna**, with a vast but undistinguished collection of works by the principal Italian and foreign artists of the 20th century. The list includes most of the stars in the firmament of modernism – Hans Arp, Umberto Boccioni, Joseph Calder, Carlo Carrà, Felice Casorati, Marc Chagall, Giorgio de Chirico, Filippo de Pisis, Raoul Dufy, Max Ernst, Emilio Greco, Vasily Kandinski, Paul Klee, Gustav Klimt, Arturo Martini, Henri Matisse, Joan Miró, Henry Moore, Giorgio Morandi, Arnaldo and Giò Pomodoro, Ottone Rosai, Alberto Savinio and Mario Sironi. There are also some 19th-century paintings by Pierre Bonnard, Camille Corot, Giuseppe de Nittis, Giovanni Fattori, Francesco Hayez and Giuseppe Pellizza da Volpedo.

On the third floor is the **Museo d'Arte Orientale**, which has a splendid collection of Japanese paintings, sculpture, porcelain, lacquers, ivories and costumes of the Edo period (1614–1868), in addition to more modest hold-

View from the terrace of the Peggy Guggenheim Collection

ings of Chinese porcelain and jades and Indonesian weapons, fabrics and shadow-theatre figures.

Exit the museum and go straight over the bridge, then down a covered portico and over another bridge. You'll come out on the Grand Canal, in front of **San Stae**, a church with a late Baroque façade by Domenico Rossi. The interior, now used for concerts and exhibitions, has 18th-century paintings by Giovanni Battista Tiepolo, Sebastiano Ricci and Giovanni Battista Piazzetta – the latter's *Capture of St James* is a masterpiece. The Salizzada San Stae, on the south side of the church, leads past **Palazzo Mocenigo**, where there is a small museum of 18th-century frescoes, paintings and furniture.

Turn right in Calle del Tentor, then left at the bridge. Almost due south, in one of the few wooded spaces in the heart of the city, is **San Giacomo dell'Orio**. This is one of the older churches of Venice, built in 1225 and altered in the 14th–17th centuries; the extant elements of the original, 13th-century building are the central apse and brick campanile. The Latin-cross interior, with a 14th-century wooden ship's-keel roof, preserves several fine works of art: in the nave, a 13th-century holy-water stoup and a Lombardesque pulpit; beneath the arch of the sanctuary, a wooden crucifix by Paolo Veneziano; in the sanctuary, a *Madonna and Saints* by Lorenzo Lotto; in the north transept, *SS Jerome, Lawrence and Prosperus* by Paolo Veronese; and in the old sacristy, a cycle of paintings by Palma Giovane.

The Frari

From the apse of San Giacomo continue southwards via Calle del Tentor to reach **Santa Maria Gloriosa dei Frari**, which rivals Santi Giovanni e Paolo as the most important church in Venice after San Marco. Built by the Franciscans between 1340 and 1443, it is a brick edifice with a lively exterior design, magnificent apses and a slightly leaning campanile of 1361–69 (the tallest after that of San Marco). The vast façade, crowned by stone pinnacles, is pierced by a marble doorway bearing sculptures by Bartolomeo Bon and Pietro Lamberti, and by Alessandro Vittoria (who did the *Resurrected Christ* at the top).

The church is entered by the doorway in the north flank, also faced in marble. The vast, solemn interior, with three aisles separated by tall pointed arches, has numerous tombs of doges and other illustrious Venetians of the 14th to the 19th century, as well as some major works of art. At the centre of the nave is the late Gothic-early Renaissance monks' choir, with a marble enclosure by Pietro Lombardo and carved and inlaid stalls. Now walk to the west end of the church. In the second bay of the south aisle is an 1852 monument to Titian; over the third altar, a statue of *St Jerome,* by Alessandro Vittoria, considered one of his better sculptures. High up in the south transept, on the right, is the Tomb of Jacopo Marcello, by Pietro Lombardo or Giovanni Buora, with the statue of the deceased on the sarcophagus supported by three caryatides. The Tomb of Beato Pacifico, on the adjoining wall, was made by 15th-century Florentine masters. Above the door to the sacristy is the Tomb of Benedetto Pesaro, by Lorenzo Bregno. In the sacristy itself are fine reliquaries displayed in an elaborate Baroque showcase; and on the altar, an enchanting triptych by Giovanni Bellini showing the *Madonna and Child with Saints Nicholas, Peter, Paul and Benedict* (signed and dated 1488), commissioned for this location and still surrounded by its original gilt wood frame. The perspective effect is truly remarkable and may distract your attention from the two angel-musicians at the bottom of the throne, which are not to be missed. Paolo Veneziano's 1339 *Madonna and Child with SS Francis and Elizabeth* has been placed at the opposite end of the sacristy.

The south apsidal chapels hold various Gothic tombs of the 14th century. In the third (the first as you come out of the sacristy) is a *Madonna and Child* by Bartolomeo Vivarini; in the first, Donatello's powerful wooden *St John the Baptist,* carved around 1450 but repainted in the 19th century. The sanctuary has a beautiful apse with large mullioned windows, before which rises Titian's magnificent *Assumption of the Virgin.* An inscription in the marble frame records that the work was commissioned in 1516 by Friar Germano, Superior of the Franciscan Monastery; the finished altarpiece was installed on 20 May 1518, in an elaborate public ceremony. This is probably the most famous painting of the Venetian Renaissance. At the time it was made, the painter's unorthodox approach to his subject – such a shapely Virgin and excited Apostles had never been seen before – was seen as scandalous; but the stir soon mellowed into praise, and by 1548 critic Paolo Pino could claim, 'If Titian and Michelangelo were one person; that is, if the draughtsmanship of Michelangelo went together with the colour of Titian, one could call that person the god of painting.' So much for religious orthodoxy.

On the south wall here is the *Tomb of Doge Francesco Foscari,* a late Gothic-early Renaissance monument by Antonio and Paolo Bregno. On the north wall, the marble facing with the *Tomb of Doge Niccolò Tron,* by Antonio Rizzo and assistants, is one of the outstanding funerary monuments of Venetian Renaissance. The first north apsidal chapel contains an altarpiece by Bernardino Licinio, who also did the Franciscan martyrs on the north wall; in the third is the *St Ambrose Altarpiece* by Alvise Vivarini and Marco Basaiti; the fourth has a triptych by Bartolomeo Vivarini over the altar and a statue of St John by Jacopo Sansovino on the baptismal font.

Over the second altar of the north aisle is Titian's *Pesaro Altarpiece,* commissioned in 1519 by Bishop Jacopo Pesaro, former admiral of the Venetian fleet, who appears at the bottom left with a soldier in armour leading a Turkish prisoner. In the opposite corner of the painting is Senator Francesco Pesaro with two other brothers, Antonio and Giovanni, and Antonio's young sons Leonardo and Nicolò. St Peter and the family patron saints Francis and Anthony stand above, forming the sides of an ideal triangle culminating in the image of the Virgin and Child. The two powerful columns, whose upper ends are lost above the top of the painting, represent the Gates of Heaven.

The lateral doorway is framed by the colossal funerary composition invented by Baldassarre Longhena for Doge Giovanni Pesaro (1669). The last bay on this side contains the *Monument to Antonio Canova,* in the form of a

Tintoretto at San Rocco

The Scuola Grande di San Rocco could be described as a veritable monument to Tintoretto's art, and the adventurous (and probably true) story behind the painting here casts light on the artist's bizarre character. Soon after the completion of the building, the Confraternity of St Roche called a competition for the decoration of the interior, inviting four leading Venetian artists of the day (Federico Zuccari, Giuseppe Salviati, Paolo Veronese and Tintoretto) to submit a proposal. The competition design had to be an oval painting of *The Triumph of St Roche*. On 31 May 1564 the committee met to judge the entries. Zuccari, Salviati and Veronese submitted drawings and sketches; but Tintoretto – with the help of the custodian of the building – arranged for the judges to find a finished picture, whipped together with characteristic impetuosity, already installed in the oval space of the ceiling. He offered this work as a gift to the confraternity and promised to paint the rest of the ceiling at no extra cost – provided he was commissioned to do the entire decorative scheme for the Scuola. Over the protests of the other artists and of a few members of the confraternity, who accused him of cheating, he won the commission.

pyramid, executed by his pupils using designs by Canova himself for a tomb of Titian. Remains of the Franciscan convent include a few rooms and the cloisters, renovated between the 16th and 18th centuries.

Scuola and Church of San Rocco

Opposite the apse of the Frari is the **Scuola Grande di San Rocco**, begun in 1516 to an initial design by Bartolomeo Bon the Younger and completed in 1560 under the direction of Sante Lombardo, then Scarpagnino. Scarpagnino is responsible for the magnificent façade, on which High Renaissance elements (on the ground floor) are tied together with foreshadowings of the Baroque taste (above). Inside, the large halls are decorated with a magnificent cycle of large paintings executed over a period of 23 years (1564–87) by Jacopo Tintoretto.

The visit begins on the upper floor, which is reached by Scarpagnino's Grand Staircase. Antonio Zanchi's 1666 *Plague of 1630* lines the walls. In the **Sala dell'Albergo** (where the chapter met) is Tintoretto's vast *Crucifixion* of 1565, universally considered his masterpiece, a work so profoundly moving that it left even the eloquent Ruskin speechless ('I must leave this picture to work its will on the spectator, for it is beyond all analysis and above all praise'). The other paintings represent scenes of the Passion (*Christ Before Pilate, Christ Carrying the Cross* and *Ecce Homo*). The famous – or infamous

– *Triumph of St Roch* shines down from the great oval in the middle of the ceiling. Set on easels are two small paintings brought here from the church of San Rocco for safekeeping: *Ecce Homo,* an early work of Titian, and *Christ Carrying the Cross,* which some ascribe to Titian and others, to Giorgione.

In the large **Sala Maggiore** the ceiling is occupied by stories drawn from the Old Testament (*Moses Drawing Water from the Rock* in the first large frame, surrounded by *Adam and Eve, God Appearing to Moses, The Pillar of Fire* and *Jonah and the Whale; The Brazen Serpent,* flanked by *The Vision of Ezekiel* and *Jacob's Ladder;* and the *Gathering of Manna,* surrounded by the *Sacrifice of Isaac, Elijah Fed by the Angel, Elisha Multiplying the Loaves* and *The Passover Feast*). On the walls are *SS Roch and Sebastian* (by the windows) and New Testament stories (*Adoration of the Shepherds, Baptism of Christ, Resurrection, Agony in the Garden, Last Supper, Miracle of the Loaves and Fishes, Resurrection of Lazarus, Ascension, Pool of Bethesda* and *Temptation*). Tintoretto executed the cycle in just five years, between 1576 and 1581, adding the altarpiece of the *Vision of St Roch* in 1588. On the sides of the altar, on easels, are an *Annunciation* by Titian and a *Visitation* and *Self-Portrait* by Tintoretto, and *Abraham Visited by the Angels* and *Agar Rescued by the Angels* by Giovanni Battista Tiepolo. In the ground floor hall are eight large canvases that Tintoretto painted in 1583–87. The *Annunciation, Flight into Egypt, St Mary Magdalen* and *St Mary of Egypt* are particularly beautiful. The statue of *St Roch* over the altar was carved by Girolamo Campagna in 1587.

Across the way is the church of **San Rocco**, with an elegant façade of 1760 decorated with sculptures by Giovanni Marchiori and the Austrian G.M. Morlaiter. The 18th-century interior has more paintings by Tintoretto, two of which are particularly significant. The powerful handling of the nudes in *St Roch in Prison,* on the south wall, is a reminder that Tintoretto originally painted his great *Crucifixion* with naked figures, adding draperies later. The privileged position of *St Roch Ministering to the Plague-Stricken* – in the sanctuary – recalls that St Roch's miraculous ability to heal those afflicted with plague was intimately tied to the enormous prestige his scuola enjoyed in Venice. The church also holds paintings by Sebastiano Ricci and Giovanni Antonio da Pordenone, and (by the main door) elegant Rococo statues of David and St Cecily by Giovanni Marchiori.

Cross back over the Rio dei Frari, then cross over the Rio di San Polo and follow the signs for San Marco to reach the old church of **San Polo**, a Byzantine foundation several times altered, which you enter by a large 15th-century Gothic doorway on the south flank. The interior, which still retains a marked medieval feeling, has three aisles on columns with a wooden ship's-keel roof and paintings by Tintoretto (west wall and first south altar), Tiepolo (second north altar) and Palma Giovane (on the walls). The organ dates from 1763. The large square behind the church, where popular feasts were once held, is overlooked by several patrician palaces, all of which have their more elaborate façades on the water. Baron Corvo stayed at the Palazzo Corner Mocenigo (No. 2128a) while writing his last book, *The Desire and Pursuit of* *the Whole;* Nos. 2169 and 2171 are Gothic palaces with finely decorated windows and balconies; next to them rises the 18th-century Palazzo Tiepolo (whose aristocratic owners were no relation to the painter). Continue walking northeast, past the churches of Sant Aponal and San Giovanni Elemosinario. In just a few minutes you'll come to the Rio degli Orefici and the Rialto Bridge.

Castello, San Giorgio and the Giudecca

Looking at the crowded quay that stretches eastwards from the Palazzo Ducale to the Giardini di Castello, you would never guess that one of the quieter and more relaxed areas of Venice lies just behind San Marco. Oddly enough, the throngs stick to the waterfront, notwithstanding the presence just a few paces inland of some of the more delightful and magnificent achievements of Venetian art and architecture.

This walk, which starts and ends at San Marco, winds its way among the major sights of the *sestiere* of Castello. The first stop is the charming little church of Santa Maria Formosa, around the corner from which stands the Fondazione Querini-Stampalia with an outstanding gallery of old masters. From here you amble over to the magnificent complex represented by Santi Giovanni e Paolo and the Scuola di San Marco, sternly guarded by Andrea Verrocchio's equestrian monument to the mercenary general Bartolomeo Colleoni. Touching upon the convent of San Zaccaria you reach the Greek Orthodox church of San Giorgio dei Greci, the Dalmatian *scuola* of San Giorgio degli Schiavoni, and San Francesco della Vigna with its splendid Palladian façade. From here you pass the imposing shipyards at the Arsenale to wander among the old boats, antique models, cannon, flags and memorabilia of the Museo Storico Navale.

Lastly, you embark for San Giorgio Maggiore and the Giudecca, in the incomparable atmosphere of which you might want to lunch or dine before boating back to San Marco. It sounds like a lot and it *is* a lot, but the distances from one sight to the next are really quite short. Walking time (including the *vaporetto*) is about three hours.

Santa Maria Formosa to San Zanipolo

From Piazza San Marco, take the Mercerie (beneath the clock tower) to the church of San Zulian, then Calle delle Bande right to **Campo Santa Maria Formosa**. Among the livelier Venetian *campi*, formerly used for open-air theatre, this pleasant square is surrounded by fine palaces: No. 5866, Palazzo Ruzzini, of 1580; Nos. 6121 and 6125–26, three Palazzi Donà – the first late 16th-century, the others 15th-century Gothic. At No 5246 is Palazzo Vitturi, an unusual example of Veneto-Byzantine architecture of the 13th century; No. 5250 is Palazzo Malipiero, a 16th-century house remodelled in the 19th century.

The church of **Santa Maria Formosa**, erected according to tradition in 639 following a miraculous apparition of the Virgin Mary in the form of a beautiful (*formosa*) maiden, was rebuilt in 1482 by Mauro Codussi in Renaissance forms. In the 16th century it received its two classical façades, and in the 17th century its Baroque campanile. The interior, whose Greek-cross plan may be a carry-over from the earlier church, combines the elegance of Renaissance ornament with the spatial values of Byzantine architecture. It preserves a *Madonna of Mercy* by Bartolomeo Vivarini, signed and dated 1473; and a polyptych with *St Barbara and Four Saints* by Palma Vecchio. St Barbara was the patron of the artillerymen who had their chapel in this church, and her valiant, resolute bearing in Palma's painting caused George Eliot to describe her as 'an almost unique presentation of a hero-woman, standing in calm preparation for martyrdom, without the slightest air of pietism, yet the expression of a mind filled with serious conviction'.

Walk all the way around the church and then south to reach Campiello Querini Stampalia, along the Rio Santa Maria Formosa. Here, in a palace of 1528, stands the **Fondazione Querini-Stampalia**, with an important library and picture gallery. The building was renovated in the 1960s to a design by Carlo Scarpa, the most prominent Italian architect of the time, and the collection was completely rearranged to meet state-of-the-art museological standards in 1995–96. The works reflect the personal taste of the founder, Count Giovanni Querini, whose interest focused on the social portraits, conversation pieces and rich furnishings of 18th-century Venice.

A Portrait by Tiepolo

The real surprise in this collection is Giovanni Battista Tiepolo's *Portrait of the Procurator Dolfin*, painted between 1750 and 1755. Tiepolo rarely showed much interest in portraiture; his imagination was attracted more by mythological or historical subjects. The sitter has only tentatively been identified as Daniele Dolfin IV (1656–1723), a captain in the Venetian navy and Procurator of the Republic for whose palace the young Tiepolo had painted a series of Roman generals. The cruel energy in the gloved hand, and the sinister, almost spectral white wig, are perfectly in keeping with the prestige of such a position. The daring perspective and the theatrically billowing draperies give the painting an expressive power so strong that it verges on caricature.

Return to Santa Maria Formosa and walk north to reach Campo Santi Giovanni e Paolo ('San Zanipolo' in dialect). Opening around the imposing Dominican church of Santi Giovanni e Paolo and the small marble façade of the Scuola di San Marco, this is the most monumental of Venetian squares after Piazza San Marco. Near the corner of the church stands the bronze equestrian monument to mercenary general **Bartolomeo Colleoni**, the last and grandest work of the Florentine sculptor Andrea Verrocchio.

The story of the statue offers an interesting anecdote. Colleoni, who had commanded the land forces of the Venetian Republic, died in 1475, leaving a considerable sum of money to erect a bronze equestrian monument in his honour. The legacy stipulated that the statue should be set up in Piazza San Marco. The authorities had no intention of glorifying a single individual in the city's main public square, however, and destined the statue for a less important site, in front of the Scuola di San Marco – thus, in a sense, fulfilling the terms of the will. Verrocchio received the commission in 1479 and completed a full-scale clay model by 1483, but died before it was cast. This work was eventually done by a Venetian bronze-founder, Alessandro Leopardi, who also designed the base on which the monument was set in 1496. In keeping with the new interests of his period, Verrocchio has abandoned the static concept of equestrian statuary expressed by Donatello in the Gattamelata monument in Padua (see page 151). The horse is strong and unruly, its veins swollen, its muscles tense. Erect in the stirrups, his torso twisted against the movement of the horse's head, the general frowns down with fierce pride, in full command of his nervous charger. Never was there a more convincing portrait of power and command than this, Verrocchio's last work. 'I do not believe that there is a more glorious work of sculpture existing in the world,' remarked Ruskin of this monument.

Santi Giovanni e Paolo or San Zanipolo is the second largest Gothic church in Venice, almost on a par with the Frari. It was begun in the mid-14th century. The apses and transept had been completed by 1368, and the church was consecrated in 1430. The austere façade, in striking contrast with the extremely ornate front of the adjacent Scuola di San Marco, has a delicately designed roofline above and, below, a large marble doorway by Bartolomeo Bon and assistants flanked by tall arches bearing sarcophagi. The right flank and polygonal apses are also quite handsome.

The interior is a feast of Venetian sculpture and painting. From the 15th century on, San Zanipolo was the traditional site of the doges' funerals, and splendid Gothic and Renaissance monuments to 25 of the republic's leaders line the walls. The most impressive of these is Pietro Lombardo's 1476 *Monument to Pietro Mocenigo,* whose family occupies the entire west wall. Two paintings are of special note: Giovanni Bellini's gentle, sensual *Triptych of St Vincent Ferrer,* flanked by SS Christopher and Sebastian (near the Lombardo tomb, in the south aisle) and Lorenzo Lotto's warm, sensitive *St Anthony Giving Alms,* in the south wing of the transept. Here also is the last surviving example of the large painted glass windows that were a speciality of Murano glassmakers, the *Window of Warrior Saints* (1515), based on designs by Bartolomeo Vivarini and Girolamo Mocetto. The Cappella del Rosario, reached from the north transept, contains ceiling paintings by Paolo Veronese. Back on the south side, the Cappella di San Domenico, adjoining the south transept, has paintings by Piazzetta in the ceiling and low reliefs of the saint's life on the walls by Giuseppe Mazza and Giambattista Alberghetti. The

Cappella della Madonna della Pace, in the south aisle, has fine paintings by Leandro Bassano, stuccoes and a Byzantine icon of rare beauty over the altar.

On the north side of Campo Santi Giovanni e Paolo is the **Scuola Grande di San Marco**, now the city hospital. The palace, largely a work of the early Renaissance, was begun by Pietro and Tullio Lombardo, continued by Mauro Codussi and completed by Jacopo Sansovino. The splendid coloured-marble façade has sophisticated trompe-l'œil reliefs in which a marvellous sense of depth is obtained from an essentially two-dimensional surface. The roofline presents arched pediments of various sizes and the main doorway has a porch with lunette by Bartolomeo Bon. From the ground floor hall you can enter the

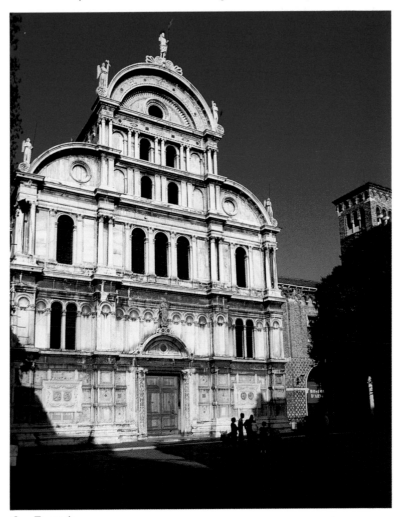

San Zaccaria

former Dominican convent of Santi Giovanni e Paolo, rebuilt by Baldassarre Longhena in 1660–75 on a 13th-century plan around two cloisters and a courtyard.

San Zaccaria, Wild Nuns and the Greek Connection

Winding southwards toward the Riva degli Schiavoni you eventually come to the quiet, sheltered Campo San Zaccaria, overlooked by the façade of its church. **San Zaccaria** was founded in the 9th century, and there are still traces (in the crypt) of the original building, where eight of the first doges were buried. The church you see today was begun during the 15th century in Gothic forms and completed in 1480–1515 by Mauro Codussi, who gave it its multi-level white stone façade, one of the first Renaissance church façades in the city. Despite the classical trabeation, columns and round-headed arches, its vertical thrust is still distinctly Gothic. It corresponds to the forms of the tall, vaulted three-aisled interior, whose ambulatory with radial chapels lit by tall windows is unique in Venice. Along the walls are numerous paintings, the most important of which is Giovanni Bellini's *Madonna and Saints* over the second north altar, signed and dated 1505. Executed when the painter was in his seventies, this is considered a pivotal work in Venetian painting's progress toward the conquest of light and colour. Off the south aisle is the late Renaissance Cappella di Sant'Atanasio, which holds paintings by Tintoretto (*Birth of the Baptist*) and Tiepolo, and inlaid choir stalls of 1455-64. From the adjoining Cappella dell'Addolorata you enter the **Cappella di San Tarasio**, formerly part of the apse of the church, where there are three carved and gilt Gothic polyptychs jointly painted by Antonio Vivarini, Giovanni d'Alemagna and Stefano da Sant'Agnese (1443). Perhaps the most impressive of these is the *Madonna of the Rosary,* with saints by Vivarini, decorative panels by d'Alemagna and a Madonna by Sant'Agnese set in a massive wooden frame of carved niches, turrets and pinnacles. On the walls are Andrea del Castagno's *Church Fathers,* executed by the Florentine artist in 1442 with the help of Francesco da Faenza. Andrea, who had been Masaccio's first pupil, was 19 years old when he brought the Tuscan Renaissance style to Venice in these paintings.

Back in the campo, a 16th-century doorway (No. 4693) marks the entrance to the former Benedictine convent, once the wealthiest and wildest in Venice. Here the city's aristocratic families sent young girls against their will, to save the expense of dowries. The more rebellious naturally refused to renounce the luxury and extravagance of patrician life, with results that are easily imagined. There is a painting by Francesco Guardi in the museum at Ca' Rezzonico (*The Parlour of the Nuns of San Zaccaria*) which shows the notoriously libertine atmosphere that prevailed in the convent, with dancing, theatre and novices making doughnuts. By a peculiar twist of fate, the convent is now a police station.

Walk away from San Zaccaria and turn right in the triangular Campo San Provolo, then follow the Fondamenta Osmarin and cross over the narrow Rio di Greci. Here, in a shady garden on the right, is **San Giorgio dei Greci**, a 16th-century church built on a design by Sante Lombardo for the Greek Orthodox community. The most important foreign church in Renaissance Venice, it has a magnificently decorated interior divided by a marble iconostasis with late Byzantine gold-ground paintings. On the north, in the rooms of the former Scuola dei Greci (now the Istituto Ellenico), is the **Museo dei Dipinti Sacri Bizantini**, which preserves some 80 Byzantine and post-Byzantine icons and various liturgical objects. One of the highlights here is a hieratic icon of *St Anastasius* by the 16th-century painter Michele Damaskinos, who is credited with having encouraged a young artist from Crete who was in Venice at the time – Domenico Theotocopuli – to absorb all he could from Tintoretto's work and then move on to Spain, where he was to establish a reputation under the name of El Greco.

Of Dalmatian Merchants and Ship-builders

The **Scuola di San Giorgio degli Schiavoni**, one block north along the canal and to the right, was erected in the early 16th century by the Dalmation confraternity, whose members were mainly merchants involved in trade with the East. The beautiful painting cycle on its ground-floor walls is one of the artistic jewels of Venice and should not be missed. Executed by Vittore Carpaccio, who worked in Venice between 1490 and 1523, the richly fantastic scenes portray episodes from the lives of three protectors of Dalmatia, SS George, Jerome and Tryphon.

Carpaccio tended to work on commissions that allowed him to indulge in his natural vocation for simple and apparently ingenuous narrative art, which in many ways recalls the *sacre rappresentazioni* that were the most widespread form of popular theatre of the time. These works, with their entrancing atmospheric power, mark the high point of his career. Most poetic of all, perhaps, is the *Study of St Augustine* (right), which depicts a scene described in the *Golden Legend:* alone in his study, the Bishop of Hippo hears the voice of his friend St Jerome (then absent in Antioch) announcing that he has died. The room is flooded with a sudden light and all movement comes to a halt (even the saint's fluffy dog is silent and still) as St Augustine interrupts his writing. The vanishing point of the perspective scheme has been shifted from the centre to the right of the painting, to coincide with the saint's pen, suspended above the page. Carpaccio never again achieved such expressive force, nor created an effect as magical as that achieved here. The painted wood ceiling and inlaid benches of the scuola are also noteworthy.

Now go down the *rio*, over the bridge, through a charming passageway with a tabernacle of the Madonna, then right to Salizzada San Francesco, which leads under an imposing portico to **San Francesco della Vigna**. This large 16th-century church, built to a design by Jacopo Sansovino, has a noble classical façade by Andrea Palladio based on a complex arrangement of superimposed temple fronts. The vast Latin-cross interior contains numerous masterpieces. Over the first altar of the south transept is the one work that can be attributed with certainty to Fra' Antonio da Negroponte, a *Madonna Adoring the Child* painted in the 1450s in a curious *retró* style; in the sanctuary are monuments to Doge Andrea Gritti and his circle, possibly by Sansovino; in the chapel on the north of the sanctuary, an outstanding ensemble of sculptures by Pietro Lombardo and pupils (1495–1510) with a fine illusionistic floor; in the Cappella Santa, entered from the north transept, *Madonna and Child with Saints* by Giovanni Bellini (signed and dated 1507); and in the fifth north chapel, another Madonna and Saints, the *Giustinian Altarpiece* by Paolo Veronese, the earliest of his masterpieces to be seen in Venice (1551).

In Campo Bandiera e Moro, almost due south near the Riva degli Schiavoni, is the late Gothic church of **San Giovanni in Bràgora**, with a distinctive linear brick façade and a low, cosy interior. Here are more masterpieces of Gothic and Renaissance painting: a *Resurrected Christ, Madonna with Saints Andrew and John the Baptist, Praying Madonna and Child* and a small panel with the *Head of the Redeemer* by Alvise Vivarini; *SS Andrew, Jerome and Martin* by Francesco Bissolo; *Constantine and St Helen* and *Baptism of Christ* by Cima da Conegliano; and a *Last Supper* by Paris Bordone. The stuccoed vault of the sanctuary is the work of Alessandro Vittoria.

Continuing eastwards you soon come to the **Arsenale**, once the greatest shipyard in the world. From here, after 1155, came the Venetian galleys, the basis of the republic's economic and political power. From here, also, comes the modern European word 'arsenal' – a corruption of the Arabic *darsina'a*, an industrial complex. Dante described this once-bustling dockyard in the *Inferno,* comparing the pitch in which he placed barterers of public offices to that boiled in the arsenal for caulking the damaged hulls of Venetian ships. The complex is usually closed to the public, except when one of the *corderie* – huge, long buildings originally designed for the storage of rigging – is being used for an exhibition. Part of the complex can be seen, however, from vaporetto No. 52, which runs along the canal inside. The land entrance is marked by a doorway of 1460, considered the first work of the Venetian Renaissance, surmounted by an attic with a large lion of St Mark attributed to Bartolomeo Bon. In 1692–94 the doorway was given a terraced porch adorned with Baroque allegorical statues; at the sides of this are two stone lions brought here from Greece (the one on the left comes from the harbour of Piraeus). Further right are two smaller lions, one from the Isle of Delos.

Walk down the Rio dell'Arsenale to reach the waterfront. You'll pass two sections of the **Museo Storico Navale** – one with historic ships, in the Officina Remi (just outside the Arsenale); the other with a beautiful model collection of typical Adriatic galleys, Venetian gondolas and other vessels – including the famed Bucintoro, the doges' ceremonial barge – in the former republican granary on the wharf at the end of the canal. When on display there is also an interesting model of the system of wooden piles on which Venice is built.

Riva degli Schiavoni, the broad, lively quay along the basin of San Marco, takes its name from the merchants of Schiavonia or Slavonia (modern Dalmatia), who here anchored their ships and carried on their business (you saw their *scuola* a few minutes ago). From Rio dell'Arsenale follow the Riva along the waterfront past the church of the Pietà (where Vivaldi was choirmaster) to reach the landing stage of vaporetto No. 9, which plies across the San Marco basin to San Giorgio and the Giudecca.

San Giorgio Maggiore

Henry James called the island of San Giorgio 'a success beyond all reason', attributing its fortune to its position, to the immense detached campanile, which seems to pin the buildings to their magnificent background, and above all to its colour. 'I do not know whether it is because San Giorgio is so grandly conspicuous, with a great deal of worn, faded-looking brickwork,' he wrote, 'but for many persons, the whole place has a kind of suffusion of rosiness.'

The most striking building on the island is Palladio's church of **San Giorgio Maggiore**, built between 1565 and 1580 over the remains of earlier churches dating back as far as the 8th century. On the right you can see a group of low red edifices, the convent, built by Baldassarre Longhena in the 17th century. The campanile is a later construction, as its neoclassical detailing suggests. It was erected in 1792 to replace an earlier one that had collapsed. The little harbour, with its twin lighthouses, was added in the early 19th century.

Palladio and his contemporaries were convinced that a harmony like that of music underlay the great buildings of the past, and that the secrets of that harmony could be unravelled by a careful study of mathematical proportions. You can see this belief at work on the façade of San Giorgio, where the triangle ideally formed by the lateral pediments reaches its apex at the base of the central pediment – an ingenious expedient that prepares the visitor, visually, for the aisled church within. Palladio's most complex church-front design, San Giorgio's classical façade was completed after the architect's death, in the early 17th century.

The interior of the church impresses more by virtue of its luminosity and spaciousness than for the complexity of its design, although it is the latter that gives rise to the former. Its remarkably sculptural quality is based on a sustained opposition between flat and rounded forms – walls, arches and vaults, engaged columns and giant pilasters – and decoration is almost totally eliminated. Its art treasures include two works by Tintoretto, the *Last Supper* and the *Gathering of Manna,* on the walls around the high altar (1594). The gift of manna to the Israelites in the wilderness provided the Old Testament parallel to the institution of the Eurcharist, and the paintings were designed to be most effective when seen by the communicant from the altar rails. In the monks' choir are stalls carved with stories from the life of St Benedict; over the altar of the winter choir is a *St George and the Dragon* by Vittore Carpaccio.

The Monastery of San Giorgio Maggiore, seat of the Fondazione Giorgio Cini, is a fine complex arranged around two cloisters. Palladio designed the refectory, where there is a *Marriage of the Virgin* by Jacopo Tintoretto; and a monumental staircase by Baldassarre Longhena ascends to the first floor, where the Library, also by Longhena, has 17th-century inlaid bookcases with over 100,000 books on the history of art. In the park is the Teatro Verde, for open-air theatre. The complex is open to the public only for special events. The campanile, reached by a lift, is 60m high and offers unsurpassed views of the city and the lagoon.

The Giudecca

The Giudecca is a long, narrow island delightfully off the beaten track. Originally known as *spinalonga* ('long spine') because of its shape, its present name probably derives from the Jewish community that lived here in the 13th century. By the 16th century it had become a place of green quietude, abounding with lush gardens, aristocratic homes and tranquil convents. Following the decline of the Venetian aristocracy and the suppression of the convents, the island was gradually given over to barracks, prisons and factories. Today its simple houses are home to many of Venice's boatmen. The quay, along the inner, southern side of the island, takes different names as it goes along, offering splendid views of the Giudecca Canal, San Marco and the Riva degli Schiavoni. The entire section from the Rio di San Biagio canal, on the island's western tip, to the church of the Zitelle, on the east, is almost tourist free and gives a sense of a simpler, original Venice.

The boat stops first at the church and convent of Santa Maria della Presentazione, usually known as **Le Zitelle** ('The Virgins'), where the nuns once made excellent Venetian lace. Its design is attributed to Palladio, though it was not built until after his death. From here it is a short walk to the main monument on the Giudecca, the church of the **Redentore**, designed by Palladio in 1577 and completed after the architect's death by Antonio da Ponte. This church, which was erected as a thank-offering after an outbreak of plague that killed more than one-third of the population, is another of Palladio's masterpieces. Its façade is a development of that of San Francesco della Vigna, which he had designed some ten years earlier, with pediments over the door and central bay and the end sections of a hidden pediment emerging on either side of the main block. As at San Francesco della Vigna (and again at San Giorgio Maggiore), the overall scheme is regulated by a complicated system of proportions. In past centuries the doge paid an annual visit to this church, crossing the canal from the Zattere on a bridge of boats – and the tradition is still kept up today, with fireworks and other events on the third Saturday in July.

In the interior, Palladio appears to have paid more attention to the visual effects than he did at San Giorgio Maggiore: there is a more harmonious relationship between the various parts, and a much better climax in the semi-circular colonnade behind the high altar. From the door the church appears as a simple rectangular basilica with an apse; but as you approach the high altar, the curves of the dome and arms gradually reveal themselves, giving a sense of elation and expansion rarely achieved by purely architectural means. Over the altars are paintings by 16th- and 17th-century painters, notably, a *Nativity* by Francesco Bassano, a *Deposition* by Palma Giovane, a Resurrection by Francesco Bassano and an *Ascension* by Jacopo Tintoretto and assistants. Over the Baroque high altar (which Palladio certainly didn't anticipate) is a crucifix between 16th-century bronze statues of St Mark and St Francis. In the sacristy are a *Madonna and Child with Angels* by Alvise Vivarini, a *Madonna and Saints* atrributed to Francesco Bissolo and a *Baptism of Christ* by Paolo Veronese.

Further west rises the church of Sant'Eufemia, originally of the 11th century, and at the end of the *fondamenta* beyond a metal bridge, the imposing Gothic-Revival mass of the Mulino Stucky, a flour mill of 1895 presently undergoing a facelift.

Beyond the Giudecca are the island of **San Lazzaro degli Armeni**, seat of an Armenian monastery founded in the 18th century by a group of monks who fled the Orient; and the **Lido di Venezia**, a busy suburban neighbourhood and bathing beach on the island separating the Adriatic sea from the lagoon. Noteworthy buildings include the Grand Hotel des Bains (1900), the setting of Thomas Mann's *Death in Venice,* and the Moorish style Grand Hotel Excelsior (1898–1908).

Canareggio

This walk takes in the *sestiere* of Cannaregio, the northwestern part of the city lying between the Grand Canal and the Lagoon. From the church of the Scalzi, next to the train station, it wanders amid busy *calli* and quiet *campi*, touching upon the Ghetto, one of the prettier areas of the city, with an interesting museum of Jewish life. Making a loop to take in four important churches – the Madonna dell'Orto, the Gesuiti, Santa Maria dei Miracoli, and

---

Mantegna's Saint Sebastian

The subject of St Sebastian seems to have held some mysterious fascination for Andrea Mantegna, who painted at least three other versions (now at the Accademia, in Paris and in Vienna); but the most powerful treatment of the theme is to be found in this Ca' d'Oro painting. The style is certainly that of his later years (1490–1500), filled with symbolic nuance: the tortured line of the drapery accentuates the idea of Christian suffering in the name of faith, and the ample use of purple-grey tones emphasises the saint's human agony. The perspective rendering of anatomy (notice the foot that steps out of the frame at the bottom of the painting) is as sophisticated as that of the artist's most famous painting, the *Dead Christ* in Milan.

Giudecca, panorama

San Giovanni Crisostomo – it ends at the splendid Ca' d'Oro, a Gothic mansion containing a beautiful and well-displayed collection of paintings, sculpture and applied arts. The two-hour walk can be combined with the boat trip to the lovely islands of Murano, Burano and Torcello (described in the following section) to make a full, but satisfying, day.

Gli Scalzi to Madonna dell'Orto via the Ghetto

The church of Santa Maria di Nazareth, usually known simply as **Gli Scalzi** (literally, 'the Barefoot') was built by Baldassarre Longhena after 1654 for a community of Carmelite monks who moved here from Rome, and its design and interior décor in fact recall those of Roman Baroque churches. Giuseppe Sardi added the white marble façade in 1680. The second south and first north chapels have vault frescoes by Tiepolo, who also painted the ceiling of the nave. This painting was destroyed by Austrian bombs in 1915, and the modern replacement dates from 1934.

The crowded Lista di Spagna leads northeastwards, crossing the broad Canale di Cannaregio by the Ponte delle Guglie. Once across the canal you turn left then immediately right through the Sottoportico del Ghetto. The street leads past a synagogue with beautifully carved doors, and over a bridge to the **Ghetto Nuovo**. Set aside from 1516 to 1797 for the city's Jewish population, this tiny, water-ringed neighbourhood is the oldest historically documented ghetto in the world. The site was originally occupied by a foundry – in Venetian dialect, *getto* – and this term was subsequently taken to describe the Jewish quarter in cities everywhere. On the whole the Venetian Jews enjoyed a relatively relaxed relationship with the republic: though they were obliged to follow certain rules that limited their social and economic activities, they maintained their religious freedom and, except for a brief period of expulsion between 1527 and 1533, they remained within the city, in this neighbourhood, until Napoleon demolished the gates of the ghetto in 1797. After this time they were allowed to live where they pleased. As the area of the ghetto was limited, the Jews were forced to build tenements that, without violating the city's height limitations, would accommodate many families. Several of the houses therefore have very low ceilings.

The **Museo d'Arte Ebraica**, in Campo Ghetto Nuovo, offers guided tours of the ghetto and of three of its synagogues, also called 'scuole' by virtue of the mixed purposes they served. The most sumptuous is the Scuola Levantina, in the Ghetto Vecchio, established in 1538 and remodelled in the 17th century, possibly to a design by Baldassarre Longhena. The museum's collections include liturgical objects and other interesting examples of Venetian Jewish art of the 17th to 19th centuries, and text boards describing the plight of Venetian Jews during the holocaust.

Cross the Campo di Ghetto Nuovo to the Fondamenta degli Ormesini and turn right. This is one of the quieter parts of the city, almost untouched by tourists. Most of the alleys on the left will lead you eventually to the beautiful Gothic church of the **Madonna dell'Orto**, founded in the 14th century and rebuilt in the 15th to hold a miraculous image of the Virgin discovered in a nearby garden (*orto* in Italian). This was the parish church of Tintoretto, who was buried in 1594 in the chapel on the south side of the sanctuary. Inside are several of his works: the *Presentation of the Virgin in the Temple* at the end of the south aisle, the *Last Judgement* and *Worship of the Golden Calf* in the choir, and the *Vision of the Cross to St Peter* and *Beheading of St Paul* in the apse. The latter are hung around an *Annunciation* by Palma Giovane, and a *St John the Baptist and Saints* by Cima da Conegliano stands over the first south altar. There is also a fine 15th-century cloister.

I Gesuiti to Ca' d'Oro

It takes some fancy footwork, down the busy Rio di Noale towards the Grand Canal and up the other side almost to the Fondamenta Nuove to reach **I Gesuiti**, the church of Venice's Jesuit community. This is an early 18th-century edifice with a lively Baroque façade based on Roman models. Like so many Jesuit churches in Italy, it has an elaborately decorated interior – in this case an extraordinary work of trompe-l'œil with green and white inlaid marbles imitating damask wall hangings and white and gold stuccoes. Over the first north altar is Titian's *Martyrdom of St Lawrence,* and in the transept on this side is an *Assumption* by Jacopo Tintoretto. Palma Giovane decorated the nearby Oratorio dei Crociferi, founded in the 13th century and renovated in the late 16th century. If it strikes you as odd that the seat of such an important order should be located so far from the mainstream of city life, you have not yet begun to understand Venetian psychology: the senate managed to keep the powerful Jesuits out of the city for a long time, and when the order finally was allowed to establish itself, it was kept as far from the centres of political and economic affairs as topography would allow.

From Campo dei Gesuiti cross the Rio Santa Caterina and follow the calli southwards to their end, near the church and campo of Santi Apostoli. Now turn left, cross the Rio Santi Apostoli and bear slightly left again. **Santa Maria dei Miracoli**, a lonely little church in the narrow Campo dei Miracoli, is one of the higher achievements of the early Venetian Renaissance. Constructed between 1481 and 1489 to enshrine a miraculous image of the Virgin, it is covered with coloured marble panels whose ingeniously complex design makes the church appear larger than it really is without disturbing the overall effect, which is undoubtedly one of harmonious tranquillity. The church is the work of Pietro Lombardo, who was assisted here by his sons Antonio and Tullio. The interior also has exquisite Lombardesque marblework and a delightful Madonna, over the high altar, by Nicolò di Pietro Paradisi. The figures of Saints in the coffered ceiling were painted by Pier Maria Pennacchi (1528). The choir loft above the entrance bears a *Madonna and Child* by Palma Giovane.

Nearby, the pleasant red and white church of **San Giovanni Crisostomo** almost fills its small campo. The last work of Mauro Codussi, it too is a masterpiece of Venetian Renaissance architecture. The Greek-cross interior preserves two important paintings – Giovanni Bellini's *St Jerome with St Christopher and St Augustine* (over the first south altar), the high altarpiece of *St John Chrysostom and Six Saints* by Sebastiano del Piombo – and an extraordinarily powerful, classically serene marble relief of the *Coronation of the Virgin* (over the second north altar) by Tullio Lombardo, who also decorated the pilasters in the chapel.

At the eastern end of the Strada Nuova, a broad thoroughfare cut in 1871 to connect Rialto with the train station, stands the plain brick church of Santi Apostoli, built in 1575 possibly to a design by Alessandro Vittoria. Some way down the Strada Nuova, but before the first bridge, Calle della Ca' d'Oro leads left to the land entrance of the **Ca' d'Oro**, the fine Gothic palace designed by Giovanni and Bartolomeo Bon and Matteo Raverti (1420–34), named the 'Golden House' after the splendid gilt decoration that used to adorn the façade on the Grand Canal. The palace is now a museum displaying the outstanding art collection of its former owner, Baron Giorgio Franchetti. Here you can see Italian and foreign paintings and Venetian marbles, bronzes and ceramics of the 15th to the 18th centuries. Highlights include Antonio Vivarini's remarkable *Polyptych with Passion Scenes* (1476–84) and Andrea Mantegna's *St Sebastian,* a splendid masterpiece of the early Renaissance; a double portrait by Tullio Lombardo and fresco fragments by Giorgione and Titian from the exterior of the Fondaco dei Tedeschi. From the ground-floor atrium, take a stroll outside in the small secret garden and stunning canal-front portico before leaving.

Murano, Burano and Torcello

To see Murano, Burano and Torcello – the three inhabited islands in the lagoon between Venice and the mainland – requires a long morning or afternoon, but it is well worth the time and trouble. Murano and Burano are known for their glass and lace, respectively. Torcello, now a romantic place with a little village counting fewer than 50 souls, is famous for its great cathedral, whose sheer splendour alone justifies the journey. Take vaporetto No. 12 from Fondamenta Nuove, easily accessed by the No. 52 from San Marco or on foot from the church of the Gesuiti. Remember to check schedules when you arrive on the islands, and to give yourself at least an hour to go to and from Venice.

Shortly after leaving the Fondamenta Nuove the boat passes the walled Island of San Michele, the cemetery of Venice and site of the city's oldest Renaissance church – the chapel of San Michele in Isola, designed by Mauro Codussi in 1469. Between Murano and Burano you'll be able to spot the cypress-girt Franciscan hermitage of San Francesco del Deserto, on a solitary little island to the southwest. The monks do allow visits, and you can hire a boat from Burano to get there if you wish.

Murano

The Venetian glass factories were moved to Murano as a safety measure in 1291 (to remove from the city the implicit risk of fire), and the town has been synonymous with exquisite craftsmanship ever since. The Venetians rediscovered this lost art in the 10th century, when merchants brought the secrets of the trade from the East, and the making of clear 'crystal' glass remained a well-kept secret until the 16th century. After a period of decline the making of artistic glass was revived at the end of the 19th century, and today the many glass factories all welcome visitors. In the 16th century Murano became a favourite retreat of Venetian intellectuals, many of whom had splendid houses

Santa Maria dei Miracoli

and luxuriant gardens on the island. Few of these remain, however, and it is difficult, today, to imagine this aspect of the island's past.

The small Grand Canal that runs betwen the town's shops and houses takes you to the **Museo dell'Arte Vetraria**, or glass museum, located in the 17th-century Palazzo Giustinian. Here, on the ground floor, are examples of antique glass ranging in date from the 2nd century BC to the 2nd century AD. Venetian glass of the 15th to 18th centuries is displayed on the upper floor; among the earliest surviving pieces is a dark blue marriage cup of 1470–80 with portraits of the bride and groom and allegorical devices in coloured enamel, ascribed to the workshop of Angelo Barovier. There are also examples of foreign glass. Modern and contemporary glass is displayed in an annexe to the museum (one ticket gives admission to both) on Rio dei Vetrai.

Murano's main architectural monument is **Santi Maria e Donato**, a splendid example of Veneto-Byzantine church type founded in the 7th century but rebuilt in the 12th century. It was originally dedicated to the Virgin Mary; St Donato's name was added when his relics were brought here from Cephalonia, in Greece, together with the bones of a dragon he supposedly slew (four of which, for sceptics, hang behind the altar). The church is known above all for its magnificent Romanesque mosaic pavement (1141), although the capitals of the columns, the Byzantine mosaic of the Virgin in the apse and the colourful wooden ancona by Paolo Veneziano in the north aisle, are also quite beautiful.

Burano, panorama

Burano

About half an hour away from Venice, this is a charming little fishing village resplendent with colour, a delightful place just to wander without any precise goal, though there are a few paintings – by Girolamo da Santacroce, Giovanni Battista Tiepolo and Giovanni Mansueti – in the parish church. In past centuries the island was a favourite haunt of painters, who were drawn by the maritime atmosphere of water, sky and sails, as well as by the colour of its walls and by the picturesque quality of its *merlettaie,* or lace-makers, who used to pursue their minute craft outside, in the sunlight, as Canaletto shows them. Lace-making in fact has been a mainstay of the island's economy since the early 16th century, and lace is still made and sold on the island. If you plan to buy some, however, be sure to get the genuine Venetian variety, which you'll learn to recognise in the lace museum at the **Scuola dei Merletti**. And don't leave Burano without strolling over to its small sister-island, **Mazzorbo**, whose pretty little canal is still lined with fishing-nets spread out to dry in the sun. Here, too, is some of the best contemporary architecture in Venice, G. De Carlo's 1986 housing project built in full respect of local vernacular forms and colours.

Torcello

Ruskin tells the early history of Torcello with uncommon poetic skill: 'Thirteen hundred years ago, the grey moorland looked as it does this day, and the purple mountains stood as radiantly in the deep distances of evening; but on the line of the horizon there were strange fires mixed with the light of sunset, and the lament of many human voices mixed with the fretting of the waves on their ridges of sand. The flames rose from the ruins of Altinum; the lament from the multitudes of its people, seeking, like Israel of old, a refuge from the sword in the paths of the sea.' In more prosaic terms it can be said that Torcello flourished between the 7th and the 13th century, when it was the insular stronghold of refugees driven from mainland Altinum by the Lombard invasions. At one time it counted as many as 20,000 inhabitants, but by the 15th century rivalry with Venice and chronic malaria had eroded its prestige and decimated its population. Now it is little more than a small group of houses in a lonely part of the lagoon, huddled in the shadow of one of the more singular and impressive churches in Venice.

The **Cathedral of Santa Maria Assunta** is a ten-minute walk from the landing stage, down a lonely canal amid fields and a few houses. This great church was founded in 639, rebuilt in 864 and again in 1008. In front of it are remains of the baptistery and a narthex enlarged in the 14th and 15th centuries. The tall detached campanile, as you will have seen from the boat, is a conspicuous landmark in the lagoon.

The stunningly beautiful interior is among the highest achievements of Christian religious architecture. Eighteen Greek marble columns with finely carved capitals separate the aisles and nave, and a superb 11th-century mosaic pavement covers the floor. Four elaborately carved screens, of Byzantine inspiration, mark the entrance to the sanctuary, surmounted by 15th-century paintings of the Virgin and Apostles. The relics of St. Heliodorus, first bishop of Altinum, are preserved in a Roman sarcophagus beneath the 7th-century high altar. Set into the wall north of the altar is an inscription commemorating the foundation of the church, considered the oldest document of Venetian history.

The most striking feature of the church, however, is the important cycle of mosaics, almost certainly fully completed by the time the mosaicists set to work on San Marco in 1156. The *Virgin and Child with Apostles* in the apse represents a break with traditional iconography, which ordinarily reserves this position for Christ Pantokrator (as at San Marco); the exception may be justified, in part, by the inscription in the arch, which begins, 'I am God and the flesh of the Mother ...' The work was probably done by craftsmen from Constantinople. In the chapel to the right of the high altar is a somewhat earlier representation of *Christ between the Archangels Michael and Gabriel with Saints Nicholas, Ambrose, Augustine and Martin,* in which the workmanship is considerably coarser.

The west wall of the church holds a vast mosaic of the *Last Judgement,* thoughtlessly restored in the 19th century when many areas were removed and replaced by copies. The most intact sections are those depicting the realm of Hell, with the seven deadly sins (Pride, Lust, Greed, Anger, Envy, Avarice and Sloth). There are many memorable details here: the tremendous energy of the angels as they drive the Proud into hellfire, the smoky burst of flame that envelops the Lustful, the chill bodies of the Greedy depicted engulfed by darkness, the sinister pallor that throws into relief the writhing serpents emerging from the eyes of the Envious.

In front of the cathedral and a little to one side is the church of **Santa Fosca**, built in the 11th century to enshrine the relics of an early Christian martyr brought to the island in 1011. This is a centrally-planned building with a projecting apse, an arcaded portico and a tiled wooden roof. It is an austere building inside and out, with little decorative detail to distract from its well-proportioned forms and space. On the grass outside is a primitive stone seat known as 'Attila's chair'.

The Palazzo del Consiglio, across the lawn, now houses the **Museo dell'Estuario di Torcello**, which contains an interesting and well displayed collection of objects tracing the history of the island and its environs. It includes some objects from the cathedral – fragments of 12th-century mosaics removed from the tympanum of the apse, and all that remains of the 13th-century silver-gilt altar frontal – as well as archaeological finds and a number of paintings from demolished churches in the area.

Practical Information

Getting There

Venice's Marco Polo International Airport is located on the mainland 13km (8 miles) north of the city. Domestic **flights** connect with Milan, Naples, Palermo, Rome and Turin; international flights with Amsterdam, Barcelona, Brussels, Copenhagen, Düsseldorf, Frankfurt, London, Lugano, Montpellier, Moscow, Munich, New York (via Milan), Nice, Paris, Stüttgart, Vienna and Zurich. Airport buses run to and from the terminal and the car park at Piazzale, and there are regular boat connections between the airport, San Marco and the Lido. If you are carrying a lot of baggage, you might want to consider a water taxi, which will take you directly to the landing nearest your hotel (expensive).

Venice Santa Lucia Station is located on the Fondamenta Santa Lucia, at the west end of the Grand Canal. The principal **trains** connect with Verona, Milan, Turin and Genoa; Bologna, Florence and Rome; and Trieste. There are direct through services to and from Basel, Bern, Geneva, Lugano, Munich, Nice, Paris, Vienna and Zurich.

All **roads** from the mainland terminate at Piazzale Roma, on the Tronchetto landfill, where there is a multi-level car park.

Tourist Information

Azienda Promozione Turistica, Castello 4421 (tel. 041 529 8711, fax 523 0399).

There are Information Offices at the train station (tel. 719 078); Giardini di San Marco (tel. 522 6356); and Lido di Venezia, Gran Viale Santa Maria Elisabetta (tel. 526 5721).

Ask your concierge for the useful (free) publication, *Un Ospite di Venezia*, listing everything you need to know to get around, including current events and emergency numbers.

Getting Around

There are two ways to get around Venice – by land and by water – and neither of them is very fast. If you manage to go from your starting point to your destination without making a wrong turn, walking is probably the most practical means of locomotion. The trouble is, Venice's maze-like street plan tends to prevent out-of-towners getting from here to there on the first try. If you wish to walk through Venice without carrying luggage, shopping bags, or other encumbrances, you can hire a *portabagagli*, or porter, to do the work for you; details in *Un Ospite di Venezia*.

The *vaporetto*, or water bus, is the most convenient way of getting around town, but it is painfully slow and, in the season (May–Oct), jam-packed with passengers. The main services are the No. 1, *accelerato*, calling at all stops on the line, Piazzale Roma-Ferrovia (the train station)-Rialto-San Marco-Lido and vice versa; the No. 52, *diretto*, is an express service calling at selected stops on the line, Lido-San Zaccaria-Piazzale Roma-Ferrovia-Fondamenta Nuove-Murano-Fondamenta Nuove-San Zaccaria-Piazzale Roma and vice versa; the No. 82 is another *diretto* calling at selected stops on the line, San Marco-Rialto-Casinò-Ferrovia-Piazzale Roma-Tronchetto-Santa Marta-Saccafisola-Zattere-Giudecca-San Giorgio-San Zaccaria and vice versa; the No. 6, *diretto*, is a fast motor boat that runs from San Marco to the Lido and back; and the Nos. 12 and 14 serve the northern lagoon: San Zaccaria-Lido-San Nicolò-Punta Sabbioni-Treporti-Burano-Torcello-Burano-Mazzorbo-Murano-Fondamenta Nuove and vice versa. Timetables are posted at most landing stages and published monthly in *Un Ospite di Venezia*. Tickets can be bought during working hours at most landing stages and from shops displaying the ACTV logo, or on board after hours. There are discounts for round-trip, 24-hour and three-day tickets. There is also a sort of frequent-flyers card, called *Carta Venezia*, which entitles holders to substantial discounts on all lines; enquire at the ACTV offices in Corte dell'Albero (near the Sant'Angelo landing on the Grand Canal), or on Piazzale Roma.

Traghetti, or gondola ferries, offer a handy way of getting across the Grand Canal without walking all the way to one of the bridges (there only three: Ponte Scalzi at the train station, Rialto and the Accademia). You'll see yellow signs marked 'Traghetto' with a gondola here and there as you wander the city. They are extremely cheap and quite a lot of fun, for in all but the roughest weather you ride standing up. Most operate from early morning until late afternoon. Furthermore, some *vaporetti* operate as *traghetti* on short, single-stop trips: cases in which a *traghetto* fare applies will appear on the tariff list at the ticket booth.

Motoscafi, or water taxis are the fastest and most exclusive vehicles in Venice. Point-to-point service in town is metered, and there are fixed rates (published in *Un Ospite di Venezia*) for the most common destinations outside the city centre.

Gondolas can be hired for a leisurely tour of the city, at standard rates or on a custom-service basis. In the latter case be sure to agree upon the duration and price of your ride before setting out.

Hotels

Surely one of the world's finest hotels, the **Cipriani**, Isola della Giudecca 10 (tel. 041 520 7744, fax 520 3930; closed Jan–Feb) is also Venice's most exclusive. It is a world unto itself, with luxuriously appointed rooms, a stunning garden and views that are hard to forget. Its position at the tip of the Isle of the Giudecca, however, makes getting downtown rather a bother. If you're in the market for a fancy place to stay, but are planning on doing a lot of sight-seeing, you're probably better off in one of the city's other luxury hotels, which are arranged in a neat row along the waterfront on either side of San Marco. The most famous of these is the **Danieli**, Castello, Riva degli

Schiavoni, 4196 (tel. 041 522 6480, fax 410017), where Marcel Proust stayed. Weather permitting, breakfast is served on the roof terrace over-looking the lagoon, the Isle of San Giorgio and the Grand Canal. Just down the quay, is the **Londra Palace**, Castello, Riva degli Schiavoni, 4171 (tel. 041 520 0533, fax 522 5032), which is less expensive and more refined than the Danieli. Still in the luxury class, it offers marvellously appointed rooms and an equally impressive roof terrace. On the other side of San Marco, in Calle Larga del 'Ascension, are the **Luna Baglioni**, San Marco 1243 (tel. 041 5289840, fax 528 7160), and the **Europa & Regina**, San Marco, Calle Larga 22 Marzo, 2159 (tel. 041 520 0477, fax 523 1533), also deservedly famous.

Moderately priced hotels abound in Venice, but good ones are few and far between. The **Flora** is nicely situated at San Marco, Calle dei Bergamaschi, 2283a (tel. 041 520 5844, fax 522 8217). It has a beautiful small garden. On the other side of the Calle Larga, at San Marco, Campiello de la Fenice, 1936, is **La Fenice et des Artistes** (tel. 041 523 2333, fax 520 3721), which really is frequented by artists (there are some original works by 20th-century masters in the lobby). On the Lido, with a pleasant garden, is **Quattro Fontane**, 16 Via Fontane (tel. 041 526 0227, fax 526 0726).

The level of comfort and service in inexpensive hotels can be downright disappointing – as is to be expected in a city, like Venice, subject to excessive demand. Three exceptions to this rule are the **Accademia**, at Dorsoduro, Fondamenta Bollani, 1058 (tel. 041 523 7846, fax 523 9152); **La Calcina**, Dorsoduro 780, Zattere (tel. 041 520 6466, fax 522 7045), where Ruskin stayed; and the **Falier**, Santa Croce, Salizzada San Pantalon, 130 (tel. 041 522 8882, fax 520 6554). All three are simple but quite good. If you're looking for an adequate place to stay but are short on cash, bear in mind that several of the city's religious communities open their convents to visitors during high season, offering very good accommodation at remarkably low prices. Details from the APT.

Restaurants

Restaurants in Venice can be entertaining in their own right, especially in the warmer months when most offer table service outside. Unlike Rome or Florence, Venice is traffic free, which makes eating outside and watching the boats – or crowds – go by remarkably like dinner theatre. **Harry's Bar**, on the Grand Canal near San Marco, at San Marco, Calle Vallaresso, 1323 (tel. 041 528 5777, fax 520 8822; closed Mon), draws three kinds of clientele: the people-watchers, who like to sit downstairs and watch the artists, musicians and movie stars walk in; the romantics, who prefer a table upstairs, by the window, where they can gaze out over the water; and of course the celebri-ties themselves, particularly abundant during the Biennali. Founded many years ago by legendary hotelier Harry Cipriani, this is still one of Venice's finest restaurants (specialities: *risotto alle seppioline, scampi alla Thermidor con riso pilaf* and a remarkable selection of desserts) – and one of its most expensive. The same impeccable level of cuisine and service, but at more moderate prices, is offered by **Harry's Dolci**, Giudecca 773 (tel. 041 522 4844, fax 522 2322), where the atmosphere is less formal and there are tables on the water in summer. In the same general neighbourhood as Harry's Bar, west of San Marco, is **La Caravella**, San Marco, Calle Larga 22 Marzo, 2397 (tel. 041 520 8901; closed Wed, except from Jun to Sep), another expensive, but excellent restaurant (specialities: *antipasto Tiziano con granseola, bigoli in salsa, filetto di branzino alle erbe*) with a distinctive maritime décor. Needless to say, all the high-end venues have extensive lists of regional, Italian and imported wines.

Moderate-to-inexpensive restaurants include **Osteria da Fiore**, San Polo, Calle del Scaleter, 2202a (tel. 041 721 308, fax 721 343; closed Sun, Mon, a few days around Christmas and in Aug), serving very good seafood; **Al Graspo de Ua**, San Marco 5094, Calle dei Bombaseri (tel. 041 520 0150, fax 523 3917; closed Mon, Tue, late Dec–early Jan and two weeks in Aug), an authentic Venetian tavern; **Ai Gondolieri**, Dorsoduro, Fondamenta San Vio, 366 (tel. 041 528 6396; closed Tue); **Antica Locanda Montin**, Dorsoduro, Fondamenta di Borgo, 1147 (tel. 041 522 7151; closed Tue evening and Wed, and a few days in Jan and Aug); and **Corte Sconta**, Castello, Calle del Pestrin, 3886 (tel. 041 522 7024, fax 522 7513; closed Sun, Mon, a few days in Jan–Feb and mid-Jul–mid-Aug), serving Venetian specialities, especially seafood, in a rustic interior and a pleasant garden court. All the above have good selections of regional and Italian and a limited selection of imported wines. Next to the Hotel La Fenice et des Artistes but under separate management, is the **Taverna la Fenice** (tel. 041 522 3856; closed Sun, Mon morning and a few days in Jan), serving skilfully prepared regional specialities and great pizza, with tables in the *campiello* in fair weather.

A good, inexpensive seafood place on Murano is **Ai Frati** (tel. 041 736694; closed Thu and Feb). On Burano are two very good trattorie, **Da Romano**, 221 Via Galuppi (tel. 041 730 030, fax 735 217; closed Tue, Sun evening and mid-Dec–mid-Feb) and **Al Gatto Nero-da Ruggero** (tel. 041 730 120, fax 735 570; closed Mon and a few days in Feb and Nov), serving Venetian specialities such as *spaghetti al nero di seppia, pesce in umido* and *biscotti di Burano* accompanied by regional wines. And if you make it all the way out to Torcello, treat yourself to a meal at the **Locanda Cipriani** (tel. 041 730 150, fax 735 433; closed Tue and Nov–Mar; expensive), known for its *insalatina novella con scampi al sesamo, tagliatelle nere con ragout di vongole e cape-sante, sorpresa di mare in crosta* and *semifreddo alla Grappa di Picolit*; or at the **Osteria al Ponte del Diavolo** (tel. 041 730 401, fax 730 250; closed Thu and all evenings except Sat, as well as Jan–Feb; moderate), where house specialities include *polipetti caldi, filetti di sogliola in salsa di zucchine, seppioline fritte* and *crespelle alla crema della casa*.

Special Events

La Biennale di Venezia organises biennial historical and documentary exhibitions in five areas: Visual Arts, Cinema, Theatre, Music and Architecture.

These events, which draw immense international crowds, usually take place in odd years, between June and September; but there is talk of switching the dates to even years to allow a super-biennale to be staged in 2000. Also important are the **Mostra Internazionale del Cinema**, on the Lido (annual, Sep) and the **Premio Letterario Campiello** (Sep). The Teatro La Fenice traditionally hosts opera in winter and classical music in spring, summer and autumn; but it was recently damaged by fire, and at the time of writing events are held in a large tent in a rather out-of-the-way position on the Tronchetto. There is good drama at the Teatro del Ridotto and Teatro Goldoni; and at any given moment there is at least one major exhibition of art or architecture going on at the Fondazione Cini, Palazzo Grassi, Museo Correr, or one of the other major venues in the city. Surviving from past ages are the popular **Festa della Sensa** (late spring), culminating in a ceremony recalling the traditional marriage between the Doge and the Sea; the great gondola race known as the **Regata Storica** in the Grand Canal (first Sun in Sep); the **Festa del Redentore** (third week in Sep), with ceremonial boat processions and fireworks; and many other feasts in the towns and islands of the lagoon. Last but by no means least, **Carnevale** draws merrymakers from all parts of the world.

Museums and Monuments

Venice's museums and galleries observe the following opening times, though changes may be made without notice.

Galleria dell'Academia: Mon–Sat 9.00–19.00, Sun 9.00–14.00 (visitors admitted until 18.00).

Palazzo Ducale: daily 9.00–19.00.

Peggy Guggenheim Collection: Wed–Mon 11.00–18.00.

Museo Civico Correr: Wed–Mon 10.00–16.00 (visitors admitted until 17.15).

Museo Fortuny: closed for restoration at the time of writing.

Ca' Rezzonico – Museo del Settecento Veneziano: Sat–Thu 10.00–16.00.

Museo Storico Navale: daily 9.00–13.00, Thu 9.00–13.00 and 14.30–17.00; closed Sun and hols.

Ca' Doro – Galleria Franchetti: daily 9.00–14.00.

Museo Archeologico: daily 9.00–14.00 (visitors admitted until 13.30).

Ca' Pesaro – Museo d'Arte Moderna: Tue–Sun 10.00–16.00; **Museo Orientale**: Tue–Sun 9.00–14.00.

Museo Dipinti Sacri Bizantini – Istituto Ellenico: daily 9.00–13.00, 14.00–17.00; closed Sun and hols.

Palazzo Mocenigo: daily 8.30–13.30; closed Sun and hols.

Monastero Mekhitarista, Isola di San Lazzaro degli Armeni: guided tours daily 15.20–17.00.

Museo della Comunità Ebraica: daily 10.00–16.30; closed Sat and Jewish hols.

Biblioteca Marciana: Mon–Fri 9.00–19.00, Sat 9.00–13.30; closed Sun and hols.

Museo della Fondazione Querini-Stampalia: Tue, Wed, Thu, Sun

10.00–13.00, 15.00–18.00, Fri–Sat 10.00–13.00, 15.00–22.00.
Scala Contarini del Bovolo: daily 10.30–18.30.
Scuola Grande di San Rocco: daily 9.00–17.30.
Scuola di San Giorgio degli Schiavoni: Tue–Sun10.00–12.30, 15.00–18.00.
Scuola dei Carmini: Mon–Sat 9.00–12.00, 15.00–18.00.
Oratorio dei Cruciferi (Gesuiti): Fri, Sat and Sun 10.00–13.00.
Basilica di San Marco: summer 9.30–17.00, Sun 14.00–17.00; **Galleria Basilica di San Marco**: daily 9.30–16.30; **Pala d'Oro e Tesoro**: Mon–Sat 9.30–16.30, Sun and hols 14.00–16.30; **Campanile di San Marco**: daily 9.30–19.00.
Chiesa di San Giorgio Maggiore: daily 9.30–12.30 and 14.30–17.30.
Basilica dei Frari: Mon–Sat 9.00–12.00, 14.30–18.00, Sun and hols 15.00–18.00.
Museo Vetrario di Murano: Thu–Tue 10.00–17.00.
Scuola di Merletti di Burano: Tue–Sat 9.00–18.00, Sun 10.00–16.00.
Museo dell'Estuario di Torcello: Tue–Sun 10.30–12.30, 14.00–17.30; closed hols.
Cattedrale di Torcello: daily 10.00–12.30, 14.00–17.00.
Convento di San Francesco del Deserto: daily 9.00–11.00, 15.00–17.00.

6. EAST OF VENICE

There is a curious feeling about the region east of Venice: you really do sense you're in another country – or perhaps more precisely, in no country at all. Trieste is an Austrian city inhabited by Italians; and in Cividale del Friuli, you can hear Slovene spoken in the streets. The presence over the centuries of Latin, Slavic and Germanic cultures in this area has left a mark so deep that it underlies everything from architecture to appetisers.

The overall atmosphere of the region is actually quite pleasant; with the notable exception of the beach resorts, tourist crowds are few and far between – even the roads are relatively unencumbered with traffic – and this is despite the fact that there are some truly memorable things to see. Aquileia is known for its late Roman and early Christian remains; Trieste is a little Vienna by the sea; Palmanova is a shining example of the ideal Renaissance city; Udine is a small treasure-chest of Venetian art and architecture; and Cividale has some of the finest vestiges anywhere of Lombard art – a real rarity. The landscape – from the marshy lowlands of the coast, a favourite stopping place of migratory birds, to the white limestone peaks of the Carnic Alps in the north – is unforgettable.

Aquileia

Established by the Romans in 181BC, **Aquileia** quickly grew to be the fourth-largest city in Italy, capital of one of the Augustan Regions – the ancient equivalent of an English county or an American state. And it is no wonder, for this affluent market town was the departure point for the roads over the Alps to the Danube basin. Devastated by Attila in the 5th century, in Byzantine times it returned to prominence, becoming the seat of a metropolitan bishop, or patriarch. Today a sleepy village of 3000 souls, it conserves considerable traces of these two moments of glory, offering some of the more remarkable vestiges of Roman and early Christian art to be found anywhere in Europe.

At the centre of the old town stands the **Basilica**, built by the first patriarch, Theodore, soon after the Edict of Constantine (AD313) established Christianity as the official religion of the Roman world. It was rebuilt to Romanesque canons by the patriarch Poppo between 1021 and 1031, and despite later alterations it is still considered one of the outstanding monuments of Romanesque architecture in Italy. The simple façade is preceded by

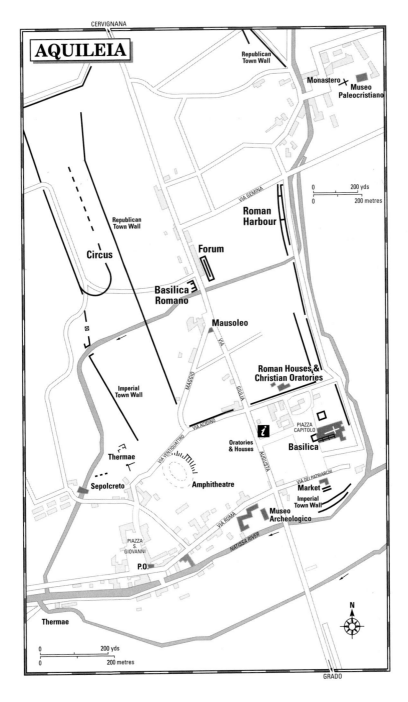

AQUILEIA

CERVIGNANA

Republican
Town Wall

Monastero

Museo
Paleocristiano

VIA GEMINA

0   200 yds
0   200 metres

Roman
Harbour

Republican
Town Wall

Circus

Forum

Basilica
Romano

Mausoleo

VIA

Roman Houses &
Christian Oratories

Imperial
Town Wall

VIA MAGGIO

VIA GIULIA

VIA ACIDINO

PIAZZA
CAPITOLO

Thermae

VIA VENTIQUATTRO

Oratories
& Houses

VIA AUGUSTA

Basilica

Sepolcreto

Amphitheatre

VIA DEI PATRIARCHI

Market

Imperial
Town Wall

PIAZZA
S.
GIOVANNI

VIA ROMA

Museo
Archeologico

NATISSA RIVER

P.O.

N

Thermae

0   200 yds
0   200 metres

GRADO

Interior of the basilica, Aquileia

a porch connecting the church to the ruined 5th-century **Baptistery** and the 9th-century **Chiesa dei Pagani** ('pagans' church'), where converts to Christianity received training in doctrine and discipline before baptism. North of the façade stands the massive campanile, an 11th-century construction with later additions.

The spacious interior is built to a Latin-cross plan with three aisles separated by pointed Gothic arches on antique columns. It is known for its 4th-century mosaic pavement, a remnant of Theodore's church, discovered in the early 20th century. This is the largest early Christian mosaic in the West, and its nine vast sections deal with pagan as well as Christian subject matter. Frescoes from Theodore's period can be seen in the apse at the end of the south aisle; and there are others, of Poppo's time (including one showing the patriarch with a model of the church) in the main apse. The elegant tribune on the steps to the sanctuary, the delicately carved altars, and the finely painted altarpieces date mainly from the Renaissance. In the crypt, below the high altar, are 12th-century frescoes depicting episodes from the lives of Christ, the Virgin Mary, and SS Hermagoras and Fortunatus. In the **Cripta degli Scavi**, entered from the west end of the north aisle, are three more sets of magnificent mosaics: from Theodore's church, from a second early Christian basilica, and from a Roman house of the Augustan age (1st century BC–1st century AD).

The **Museo del Patriarcato**, opposite the Basilica at 7 Via Patriarca Popone, merits a visit if you are interested in learning more about the Patriarchate of Aquileia. Unfortunately it is open only for special events. Highlights include a 14th-century reliquary bust of Santa Ermacora; a 13th-century painted wood statue of the Madonna del Latte; 12th- and 13th-century reliefs depicting the life of Christ and St Thomas of Canterbury; and an 11th-century crosier.

In the vicinity of the basilica are several archaeological excavations, with remains of Roman private homes and early Christian oratories, foundations of a market and traces of the town walls, an amphitheatre and baths, and a small family necropolis (the 'Sepolcreto'). Other conspicuous Roman remains include a large mausoleum (moved here from the outskirts of town in the 1950s), traces of the forum and the Roman basilica (or town hall), the circus, and a fine stretch of Roman road. The modern highway follows the course of the *cardo maximus,* the principal north–south thoroughfare of the ancient city.

The material unearthed in these and other excavations conducted in the area over the last two centuries are displayed in the **Museo Archeologico Nazionale**, at 1 Via Roma. This is one of Italy's leading museums of Roman antiquities, and you should not leave town without at least a quick look inside. The well-displayed collections include examples of Roman architecture, sculpture, inscriptions, and mosaics; a remarkably well conserved Roman ship; and many unique specimens of glass, amber, and cut stone.

Behind the basilica, the cypress-lined **Via Sacra** winds northward along the Natissa, once a river navigable as far as Grado, but now little more than a stream. The walkway is flanked by architectural fragments, altars, and other material brought to light during excavations in the environs. Here may be seen the remains of a river port unearthed in the late 19th century and dating in its present form from the 1st century AD. The quay has two levels (for large and small ships) and remains of 3rd-century walls. Further north the former **Benedictine Monastery of Santa Maria** stands over the remains of another large early Christian basilica dating from the 4th or 5th century, with extensive remains of a 5th-century mosaic pavement. The complex houses the **Museo Paleocristiano**, with sarcophagi, mosaics, tomb inscriptions, and other material representing the early Christian era in Aquileia. A fragment of Roman road can be seen in the square in front of the monastery.

Grado

The historic centre of **Grado** is a town of narrow lanes and little squares on a small island at the edge of the lagoon to which it gives its name. In ancient times it was the seaport of Aquileia, and many of that city's wealthier citizens had beach houses here. It reached its greatest prosperity after the 6th century, when the patriarchate of Aquileia split in two, the second patriarch taking up residence in Grado. The rival sees were eventually reunited and moved to Venice, and by the 15th century, when the title was abolished altogether, the town was well into its decline. Since the 19th century Grado has been a popular seaside resort – *ad aquas gradatas,* the Latin expression from which the name comes, alluding, perhaps, to the gentle slope of its sandy beach.

In the centre of the old town is the **Cathedral of Sant'Eufemia**, built in the 6th century on the site of a small 4th- or 5th-century basilica, in the style of the great churches of Ravenna. The campanile, with a distinctive pointed steeple, is crowned by a 15th-century statue of the archangel Michael. The interior follows the classical basilican plan, with three aisles separated by antique Roman columns with fine capitals, a large apse, and a magnificent mosaic pavement dating from the 6th century. The 11th-century ambo has reliefs with symbols of the Evangelists and an unusual Moorish dome. The sanctuary is surrounded by a 6th-century pluteus; on the high altar is a silver altarpiece of 1372, and in the apse, 15th-century fresco and panel paintings. More mosaic pavements can be seen around the altar and near the entrance to the sacristy.

North of the basilica is the 5th-century **Baptistery**, an ocatgonal building with a hexagonal font; and further north, the small basilica of **Santa Maria delle Grazie**, a 4th- or 5th-century church reworked in the 6th century, with a mosaic pavement and a carved transenna of the same period. In the small garden of Piazza della Vittoria you can see traces of foundations and remains of the mosaic pavement of another 4th- or 5th-century Christian basilica; nearby are sarcophagi of the same period. The **Lagoon of Grado** – a maze of channels, dunes and *mote* (islands) punctuated by *casoni* (straw and cane huts) – provides a cosy winter home to herons, cormorants, swans, teal, and swamp hawks.

Trieste

There is an element of truth in James Joyce's turn of phrase, 'And trieste, ah trieste ate I my liver' (from *Finnegans Wake,* 1939): **Trieste**, which sounds so like *triste*, the Italian word for 'sad', has a melancholy air about it that even the bright summer sun is unable to dissipate. Sometimes it is quite enjoyable – for example, on a cold winter's day, when the icy *bora*, racing down the Adriatic at well over 60km/h, whips the snowflakes through the air like so many tiny needles, and the warm, wood-panelled interiors of the city's *Jugendstil* cafés are at their most welcoming. 'We are the furthest limit of Latinity,' a recent mayor of Trieste was quoted as saying, 'the southern extremity of Germanness.' And the city's mixed heritage may be responsible for this undefinable malaise, the consequence of being an 'outsider' in both cultures.

Modern Trieste, an important seaport and a lively provincial capital, nestles on an attractive gulf surrounded by low limestone hills. Most of what you will see here was built in the late 18th and early 19th centuries when, thanks to tax breaks and other incentives offered by Austrian Emperor Charles V and his daughter, Maria Theresa (who wished to establish an Adriatic port that would rival the power and prestige of Venice), the small town that Trieste had been in earlier centuries increased tenfold in size and population. Salty dogs will be pleased to know that the first screw-propelled steamer in Europe, the *Civetta*, was tested in Trieste's roadstead in 1829.

The Old City

The old quarter of the city lies on the hill of San Giusto, at the top of which stand the cathedral and castle. The **Cathedral**, dedicated to St Justus, is the fruit of a 14th-century union of two earlier churches, San Giusto (on the south) and Santa Maria Assunta (on the north). The simple façade, with a

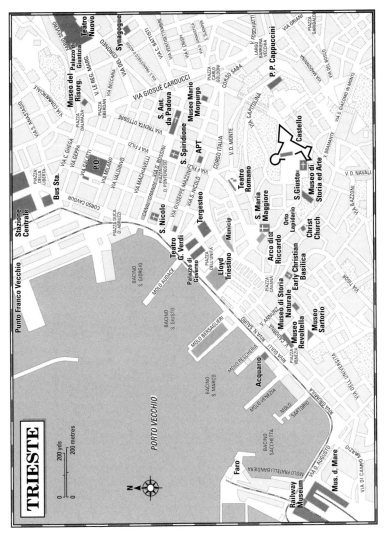

single, large gable, is graced by a large 14th-century rose window; the posts of the main doorway incorporate elements of a Roman tomb. The campanile, also of the 14th century, resembles a defensive tower. It stands on the remains of the vestibule of a Roman temple. A Byzantine-Romanesque statue of the patron saint occupies a Gothic aedicule on the south side.

Inside, the cathedral has five asymmetrical aisles divided by columns with fine capitals. The 16th-century ship's-keel ceiling of the nave was reconstructed in 1905; also modern is the central apse, with a mosaic inspired by fragments of the original. In the south apse you can see original blind arcading, frescoes of the 13th century and, on the ceiling, a remarkable late 13th-century mosaic depicting *Christ between SS Justus and Servulus*. The floor preserves remains of the mosaic of the original 5th-century basilica. Twelfth-century Venetian mosaics of the *Madonna between Archangels Michael and Gabriel,* with *Apostles* below, look down from the ceiling of the north apse. In the north aisle is the entrance to the baptistery, with a 9th-century font.

At the foot of the castle stretches the area known as the Platea Romana, with remains of the basilica of the Roman forum (2nd century AD) and of the so-called Tempio Capitolino (1st century AD). The **Castello**, as it appears today, was constructed between 1470 and 1630 on the site of an earlier Venetian fortress, which in its turn rose on the probable site of a prehistoric fortification. Restored and adapted as a museum and open-air theatre (plays are staged on summer evenings in the courtyard) in the 1930s, it offers fine views over the city and gulf. The square 15th-century tower and the adjoining building house the Museo del Castello, with arms and armour, furniture, paintings and tapestries.

From the steps before the cathedral, the tree-lined Via della Cattedrale will take you to the **Museo di Storia ed Arte e Orto Lapidario**, the most important museum in Trieste. Here antique and medieval sculpture and inscriptions, Egyptian antiquities, prehistorical and protohistorical material, Greek and Italic antiquities (pottery, glass, bronze and jewellery and coins), and drawings and prints are displayed in a pleasant building and a lovely garden. The street ends at the Arco di Riccardo, a vaulted Roman gate of the 1st century AD, dedicated to Augustus.

Borgo Teresiano

Extending along the waterfront north of the San Giusto hill is the **Borgo Teresiano**, the quarter developed by Maria Theresa in the 18th century. Its southern limit is marked by the large, dramatic Piazza dell'Unità d'Italia, which was created in the 19th century by filling in the old Roman harbour. Facing the sea is the eclectic façade of the Palazzo Comunale (1875). To the north stand the Palazzo del Governo, designed in 1904 by the Austrian architect Emil Artmann, and the historic **Caffè degli Specchi**, a good place to take a break. (Coffee is particularly delicious in Trieste, which imports more than any other port in the Mediterranean.) To the south, the seaward side of the

Borsa, detail of the exterior, Trieste

square is dominated by the imposing Renaissance-revival Palazzo del Lloyd Triestino, by the Viennese architect Heinrich Ferstel (1880–83), who also designed the two allegorical fountains. Next door stands another Renaissance-revival building, today a hotel, and next to this, the elegant Palazzo Pitteri (1785), in a style somewhere between the Baroque and the neoclassical.

A short walk northwards along the waterfront brings you past the Teatro Verde, the city's main concert hall (1801) and the church of San Nicolò dei Greci, built in 1784–87 by the Greek Orthodox community and possessing a composite neoclassical façade with twin campanili by Matteo Pertsch (1819–21) and a magnificent silver iconostasis. Keeping the gulf on your left, you soon come to the **Canal Grande**, constructed in 1750–56 to provide a safe harbour for merchant vessels and to allow cargo to be unloaded directly into the warehouses of the Borgo Teresiano. On the southwest corner is Matteo Pertsch's Palazzo Carciotti (1802–05; now the port authority), a neoclassical building with a hexastyle façade and a balustrade with statues. On the opposite corner stands Palazzo Aedes, a work of the Viennese Secession architect Arduino Berlam (1926–28). At its far end, the Canal Grande is spectacularly concluded by Pietro Nobile's neoclassical church of Sant'Antonio Nuovo (1827–42). In Piazza Ponterosso, half-way down on the right, the house at No. 3 was the first home of James Joyce and his wife Nora, who lived in Trieste from 1905 to 1915 and again in 1919–20. The **Museo Scaramangà di Altomonte**, across the canal at 1 Via Filzi, houses a small but important collection documenting the history of art in Trieste.

The area of the Borgo Teresiano between the Canal Grande and the Corso Italia, four blocks south, is a genuine gold mine of early modern architecture. If you are fond of this period, or just interested in meeting the grandparents of today's architectural styles, take a look at Romeo Depaoli's Casa Smolars (1906–07), at the corner of Piazza della Repubblica and Via Dante; the Casa Fontana (5 Via Mazzini, at the corner of Via Roma; the bank at 9 Via Roma; and the Casa Bartoli (7B Piazza della Borsa), a mansion designed in the Italian variant of *art nouveau* known as the Liberty style, by Max Fabiani (1905).

Along the Corso Italia are several buildings by major architects of the period between the wars, notably the Casa delle Assicurazioni Generali (No. 1–3) and the Banco di Napoli (No. 5), by Marcello Piacentini (1935–39) and the *grattacielo* ('skyscraper') by Umberto Nordio (1936; in Largo Riborgo), as well as interesting remnants of the old Austro-Hungarian *corso* – the neoclassical Casa Steiner (No. 4) by Matteo Pertsch (1824), the Tuscan Revival Casa Ananian (No. 12) by Giorgio Polli (1905), and the building at the corner of Piazza Goldoni (No. 22), with a Liberty gable end, by Romeo Depaoli (1908).

At the foot of the San Giusto hill, just south of Largo Riborgo, excavations in 1938 brought to light remains of a 6000-seat Roman theatre dating from the early 2nd century AD; a small antiquarium displays finds from the excavations. Just one block east, on the site of the former Polish Ashenazic synagogue, is the **Museo della Communità Ebraica** (7 Via del Monte), created in

1993 to hold the collections of Jewish art and culture of the Triestine community, particularly sacred vessels and vestments from the synagogue.

House-museums

A peculiar feature of Trieste is the unusual number of old mansions that have been turned into museums. A stately Eclectic townhouse by Giovanni Berlam (1875), just off Corso Italia at 5 Via Imbriani, houses the **Museo M. Morpurgo de Nilma**, with furniture, paintings, miniatures, prints, ceramics, porcelain, and a library – all in a fascinating *fin-de-siècle* bourgeois setting.

The **Museo Revoltella** (27 Via Diaz) occupies a Renaissance-revival building designed by Friedrich Titzig (1852–58) and enlarged (1960–92) by Carlo Scarpa; it has a gallery of modern art with works by 19th- and 20th-century Italian and European masters, notably sculpture by Antonio Canova and Jean Antoine Houdon and paintings by Francesco Hayez, Domenico Induno, Francesco de Nittis, Gaetano Previati, Felice Casorati, Renato Guttuso, and Lucio Fontana. The terrace of the new wing enjoys an excellent view over the city.

The **Civico Museo Sartorio** (1 Largo Papa Giovanni XXIII) is located in an 18th-century mansion remodelled in 1820–38 by Nicolò Pertsch. On the ground floor are Italian and European maiolicas and porcelains, Triestine ceramics and rooms for temporary exhibitions. The first floor has rooms furnished in the Gothic-revival and Biedermeier styles, and paintings of the 17th to the 19th century (notably by Tiepolo and his followers). On the second floor are rotating exhibitions of paintings from various Triestine collections.

The best of Trieste's house-museums is reached by a short drive or bus ride. The **Castello di Miramare**, situated 8km (5 miles) northwest of the city along Highway 14 and surrounded by a large formal garden, was built to an English Renaissance-revival design by Karl Junker (1855–60) for Archduke Maximilian of Austria. Maximilian lived here until 1864, the year in which he accepted the Impereial crown of Mexico; and from 1931 to 1936 the mansion was the home of Amedeo di Savoia. It rises in a splendid position at the end of a promontory and, with its furniture, paintings, porcelains and ivories, is one of the more remarkable examples of a 19th-century aristocratic residence. The small Castelletto, where Maximilian lived while the castello was being built, houses the *Centro di educazione all'ambiente marino di Miramare*, with a museum of the marine environment. The sea around the promontory is now a marine reserve. The road to Miramare passes the **Faro della Vittoria**, a lighthouse and memorial to seamen who died in World War I, designed in the 1920s by Arduino Berlam and today a popular viewpoint.

A sadly significant place is the **Risiera di Santa Saba**, in the industrial district south of the city, at 1 Ratto della Pileria. This former rice-hulling plant was the only Nazi death camp in Italy. Some 5000 prisoners are believed to have been executed here between the German invasion of Italy in 1943 and the liberation of Trieste by Tito's Partisans in 1945. It is now a national monument, with death and detention cells, a permanent photographic exhibition and a library.

Palmanova

The area between Trieste and Udine holds little of interest, with the notable exception of **Palmanova**, a marvellously preserved, star-shaped town built in 1593 to defend the eastern frontier of the Venetian Republic. It is one of the few brick-and-mortar examples of that order and symmetry which Renaissance culture considered a fundamental feature of the ideal city. Its centre is the hexagonal Piazza Grande, dominated by the **Cathedral**, whose design has been attributed to Vincenzo Scamozzi. From this hub six streets radiate in a spoke-like pattern, three leading to the city's monumental gates. The town itself is most interesting for its 16th-century ambience, but there are also two small musems, the **Civico Museo Storico** (4 Borgo Udine), with weapons, documents and memorabilia ranging from the foundation of the city to World War I; and the **Museo Storico Militare** (in Borgo Cividale, next to the gate), with military uniforms from 1593 to World War II. Guided tours of the fortifications (in Italian) are led from the latter.

Udine

Udine is a prosperous, middle-class town, the second city of Friuli-Venezia Giulia and without a doubt the one with the greatest potential for future development. It was a frontier post of the Roman Empire, and in the Middle Ages its castle protected the fertile lowlands extending from the Adriatic to the Alps from the incursions of the Huns. In the 13th century Patriarch Berthold of Andrechs moved his residence here from Aquileia, marking the beginning of a period of growth of which few traces remain, but which made Udine an important regional capital. In 1420 the city and its territory were annexed to the Venetian Republic. They passed to the Austro-Hungarian Empire after the fall of the Venetian Republic and the brief Napoleonic interlude; and to the Kingdom of Italy after the Second War of Independence (1866).

Piazza della Libertà to the Castle

The centre of town life is still the Venetian Piazza Nuova, now called **Piazza della Libertà**. Set at the foot of the castle hill, this 16th-century square is considered one of the most beautiful urban complexes in Italy. The **Loggia del Lionello**, on the northeast side, is the town hall. It was built in 1448–56 by Bartolomeo delle Cisterne to a design by the Udinese goldsmith, Nicolò Lionello, in Venetian Gothic forms. Faced with alternating bands of white and pink stone, it has a first-floor loggia with balustrade, mullioned windows, and a niche on one corner holding a 15th-century statue of the Madonna. The adjacent **Porticato di San Giovanni** is a spectacular Renaissance creation of Bernardino da Morcote (1533): a long portico on slender columns, surmounted by the elegant **Torre dell'Orologio** (1527), built to resemble the clock tower of Venice, with a lion of St Mark and two *mori* (moors) who strike the hours. A taller, broader arch at the centre marks the **Cappella di San Giovanni**, now a war memorial. On the raised pavement before the portico is a statue (1819; left) representing *Peace,* presented to the city by Emperor Francis I to commemorate the passage of Udine under Austrian sovereignty; also here are statues of *Justice* (1614) and *Hercules and Cacus* (popularly called Florean and Venturin), and a 15th-century colonnade with another lion of St Mark and a fountain of 1542.

The **Castello**, built over the ruins of the castle of the patriarchs of Aquileia, was begun in 1517 to a design by Giovanni da Udine, a pupil of Raphael. To reach it, you walk beneath the Arco Bollani, designed by Andrea Palladio, and climb the Salita al Castello (1563), flanked by the graceful Venetian-Gothic Porticato Lippomano (1487). The rooftop 'observatory' offers splendid views over the plain, the mountains and the sea. The castle is home to the **Civici Musei e Gallerie di Storia e Arte**, a complex of several museums and galleries.

The **Galleria d'Arte Antica** has Italian paintings ranging from the late Middle Ages to the 19th century, including several works by Tiepolo (*Strength and Wisdom, Consilium in Arena*). Particularly interesting are the 14th-century Friulan primitives, the 15th-century Scuola Tolmezzina, and the

Piazza della Libertà, Udine

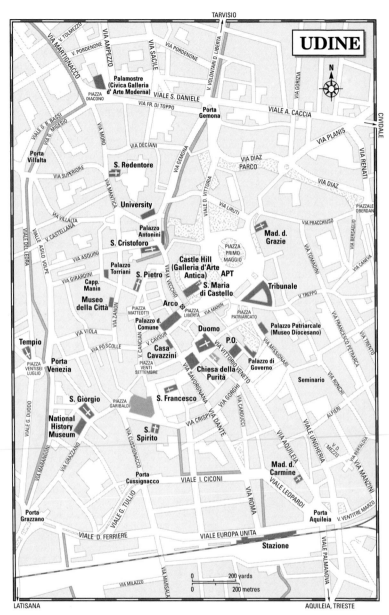

paintings by Vittore Carpaccio (*Christ and the Instruments of the Passion*), Giovanni Antonio da Pordenone (*Madonna della Loggia; Eternal Father*), Palma Giovane (*St Mark Placing Udine under the Protection of St Ermacora*), Caravaggio (*St Francis Receiving the Stigmata*), Luca Carlvarijs (*Plan of the City of Udine*), and Marco and Sebastiano Ricci (*Landscape*).

The **Museo Archeologico** presents material assembled over the past 200 years from sites in Udine and its environs, notably finds from the Mesolithic to the Iron Age from Cassacco, from Sammardenchia and from excavations in Via del Mercato Vecchio and on the castle hill in Udine; Roman-age material from excavations in town, from Aquileia and from Sevegliano; Lombard weapons; and local and imported ceramics and glass from the Middle Ages and the Renaissance. There are also extensive collections of coins (50,000 pieces, some very rare, of Roman, Byzantine, barbarian, and medieval origin, including the fabulous Collezione Colloredo Mels); Roman ambers, precious stones, glass, perfume vases and gold, from Aquileia; and cut gems from the Roman age and the 18th and 19th centuries.

The Gabinetto dei Disegni e delle Stampe exhibits, on a rotating basis, a selection from the enormous collection (some 10,000 pieces) of works by Friulan and Venetian printmakers and Italian and foreign old masters. The first-floor Salone del Parlamento hosts Tiepolo's *Triumph of the Christians over the Turks* and other fine paintings.

The Cathedral Area

The **Cathedral**, located one block southeast of Piazza della Libertà, preserves its original 14th-century Gothic appearance, particularly in the fine central doorway with its carved lunette, deep splays, and sharp cusp, and in the other great doorway on the north flank, by the campanile (1390). A third, Renaissance doorway graces the south flank. The unfinished campanile was begun in the 15th century over an octagonal baptistery built a hundred years earlier. The three-aisled interior has paintings by Tiepolo on the south side (*Trinità,* in the first chapel; *SS Hermagoras and Fortunatus,* in the second; *Resurrection* and frescoes in the fourth). The stuccoed Baroque complex of the sanctuary and crossing is preceded by two organs with painted parapets; its spectacular tone is maintained by the large marble high altar with statues (1717) and, at the ends of the arms of the transept, two colossal tombs of the prominent Manin family (18th century).

A door on the left leads to the **Museo del Duomo**, which includes the 14th-century Cappella di San Nicolò, frescoed with episodes from the *Life of St Nicholas* by Vitale da Bologna in 1348–49; panel paintings by the Maestro dei Padiglioni, his pupil; and the old **Baptistery**, beneath the campanile, with a beautiful vaulted ceiling and the sarcophagus of Beato Bertrando, with fine reliefs of the Lombard-Venetian school (1343).

The 18th-century Oratorio della Purità, across the square from the south flank of the cathedral, has an altarpiece and ceiling painting by Giovanni Battista Tiepolo and chiaroscuro mural paintings by his son, Gian Domenico. The cathedral sacristan will open it for you.

A couple of blocks northeast of the cathedral, in the shady Piazza Patriarcato, stands the stately **Palazzo Arcivescovile**, built between the 16th and the 18th century and flanked by the church of Sant'Antonio Abate. Here, in the second-floor gallery, are the finest fresco paintings in Udine and G.B.

Salita al Castello, Udine

Tiepolo's earliest masterpieces (1726–28), representing *Old Testament Scenes*. The other rooms, frescoed by Tiepolo (on the stairs, *Fall of the Angels;* in the Sala Rossa, *Judgement of Solomon and Four Prophets*) and by Giovanni da Udine, also merit a glance, as does Dionisio Delfino's Library of 1709. The building will soon host a **Museo Diocesano d'Arte Sacra**, with artworks and artefacts from the early Christian and medieval periods to the 19th century, removed for safe-keeping from the churches of Udine and Aquileia.

Other City Centre Sights

A good place to stop for coffee is the historic **Caffè Contarena**, with Liberty décor and furniture (1925), beneath the portico on Via Cavour, directly behind the Loggia del Lionello. The building, the monumental Palazzo degli Uffici Municipali, was designed by Raimondo d'Aronco, in an eclectic Liberty style, in 1911. One block north of Via Cavour is the elegant Via Rialto, today reserved for pedestrians, which runs along what was once the main axis of the medieval *villa Udin*.

Turning right at the end of the street, you soon come to Piazza Matteotti (Piazza San Giacomo for the Udinese), perhaps the oldest of the city's squares, with low porticoes on columns and a fountain by Giovanni da Udine (1542). On the west side stands the 14th-century church of **San Giacomo**, with a lively Lombardesque façade designed by Bernardino da Morcote (early 16th century), and 17th- and 18th-century paintings inside. One block further west (reached by a passageway next to the church) Via Zanon, flanked by one of the characteristic little canals the Udinese call *rogge*, is lined with fine palaces mostly of the 18th century; at the corner of Via dei Torriani is the **Torre di Santa Maria**, a remnant of the 13th-century town wall. Behind the tower and beyond the austere façade of Palazzo Torriani (No. 4) is the 18th-century **Cappella Manin**, a gem of Baroque architecture, whose hexagonal interior has fine sculptures and high reliefs by G. Torretti.

On the northwest corner of Piazza della Libertà begins the handsome Via Mercatovecchio, the traditional site of the evening promenade. The city's first marketplace, it is still the main shopping street. Broad and slightly curved, it is flanked by porticoed buildings, notably the monumental **Monte di Pietà**, today a bank, which has a façade of 1690 and a chapel, at the centre, with fine wrought-iron work and frescoes by Giulio Quaglio (1694). Continuing north you come to the **Palazzo Antonini** (3 Via Gemona), today the Banca d'Italia, built after 1570 to plans by Palladio. Almost opposite, to the north-west, is the 17th-century Palazzo Antonini-Cernazai, now occupied by the University Faculty of Languages.

At the northern edge of the city centre stands the **Galleria d'Arte Moderna**, with a collection focusing on Italian artists of the 20th century. On the first floor are: a section devoted to modern and contemporary architecture (including some original drawings by Raimondo d'Aronco); works by the well-known Italian modernists Arturo Martini, Mario Mafai and Felice Casorati; and a small collection of American art of the 1070s, notably by

Casorati; and a small collection of American art of the 1070s, notably by Willem de Kooning. The ground floor is mainly devoted to the Astaldi Collection of modern masters, with works by Gino Severini, Giorgio de Chirico, Savinio, Mario Sironi, Giorgio Morandi, Massimo Campigli, Ottone Rosai, Fausto Pirandello and Carlo Carrà.

Around Udine

The environs of Udine are known for their natural beauty – a combination of dark forests, rolling farmland and carefully tended vineyards. Scattered around are a number of castles and patrician villas, the most impressive of which is at **Passariano**, 30km (18½ miles) southwest. This tiny hamlet adjoins the magnificent buildings and park of the **Villa Lodovico Manin**, erected in the 16th century as a country house for the last of the Venetian doges and rebuilt on the present, grand scale in the 17th and 18th centuries. The manor house, with three storeys and an attic, is flanked by long, perpendicular *barchesse,* or farm buildings; in front, a large porticoed exedra encloses a vast lawn. Napoleon stayed here in 1797, before signing the Peace of Campoformio, by which Udine and its province were awarded to Austria. Now a school for art conservators, the villa is also used as a venue for exhibitions of art and antiques. The vast, Rococo park has rare plants, ponds and statues.

Cividale del Friuli

This pleasant town stands on the banks of the River Natisone, on a site which once marked the meeting-point of Venetic and Celtic cultures. Known to the Romans as *Forum Julii,* it became a *municipium* in the Augustan age, an episcopal seat in the 5th century, and an important fortress under the Lombards. In the 8th century its name was changed to *Civitas Austriae* and it became the seat of the patriarch of Aquileia, a position it retained until 1031.

Piazza del Duomo stands on the site of the ancient Roman forum, enclosed on one side by the north flank of the **Cathedral**. The church was begun in 1457 in the Venetian Gothic style to plans by Bartolomeo delle Cisterne, but it was rebuilt in the 16th century in Renaissance forms by Pietro and Tullio Lombardo, whose design is particularly evident in the interior. It has a simple stone façade with three pointed Gothic doorways (the central one is a work of Jacopo Veneziano, 1465), and is flanked by a Baroque campanile. In the north apsidal chapel are a *Last Supper* and *Martyrdom of St Stephen* by Palma Giovane. Above the high altar is the gilt-silver *Altarpiece of Patriarch Pellegrino II* (1195–1204), a masterpiece of medieval silversmithing showing the Virgin in the company of Gabriel, Michael, saints, prophets and the patron himself. The third south bay gives access to the **Museo Cristiano**, where exhibits include the octagonal aedicule of the 8th-century baptistery; the beautiful altar carved for Ratchis, Duke of Cividale and King of the Lombards (also from the 8th century); a marble patriarchal throne of the 11th century; fragments of a 7th- to 8th-century balustrade and ciborium; and detached frescoes from the Tempietto Longobardo (described below).

Facing the cathedral and preceded by a copy of the statue of Julius Caesar in the Campidoglio in Rome, is the 14th-century **Palazzo Comunale**, with the pointed arches and mullioned windows typical of Gothic public buildings. At the end of the square stands the late 16th-century **Palazzo dei Provveditori Veneti**, built to a design by Andrea Palladio. Inside is the **Museo Archeologico Nazionale**, with very important collections of prehistoric, Roman and medieval archaeology, jewellery and miniatures. The best displays on the ground floor are the Roman, Byzantine and medieval inscriptions, reliefs, and architectural elements; and the fragments of Roman and early Christian mosaic pavements, including a representation of a marine deity (1st–2nd century AD). The extraordinary Lombard items, from necropolises near Cividale and throughout the Friuli, are displayed on the first floor. Highlights include a reworked Roman sarcophagus and the burial treasure (weapons and gold) of Duke Gisulfo (mid-7th century); tomb treasures from the necropolis of Santo Stefano in Pertica (7th century); goldsmith's work (*Croce* (cross) *di Invillino*, from the 8th–9th century); weapons, tools, and utensils. Also noteworthy are the 8th-century *Psalter of St Elizabeth* with Saxon miniatures, and the late 13th-century *Veil of Beata Benvenuta Boiani*, embroidered with religious scenes.

A passage on the south side of the museum leads into Via Monastero Maggiore, which winds through the medieval quarter, passing beneath two gates to reach Cividale's most unusual monument, the **Tempietto Longobardo**. More properly called the Oratorio di Santa Maria in Valle, this is a singular church of the 8th and 9th centuries situated on a cliff above the Natisone and reached by a walkway along the river. The interior is a rectangular hall covered by barrel vaults and terminating in a three-apsed sanctuary separated from the nave by a screen. It is decorated with fine stucco-work, ranging in date from the 8th to the 11th century, and frescoes of the 11th century; the wooden choir stalls are from the 14th century.

Across the square from the Tempietto is the small 15th-century church of **San Biagio**, with remains of contemporary frescoes on its façade and inside. In a private garden on Via Monastero Maggiore is the Ipogeo Celtico, a system of tunnels cut in the rock on the bank of the Natisone, believed to have been the burial place of Celtic chieftains of the 5th to the 2nd centuries BC. From here you might want to take a stroll over the **Ponte del Diavolo**, or 'Devil's Bridge', built to join the high rocky banks of the Natisone in the mid-15th century, and destroyed and rebuilt during World War I. The views are extraordinary.

Detail of the Piazza della Libertà, Cividale del Friuli

Practical Information

Getting There

By **road**, Autostrada A4 runs from Venice to Trieste, not far from the Adriatic shore. Near Palmanova it links up with Autostrada A23, which winds northwards via Udine to Austria.

There is a direct **rail** service from Venice to Trieste (some trains continuing on to Slovenia, Croatia, Hungary, Ukraine, and Russia (via Villa Opicina), and from Venice to Udine (continuing on to Vienna and Prague). Branch lines run from Trieste to Udine, and from Udine to Conegliano, Cividale, Palmanova and Cervignano (the latter is also on the Venice–Trieste line), from which buses shuttle passengers to Aquileia and Grado.

Tourist Information

AQUILEIA Piazza Capitolo (tel. 0431 91087 – summer only).

CIVIDALE DEL FRIULI 4 Largo Bioani (tel./fax 0432 731461).

TRIESTE 20 Via San Nicolò (tel. 040 679 6111, fax 679 6299); at the train station (tel. 040 420 182)

UDINE 7 Piazza I Maggio (tel. 0432 295 972, fax 504 743).

Hotels

CIVIDALE DEL FRIULI
The **Locanda al Castello**, 20 Via del Castello (tel. 0432 733 242, fax 700 901; closed Nov), is a former Jesuit convent with just ten rooms, in a quiet, wooded setting. The **Roma**, Piazza Picco (tel. 0432 731 871, fax 701 033), is centrally located and comfortable. Both are inexpensive.

TRIESTE
The finest hotel is the **Duchi d'Aosta**, 2 Via dell'Orologio (tel. 040 7351, fax 366 092), offering turn-of-the-century Austrian style and ambience. The restaurant, **Harry's Grill**, is likewise one of the best in town; both are expensive. The **San Giusto**, 3 Via C. Belli (tel. 040 762 661, fax 734 477), is a bit out of the way (on the landward side of the hill of San Giusto), but very pleasant. The **Abbazia**, 20 Via della Geppa (tel. 040 369 464, fax 369 769), near the train station, is comfortable and practical. Both are moderately priced.

UDINE
The **Ambassador Palace**, 46 Via Carducci (tel. 0432 503 777, fax 503 711), generally considered the top venue, occupies a historic building midway

between the cathedral and the train station; and the **Astoria Hotel Italia**, 24 Piazza XX Settembre (tel. 0432 505 091, fax 509 070), elegant with a good restaurant, stands in the heart of the old town. Both are moderately priced. Somewhat less expensive are the **Friuli**, 24 Viale Ledra (tel. 0432 234 351, fax 234 354), a comfortable place a few blocks west of the city centre, and the **Là di Moret**, 276 Viale Tricesimo (tel./fax 0432 545 096), an excellent hotel with a renowned restaurant, unfortunately somewhat distant from the city centre and across town from the station.

Restaurants

AQUILEIA
The best restaurant is actually outside of town: **La Colombara**, Località La Colombara, on the road to Grado (tel. 0431 91513, fax 919560; closed Mon and Jan), is an inexpensive place specialising in seafood, accompanied by regional and Italian wines. Try the *sardelle in savor* and *seppioline ai peperoni; spaghetti alla busara* and *ravioli di pesce alla granseola; boreto alla graesana* and *calamari ripieni ai carciofi.*

CIVIDALE DEL FRIULI
Cividale offers several good restaurants. **Al Fortino**, 46 Via Carlo Alberto (tel. 0432 731 217, fax 731 192; closed Mon evening and Tues and a few days in Jan and Aug), serves traditional fare accompanied by mainly regional wines, in a setting featuring fragmentary 14th-century frescoes and a great fireplace. **Alla Frasca**, 8a Via de Rubeis (tel. 0432 731 270; closed Mon and in Feb), is a popular trattoria with garden seating in summer. **Zorutti**, 9 Borgo di Ponte (tel. 0432)731 100), is another good trattoria with cosy rooms and fireplaces, in an 18th-century building. All three are quite inexpensive.

GRADO
The **Tavernetta all'Androna**, Calle Porta Piccola 4 (tel. 0431 80950, fax 83185; closed Tue and Dec–Feb) is a traditional restaurant with an innovative twist: recommended are the *carpaccio di branzino* and *scampi gratinati al basilico; riso al nero di seppia* and *brodetto alla gradese con polenta; orata con alici e capperi* and *fritto misto alla marinara.* There is also a good selection of regional, Italian and imported wines. Fairly pricey.

TRIESTE
Trieste offers several excellent choices. The **Antica Trattoria Suban**, 2/D Via Comici (tel. 040 54368, fax 57920; closed Mon, Tue, ten days in Jan and two weeks in Aug), is an outstanding restaurant established in 1865 and serving traditional regional cuisine. The i*nsalatina tiepida con petto d'oca all'aceto balsamico* and *palacinche alla mandriera; stinco di vitello arrosto con patate al tegame* and *petto d'anatra al Tocai* are particularly delectable, and there is a good selection of regional, Italian and imported wines. **Ai Fiori**, 7 Piazza Hortis (tel. 040) 300 633; closed Sun, Mon and three weeks in Jul), is a

family-run restaurant offering a creative approach to seafood. Specialities include *orzo,* **caviale,** *cavolo capuccio e canestrelli* and *insalatina di seppie, carciofi e funghi; zuppa di asparagi e scampi* and *spaetzle di grano saraceno con calamaretti e peperoni; trancio di dentice alle zucchine e olive and branzino al finocchio.* Don't miss the interesting choice of cheeses (including a delicious Montasio), or the home-made ice-cream and desserts. **Al Bragozzo**, 22 Riva Nazario Sauro (tel. 040 303 001, fax 823 863; closed Sun, Mon and a few days in Jul), is another creative seafood restaurant with an elegant ambience. The best dishes are those invented by the house: *stuzzichini del Bragozzo; ravioli del Bragozzo, spaghetti alla Giorgio; pesce nobile al cartoccio* and *pesce bianco al tocio rosso con crostino.* Home-made desserts and a considerable selection of regional and Italian wines guarantee an enjoyable meal. **Al Granzo**, 7 Piazza Venezia (tel. 040 306 788, fax 410 157; closed Wed), is a traditional seafood restaurant established in 1923 and offering excellent *granseola alla triestina* and *moscardini caldi con polenta; spaghettini con calamaretti freschi* and *tagliolini con gamberetti e curry; astice alla busara con spaghetti, scarpena all'istriana*, and home-made apple strüdel. All of the above restaurants are moderately priced. **Allo Squero**, 42 Viale Miramare (tel. 040 410 884;closed Mon and Feb), is a good, inexpensive trattoria drawing a strong local crowd. Try the *sardoni in savor* and *seppe e folpi in insalata; zuppa di pesce* and *taglierini al granchio;* grilled *orata* or *branzino* and *scampi alla busara.*

UDINE
Among the better restaurants is **Alla Vedova**, 9 Via Tavagnacco (tel./fax 0432 470 291; closed Sun evening and Mon, and a few days in Aug). Established in 1887, its strong points are game dishes, home-made wine, and a distinctive ambience. Try the *prosciutto di San Daniele* and *arrotolato di costa di maiale; risotti all'anatra selvatica* and *orzotto alla salsiccia; capriolo in salmì* and *lombo di cervo brasato con purea di mele;* the local cheeses (*latteria friulano*, Montasio), and fresh berry tarts. There is a good selection of regional, Italian, and imported wines. The **Vitello d'Oro**, 4 Via Valvason (tel./fax 0432 508 982; closed Wed and a few days in July), is a popular trattoria serving local specialities, particularly (despite the name – the 'Golden Calf') seafood, around a great fireplace. Strong points include *zuppetta di vongole* and *capesante gratinate; risotto con frutti di mare* and *orzo e fagioli; rombo alle verdure* and *salmone al pepe rosa.* There is fresh and aged Montasio cheese, and a good *budino diplomatico* – all served with regional, Italian, and international wines. Both are moderately priced.

There are also some great eating places in the environs of Udine. At **REANA DEL ROIALE**, 8km north (5 miles), **Da Rochet** (tel. 0432 851 090; closed Tue, Wed, and mid-Jul–mid-Sep), is a country restaurant in a lovely position, with garden seating in the summer; it serves local specialities, notably ravioli al Montasio con erbe fini and orzo e silene; sformato di tacchina al Montasio and filetto di trota all'arancia. At **TRICESIMO,** 10km (6 miles) north, is the **Antica Trattoria Boschetti** (with rooms), 10 Piazza

Mazzini (tel. 0432 851 230, fax 852 216; closed Sun evening, Mon and two weeks in Jan and Aug). Truly antique (est. 1830), this elegant restaurant serves personal variations on local specialities, such as *orzetto con fagioli* and *raviolini al Montasio; fegato alle mele* and *agnello in sfoglia di patate.* The chocolate meringue and fruit tarts are not to be missed, and there is a good selection of regional and Italian wines.

At **TOLMEZZO,** 50km (30 miles) north by the Udine–Tarvisio Autostrada, a good place to stop for lunch if you are headed for the Dolomites or points north, is the **Roma** (with rooms), 14 Piazza XX Settembre (tel. 0433 2081, fax 43316; closed Sun evening, Mon, and one week in June and November). Here you'll find exceptional interpretations of regional specialities – *pindule di cjavrul* and *rane con radicchio di campo; cjalsons* and *bleons di cjanal; filetto di coniglio in crosta* and *oca bollita con mostarda; malga, Gyalins di Sigilet,* and other local cheeses; *sfogliatine di frutti di bosco* and *biscotti di Carnia con zabajone al Picolit* – all served with fine regional, Italian and imported wines. All are moderately priced.

Special Events

TRIESTE
Festival Internazionale dell'Operetta (international operetta festival, Jun–Aug); **Light and Sound show,** Castello di Miramare (Jul–Aug); **Mostramercato dell'Antiquariato** (antiques fair; late Oct–early Nov), at the Stazione Marittima; **Barcolana** (sailing regatta, second Sun in Oct).

Museums and Monuments

AQUILEIA
Basilica: daily, Apr–Sep 8.30–19.00; Oct–Mar 8.30–12.30, 15.00–18.00; **Campanile** 9.30–12.00, 15.00–18.30.
Museo del Patriarcato: open for temporary exhibitions only.
Archaeological areas: daily 9–dusk.
Museo Archeologico Nazionale: Mon 9.00–14.00, Tue–Sun 9.00–19.00.
Museo Paleocristiano: daily 9.00–14.00.

CIVIDALE DEL FRIULI
Museo Cristiano: 9.30–12.00, 15.00–18.00, summer 9.30–12.00, 15.00–19.00; Sun and hols 9.00–12.00, 15.00–19.00, summer 9.00–18.30.
Museo Archeologico Nazionale: daily 8.30–14.00.
Tempietto Longobardo: Apr–Sep 10.00–13.00, 15.30–18.30; Oct–Mar 10.00–13.00, 15.30–17.30.

PALMANOVA
Civico Museo Storico: Thu–Tue 10.00–12.00, 16.00–19.00.
Museo Storico Militare: Mon–Sat 9.00–12.00, 14.00–16.00; summer 9.00–12.00, 16.00–18.00; Sun and hols 9.00–12.00.

TRIESTE
Castello: daily 9.00–17.00, Apr–Sep 9.00–19.00.
Civico Museo del Castello: Tue–Sun 9.00–13.00
Civico Museo di Storia ed Arte e Orto Lapidario: Tue–Sun 9.00–13.00.
Museo Scaramangà di Altomonte: Tue–Fri 10.00–12.00.
Antiquarium: Thu 10.00–12.00.
Museo della Communità Ebraica: Sun 17.00–20.00, Tue 16.00–18.00, Thu 10.00–13.00.
Civico Museo M. Morpurgo de Nilma: Tue–Sun 10.00–13.00.
Civico Museo Sartorio: Tue–Sun 9.00–13.00.
Risiera di Santa Saba: Tue–Sat 9.00–18.00, Sun 9.00–13.00.
Castello di Miramare: Nov–Feb 9.00–16.00, Mar–Oct 9.00–17.00, Apr–Sep 9.00–18.00. **Garden**: 9.00–dusk.
Faro della Vittoria: Apr–Sep 9.30–11.30, 15.30–18.30; Oct–Mar hols only, 10.00–15.00.

UDINE
Civici Musei e Gallerie di Storia e Arte, **Museo Archeologico**: daily (except Sun afternoon and Mon) 9.30–12.30, 15.00–18.00.
Museo del Duomo: open as the cathedral.
Palazzo Arcivescovile: Wed–Sun 10.00–12.00, 15.30–18.30.
Galleria d'Arte Moderna: daily (except Sun afternoon and Mon) 9.30–12.30, 15.00–18.00.

7. *NORTH OF VENICE*

North of Venice begin the prealpi, the foothills of the Alps, sprinkled with beautiful old towns and imposing villas and castles where Venetian notables like Caterina Cornaro and Cardinal Bembo sought respite from the summer heat. The first thing you'll notice here is the air – crisp and fragrant with mountain breezes in spring and autumn, but noticeably 'lighter' than that of Venice even in the warm summer months. The cultural and economic capital of the area is Treviso, a lively town whose nearness to Venice (less than half an hour away by train) causes most visitors to overlook it. A genuine shame. Further north are the almost unbearably pleasant towns of Castelfranco and Asolo, and the distinctly alpine centres of Feltre and Belluno, backed by one of the Eastern Alps' fabulous nature reserves. Everywhere in the region the countryside is extremely attractive.

Treviso

A city of porticoed streets and fine old houses situated at the confluence of two rivers, **Treviso** is known for its medieval atmosphere and for the picturesque canals that flow through and around the old centre, giving the town its nickname, 'Little Venice'. Gardens are everywhere, and are particularly lush. A flourishing manufacturing and agricultural centre, Treviso is home to a number of leading Italian entrepreneurs, and its high standard of living is clearly evident.

Though a palaeo-Venetic settlement and a Roman *municipium,* called *Tarvisium,* existed on more or less the same area the old city occupies today, Treviso reached its greatest prosperity in the Middle Ages. It was the centre of a Lombard duchy, then the capital of a Carolingian *marca,* or frontier buffer zone, a free commune, a seigniory (lord's domain) and, after 1389, a component of the Venetian Republic. Old prints showning Treviso as a fortified city bear witness to the importance that Venetian military planners gave to its strategic location, on the northwestern border of their republic. The town walls were considered impenetrable, and their impression of strength was enhanced by the fact that they were pierced by just three gates: Porta Altinia,

Porta Santi Quaranta and Porta San Tomaso. Only the 18th-century agricultural revolution and the consequent construction of patrician residences in the countryside to the north, brought expansion outside the walls.

Piazza dei Signori to the Cathedral

Since Roman times, the political and social centre of the city has been the beautiful **Piazza dei Signori**, with palaces built in the 13th century on the site of the Roman forum. The most important of these is the **Palazzo dei Trecento**, named after the 300 members of the Greater Council. It was built on the east side of the square in 1210 and has a ground-floor loggia of 1552 on the main façade. An external staircase and another 16th-century loggia grace the flank facing Piazza Independenza. On the north side of the square is the **Palazzo del Podestà** (now the Prefecture), surmounted by the Torre Civica, which the Trevisans call *Il Campanon* ('The Big Bell'). Both were rebuilt in the 19th century in a Gothic-revival style. Next door is the **Palazzo Pretorio**, with a rusticated façade of the 17th century.

In a little square behind these buildings is the **Monte di Pietà**, which incorporates the 16th-century Cappella dei Rettori, a small chapel with gilt-leather wall coverings of the 17th century, frescoes and canvases, and a fine ceiling. On your right as you return are **Santa Lucia** and **San Vito**, two adjoining churches of medieval origin. The more interesting is Santa Lucia, a 14th-century building containing frescoes by Tomaso da Modena and his school (*Madonna delle Carceri*), and 14th- and 15th-century sculptures, notably busts of *Saints* on the balustrade. San Vito, built in the 11th and 12th centuries and rebuilt in 1568, conserves a Byzantine-Romanesque fresco of the 12th or 13th century depicting *Christ among the Apostles*.

Views of considerable charm are offered along the Calmaggiore, the street that joins Piazza dei Signori with Piazza del Duomo. The street is lined with 15th- and 16th-century townhouses, many with porticoes and frescoed façades. Just before meeting Piazza del Duomo it passes (left) the church of **San Giovanni Battista** or baptistery, a Romanesque building of the late 11th and early 12th centuries with pilaster strips, small blind arches, a 14th-century relief on the gable, Roman-age friezes at the sides of the doorway and, within, some fresco fragments of the 12th to 14th century in the apses. Behind rises the massive 11th- and 12th-century campanile, unfinished at the top.

The **Cathedral of San Pietro** was founded in the late 12th or early 13th century, but its present form has little in common with the original church. The apses were rebuilt in the 15th and 16th centuries to a design by Pietro Lombardo, the central structure was altered in the 18th century, and the façade with its Ionic hexastyle porch was added in 1836.

The three-aisled interior, covered by seven lead-and-copper domes, contains an *Adoration of the Shepherds* by Paris Bordone, a statue of *St John the Baptist* by Alessandro Vittoria and a marble relief of the *Annunciation* by Lorenzo Bregno (or Antonio Lombardo). The **Cappella dell'Annunziata**, at the

Treviso, panorama

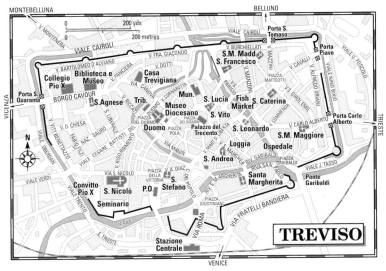

end of the south aisle, was built to a design by Martino Lombardo in 1519 for the Malchiostro family. In the vestibule are several sculptures, notably an *Adoration of the Shepherds* and *St Lawrence and Saints* by Paris Bordone and a *Madonna and Child with Saints* (the 'Madonna of the Flower') by Girolamo da Treviso il Vecchio. Titian's splendid *Annunciation* hangs over the altar, and the walls have frescoes by Giovanni Antonio Pordenone and assistants. In the sanctuary, designed by Pietro Lombardo and his sons, are the monument to Bishop Giovanni Zanetto, by Pietro, Antonio and Tullio Lombardo, and the sarcophagus of SS Teonisto, Tabra and Tabrata, with carved portraits attributed to Tullio Lombardo. In the Cappella del Santissimo Sacramento (on the north; 1513) are more Renaissance sculptures, by Pietro and Tullio Lombardo and Lorenzo Bregno. Beneath the sanctuary extends the 12th- and 13th-century Romanesque crypt, with mosaic pavement fragments and remains of frescoes. The capitals on the columns were taken from earlier buildings.

Flanking the cathedral is the Bishop's Palace, built in the 12th and 13th centuries and later altered, with a large hall frescoed by Benedetto Calieri. The **Museo Diocesano di Arte Sacra** (9 Via Canoniche), located in the recently restored Canoniche Vecchie, displays paintings, sculpture, and liturgical items. Highlights include the *Arca (Tomb) del Beato Enrico,* acquired by the commune in 1315; several marble reliefs from the cathedral (notably a 13th-century Enthroned Christ); a detached fresco by Tommaso da Modena, and tapestries and objects from the cathedral treasury.

Going West and South

The continuation of Via Calmaggiore, Via Canova, leads over a small canal and past a pleasant garden to the **Museo della Casa Trevigiana** (No. 38). Occupying the Casa da Noal, a 15th-century Gothic mansion, it contains medieval and Renaissance marbles and terracottas, wood sculptures of the 15th to 18th century, furniture, ceramics, wrought iron, weapons, and antique prints and musical instruments, shown on a rotating basis. Next door (No. 40) is the Casa Robegan, a Renaissance townhouse decorated with faded 16th-century frescoes. More old homes, some with 15th- and 16th-century frescoes, stand in the nearby Via Riccati.

Continuing westward, you soon reach the **Museo Civico Luigi Bailo**, which displays the municipal collections of art and archaeology. In the archaeological section are Copper, Bronze, and Iron Age objects (axes, fibulae and swords), Roman material (sarcophagi, tablets, sculpture, portraits and small bronzes) and early Christian and Byzantine sculpture. In the picture gallery are paintings, frescoes, and statues of the 12th through the 20th century, with works by Giovanni Bellini (*Madonna*), Cima da Conegliano, Girolamo da Treviso and Girolamo da Santacroce, Titian (*Portrait of Sperone Speroni*), Lorenzo Lotto (the famous *Portrait of a Dominican*), Jacopo Bassano (*Crucifixion*), Giovanni Antonio da Pordenone, Francesco Guardi (*View of the Isle of San Giorgio*), Gian Domenico Tiepolo, Pietro Longhi and Rosalba Carriera (three portraits). There are also 19th-century works by Francesco Hayez and Antonio Canova, and sculptures and drawings by the 20th-century Trevisan artist Arturo Martini. A section of the museum housed in the former Gothic church of Santa Caterina dei Servi contains an important cycle of detached frescoes by Tommaso da Modena and a fragmentary *Madonna* by Gentile da Fabriano.

From here it is a short walk southwards to the 14th-century Dominican church of **San Nicolò**, with a fine rose window and doorway on the façade, slender windows on the flanks and three tall polygonal apses. The vast three-aisled interior, with a beautiful ship's-keel ceiling, has frescoes by Tommaso da Modena and his school on the columns and other paintings ranging from the 16th to the 18th century. In the south chapels are a finely carved altar of Lombardesque workmanship, a large fresco of *St Christopher* attributed to Antonio da Treviso (1410), and a 16th-century organ with painted shutters. In the apse are a *Sacra Conversazione* begun by Fra' Marco Pensaben and completed by Giovan Gerolamo Savoldo (1521), a 17th-century memorial to St Benedict XI and (left) the 16th-century tomb of Agostino Onigo, incorporating a fresco attributed to Lorenzo Lotto.

Next to the church is the former convent of San Nicolò, now the **Seminario Vescovile**. The complex is connected by cloisters to the 14th-century chapter house, which is decorated with charmingly realistic frescoes (1352) by Tommaso da Modena of 40 eminent Dominians. The Abbot of Cluny wears on his nose the first pictorially documented pair of eyeglasses. The complex also houses two small museums, the Museo Etnografico Dino Grossa, displaying articles from the Venezuelan Amazon; and the Museo Zoologico Giuseppe Scarpa, with Italian fauna and exotic reptiles.

Around Treviso

A full morning or afternoon is needed to explore the environs of Treviso. At **Istrana**, 10km (6 miles) west on the road to Castelfranco Veneto, the magnificently furnished **Villa Lattes** contains collections of Oriental art, automata and carillons. **Conegliano**, 28km (17 miles) north on the road to Belluno, is the birthplace of Giovanni Battista Cima, called Cima da Conegliano, whose magnificent *Madonna and Saints* (1493) stands over the high altar of the 14th-century **Cathedral**. The imposing **Castle** commands a wonderful view over the surrounding countryside; inside is the **Museo Civico**, with a collection of local paintings, including works by Pordenone and Girolamo da Santacroce. The area around Conegliano is known for its excellent wines and the town, for its gourmet restaurants.

Belluno

The old town of **Belluno** stands on a rocky eminence at the point where the River Ardo flows into the Piave – a position that protected it over the centuries both from foreign incursions and from seasonal floodwaters. Here you immediately feel the nearness of the Alps (the Dolomiti Bellunesi, the most southerly of the Dolomite ranges, rise just to the west), and of the forests that have long been the city's principal asset. From Belluno, in fact, came the piles on which Venice is built; and something of the deep greens and browns of the Alpine woodlands can be seen in the paintings of Sebastiano Ricci and his nephew Marco, who were born here in 1659 and 1679, respectively. The wood-sculptor Andrea Brustolon was also a native.

Founded in palaeo-Venetic times (the place name *Belunum* seems to be of Celtic origin), Belluno was a Roman *municipium,* the residence of a civil and military functionary called a *sculdascio* in the Lombard period, and the seat of a count in Carolingian times. As early as the 9th century, temporal power over the city was held by its bishops, who retained control until the formation of the commune after 1200. In the 13th and 14th centuries the city lost its independence first to the Trevisan seigniories, then to the dukes of Austria and the Visconti. The beginning of Venetian rule, in 1404, brought renewed security and a vast building programme that spared only a few medieval monuments.

The spacious, park-like Piazza dei Martiri, dedicated to the victims of a Nazi massacre of 1944, is the centre of city life. It stands on the north edge of the old town, just a few blocks from the religious and civic buildings lining Piazza del Duomo.

The **Cathedral** is a 16th-century edifice designed by Tullio Lombardo, with an unfinished façade and a detached campanile by the Baroque architect Filippo Juvarra (1743). The luminous interior has paintings by Jacopo Bassano (third south altar) and Palma Giovane (fourth south altar). The two small marble statuettes in the first north chapel are attributed to Tullio Lombardo. The **Baptistery**, also called Santa Maria delle Grazie, dates from the 16th century.

A closer-than-usual relationship between civil and religious power might explain the location, on the north side of the square, of the 19th-century town hall and of its historic predecessor, the **Palazzo dei Rettori** (now the Prefecture), a Venetian Renaissance building of 1491 with porticoed façade, mullioned windows, central loggias, and an imposing clock tower (1549) over the eastern corner. The former palace of the Bishop-Counts (1190), opposite, has been completely rebuilt, the Torre Civica being the only vestige of the original structure.

One block east of the cathedral, at 16 Via Duomo, is the **Museo Civico**, arranged in the 17th-century Palazzo dei Giuristi. Here you can see the usual pre-Roman and Roman antiquities, as well as a picture gallery with works by Bartolomeo Montagna, Palma Giovane, and Sebastiano and Marco Ricci, coins and seals, jewellery and prints.

The street continues to Piazza delle Erbe or del Mercato, on the site of the Roman forum. It has a fountain of 1410 at the centre and porticoed Renaissance buildings all around, the finest of which is the **Monte di Pietà** (1531), adorned with coats of arms and inscriptions. Here you have a choice: continuing north along Via Rialto and, beyond the ancient Porta Doiona, Via Roma, you come to the late Gothic church of **Santo Stefano** (1468), with a large 15th-century doorway on the side. The Cappella Cesa, within, has frescoes by Jacopo da Montagnana (c 1487) and painted wood statues of Matteo, Antonio, and Francesco Cesa by Andrea Brustolon, over the altar. To the south, Via Mezzaterra – the main thoroughfare of the city, lined with Venetian-style townhouses – and Vicolo San Pietro lead to the Gregorian church of **San Pietro**, a 14th-century edifice rebuilt in 1750, with a bare façade and, inside, paintings by Sebastiano Ricci (over the high altar) and Andrea Schiavone (former organ shutters), and two wooden altar panels carved by Andrea Brustolon. The adjacent seminary encloses two cloisters, of which the oldest (15th–16th century) has a frescoed lunette attributed to Jacopo da Montagnana. Via Santa Maria Battuti, which flanks the seminary, continues south to the medieval Porta Rugo, which affords a magnificent view of the Dolomites and the Piave valley.

The Dolomiti Bellunesi Nature Reserve

The **Parco Naturale delle Dolomiti Bellunesi** was established in 1990 by joining eight existing nature reserves. Extending over 29,000 hectares, the park takes in the last southern ramifications of the Dolomites, including the great limestone massifs of the **Talvena** (2542m), the **Schiara** (2565m), the **Monti del Sole** (2240m), and the **Alpi Feltrine** (Sas de Mura, 2550m). These mountains join typically alpine landscapes, characterised by bold peaks and powerful vertical walls, with the grassy meadows and shady forests and valleys of the *prealpi*. Their geological history is linked to mountain-building processes that raised the sea floors of the Mesozoic and Tertiary periods (some 65 million years ago), whose sediments compose most of the rock here. Over time, glaciers carved cirques (deep, steep-walled basins shaped like half a bowl) and grooves or furrows on the mountain walls, and the waters dug dolinas (depressions) and caverns in the limestone, some as deep as 960m. The incessant action of the mountain streams has created immense waterfalls.

The vegetation of the park is made up of magnificent beech woods and broad-leafed deciduous forests, which yield at higher altitudes to firs and larches, and above the tree line to scrub pine and rhododendron. The flora, which counts over 1500 species and is one of the prime assets of the park, includes numerous native species and rarities such as *Delphinium dubium, Sempervivum dolomiticum, Alyssum ovirense, Geranium argenteum, Astragalus sempervirens* and *Cortusa matthioli*. Along with the classic Alpine flowers – edelweiss, gentian, rhododendron, and so forth – the southern slopes support thermophile species which, in particularly favourable positions, grow at altitudes much higher than might be expected. Such is the case, for instance, of the striking *Iris cengialti,* which in some areas of the Alpi Feltrine can be found as high up as 1700m.

The fauna of the Dolomiti Bellunesi includes large colonies of chamois, deer, and roe-deer. Hunters have stocked the area with mouflon (wild sheep), which in addition to damaging the forests have entered into competition, in the food cycle, with these native animals. The royal eagle, various owls, kestrel, grouse, and white partridge inhabit vast areas of the park. Reptiles include the alpine asp and the common salamander. Among the numerous insects are certain native species of coleoptera (beetles) such as *Orotrechus pavionis, Orotrechus theresiae* and *Neobathyscia dalpiazi.* Less endemic but much more bothersome are ticks (*Ixodes ricinus* and *Ixodes dammini*), which show a particular predilection for hikers in shorts.

Walk: To the Piani Eterni

Departure point: Albergo Alpino Boz (660m), in Val Canzoi, reached via Soranzen, north of Feltre. Time: 6–7 hours Difficulty: moderate

From the Albergo Boz a road (closed to vehicular traffic) climbs steeply to the dam on the Lago de la Stua (696m) and follows the left bank of the lake until it crosses the affluent of this little lake, the Torrente Caorame. Soon after, on the right, you join the mule path for the Piani Eterni (Trail 802), which climbs first through beech woods and then crosses a glen. At 1417m you encounter a fork in the trail: continue right along the mule path, which continues to climb in a southeasterly direction to the slopes of the **Pala del Lenzuoletto** (1797m), where it turns northwards in a broad curve to reach the highland known as the **Piani Eterni** (Eternal Plains), at an altitude of 1755m. On this limestone plateau, covered with meadows and low bushes, are numerous dolinas, caverns and abysses, some of which reach a depth of several hundred metres. Continuing northwards on Trail 802, you reach the Casera Erera (1708m) and, just beyond, the Casera Brendol. From here you can descend along the Val Porzil along another trail that returns to the mule path at the fork at 1417m.

Feltre

Feltre was a Roman centre, probably a *municipium,* and before that it may have been a Raetian community on the Via Opitergium-Tridentum. In the Middle Ages it was a free commune and a seigniory of various families before coming under Venice in 1404. The Venetian heads of state dated their dispatches *ex cineribus Feltri,* 'from the ashes of Feltre', after forces of the Holy Roman Empire sacked the city twice (in 1509 and 1510) during the War of the Cambrai League. The architectural uniformity of the city centre, Feltre's most distinctive asset, is a direct consequence of this double debacle and of the ambitious programme of reconstruction that followed it.

The old walled city has numerous 16th-century buildings with projecting roofs and façades bearing frescoes or graffiti. Almost all the city gates date from the Renaissance. The porticoed Via Mezzaterra begins at the 16th-century Porta Imperiale, or Castaldi, and runs uphill through the old city to the Renaissance **Piazza Maggiore**. This is laid out on several levels. On the north side stands the church of San Rocco (1599); the fine fountain in its fore-court is attributed to Tullio Lombardo (1520). On the west is the 19th-century Gothic-revival Palazzo Guarnieri; and on the south, the unusual **Palazzo della Ragione** or **del Municipio**, actually two buildings meeting at the corner – the one with the rusticated arcade (1558) is the former **Palazzo dei Rettori Veneti**, attributed to Palladio. Inside is a small wooden theatre of 1802. Above the square rises the **Castello** with its square keep, a Roman watchtower rebuilt in the Middle Ages.

The continuation of Via Mezzaterra, called Via Luzzo, is lined with inter-esting houses. Note especially No. 3, Palazzo Banchieri, with a graffitied façade; no. 13, Palazzo Pasole, and No. 23, Palazzo Villabruna, a Venetian-Gothic-revival building now home to the **Museo Civico**. The museum has an archaeological section with palaeo-Venetic and Roman antiquities; a histor-ical section with memorabilia, and a picture gallery with a small portrait by Gentile Bellini, a triptych by Cima da Conegliano, a *Resurrection of Lazarus* by Palma Giovane and four views by Marco Ricci. There are also works by the native artists Pietro Mariscalchi and Morto da Feltre. Outside the walls at the northeast end of the town is the 15th-century church of the **Ognissanti**, with a 9th- or 10th-century campanile, fragmentary frescoes on the outside and a *Madonna with SS Victor and Nicholas of Bari* by Tintoretto within.

From Piazza Maggiore Via del Paradiso leads past the elaborately deco-rated Monte di Pietà to the **Galleria d'Arte Moderna Carlo Rizzarda** (8 Via del Paradiso), situated in the 16th-century Palazzo Cumano. This is less inter-esting for the wrought-iron works of the founder, Carlo Rizzarda, than for its

19th- and 20th-century Italian paintings and sculpture by Giovanni Fattori, Francesco Paolo Michetti, Carlo Carrà and Arturo Tosi.

Outside the walls, to the south, is the **Cathedral of San Pietro**. Its present appearance dates from the 16th century, notwithstanding the 14th-century Gothic apse and campanile. The three-aisled interior, with its 9th-century crypt, conserves paintings of the *Adoration of the Shepherds* and *St John the Baptist* by Pietro Mariscalchi, the *Tomb of Andrea Bellati* by Tullio Lombardo (in the sanctuary), the 13th-century Throne of Bishop Vilata (at the end of the north aisle), a fine Byzantine crucifix of 542 (in the Archivio Capitolare), and other interesting artworks. Behind the cathedral steps, ascend to the **Baptistery of San Lorenzo**, with a 15th-century apse, a 17th-century doorway on the façade, and a Renaissance doorway on the side. Inside are a baptismal font of 1399 with a Baroque wooden cover, and paintings by Leandro Bassano and other artists of the 16th and 17th centuries. Remains of an early Christian baptistery have been found nearby.

Around Feltre

A pleasant excursion can be made to the **Santuario dei Santi Vittore e Corona**, 4km (2½ miles) southeast of Feltre. This is a Byzantine-Romanesque church of 1096–1101 with a narrow façade adorned with chiaroscuro frescoes. The three-aisled interior has 13th- to 15th-century frescoes (some of which are thought to be by the school of Giotto) and 11th-century sculptures. The adjoining convent of 1494 has more frescoes in the cloister. Other points of interest in the environs are the 15th-century church of **Santa Maria Assunta** at **Lentiai**, with coffered ceiling and paintings by Palma Vecchio; and the **Villas Bovio, Martini e Moro**, and **Mauro**, dating from the 17th and 18th centuries, at **Soranzen**.

Asolo

Asolo lies to the south of Feltre and east of Bassano del Grappa. In the Renaissance it was famous as the home of Caterina Cornaro, the Venetian noblewoman and Queen of Cyprus who traded her island dominion to the Venetian State in exchange for a substantial income and this charming town, pleasantly situated among the foothills of the Alps. Caterina lived in the castle from 1489 to 1509, and her court drew Venetian patricians and intellectuals, initiating a tradition that Robert Browning, Henry James, Eleonora Duse (who is buried here), and Ernest Hemingway would continue in later centuries. '*Vago molto e di maravigliosa bellezza*' ('quite graceful, and wonderfully beautiful') is how Cardinal Bembo described Caterina's formal gardens; and his opinion might well be extended to Asolo as a whole. The old town,

Asolo, the old town, detail

reached by bus from the main highway and car park, is a medley of 15th- to 18th-century houses whose simple elegance is still quite impressive.

In the central Piazza Maggiore is the 15th-century **Loggia del Capitano** with a fine portico and frescoed façade of 1560. Once the seat of municipal government, today it hosts the **Museo Civico**, with palaeontological and archaeological collections, historical memorabilia, and 15th- to 20th-century paintings and sculpture. On a lower level is the **Cathedral of Santa Maria Assunta**, an 18th-century church containing an important painting, Lorenzo Lotto's *Virgin and Saints* of 1506. The medieval clock tower was originally part of Caterina's castle, torn down in the early 19th century. Overlooking all is the **Rocca**, a polygonal fortress with high, massive walls incorporating some fragments of pre-Roman fortifications. The view over the town and the surrounding countryside is well worth the walk up.

Around Asolo

If you're travelling by car, take a few hours to explore the magnificent countryside around Asolo. The landscape – a harmonious ensemble of handsome farms and vineyards – is enchanting, and it is dotted with fine old villas, such as the 18th-century **Villa Falier**, on the outskirts of the town, visited for its lovely park; the 17th-century **Villa Rinaldi Barbini** at **Casella**, an exuberant Baroque creation decorated by Andrea Celesti and Pietro Liberi; and the stupendous **Villa Barbaro** (now Villa Luling Buschetti) at **Maser** This villa, designed by Palladio in 1557 for Daniele Barbaro, Patriarch of Aquileia, is one of the architect's highest achievements: following the traditional plan of the Venetian Renaissance farm, it has a central manor house with engaged Ionic columns and carved tympanum, and symmetrical porticoed *barchesse*, or working wings. The interior contains spectacular frescoes by Paolo Veronese and stucco decorations by Alessandro Vittoria. Palladio also designed the small, cylindrical tempietto nearby.

Bassano del Grappa

Situated where the River Brenta emerges from the hills, **Bassano** is a pleasant town of arcaded streets and old houses, many of which have frescoed façades. First documented in the 10th century, it was united with Venice in 1402. It was home to a family of well-known painters – the Da Ponte, called Bassano after this, their birthplace. The Austrians were defeated here by Napoleon in 1796, and by the Italians in 1917–18. The city suffered severe damage in the latter campaign, which was fought on nearby Monte Grappa; but this and the recent flourishing of small industries have done little to mar the integrity of the city centre, which is still one of the finest in the region. Shoppers will be pleased to know that there is a strong tradition here in wrought iron and ceramics. Bassano is known also for its produce, especially asparagus and *porcini* mushrooms, and of course for its *grappa* (brandy), the best in Italy.

The northernmost part of the historic centre, including the 15th-century **Cathedral** (with paintings by members of the Bassano family), stands inside the walled complex of the **Castello Superiore**, which dates as far back as 900–950 but was enlarged and fortified in the 13th, 14th, and subsequent centuries. A tower of the old fortress serves as the base of the campanile. The area to the south of this, occupied in part by the 14th-century **Castello Inferiore**, develops around three adjacent squares, Piazza Garibaldi, Piazza della Libertà, and Piazzetta Monte Vecchio.

In Piazza Garibaldi stands the former Franciscan church of **San Francesco**, a Romanesque-Gothic building with an elegant vestibule of 1306 and a graceful campanile. It conserves remains of 15th-century frescoes and, in the apse, a painted wooden crucifix of the 14th century. A door on the right of the porch leads to the **Museo Civico**, housed in the former monastic buildings. In the beautiful 17th-century cloister (partly rebuilt) are a collection of Roman and medieval inscriptions and another of ceramics. The archaeological section includes protohistoric material of the Angarano culture (11th century BC); Greek, Italiot, and Roman finds; and antique coins. The print and drawing cabinet (with works by Vittore Carpaccio, Lorenzo Lotto, Gian Lorenzo Bernini, Giovan Battista Tiepolo, Francesco Guardi and Antonio Canova) is famous for the Remondini collection of 17th- to 19th-century popular prints. On the first floor is the picture gallery, with paintings by Jacopo Bassano (*Flight into Egypt; Baptism of St Lucilla, St Martin and the Beggar*), Francesco and Leandro Bassano, Michele Giambono and Guariento. There are also numerous works from the 17th and 18th centuries, by Francesco Maffei, Marco Ricci, Giovan Battista Tiepolo, Pietro Longhi and Alessandro Magnasco. The last rooms are dedicated to Antonio Canova (casts and models); to painters of the 19th century; and to Tito Gobbi (1913–84), the great baritone, who was born here.

In the neighbouring Piazza della Libertà are the **Loggia del Commune** (1582) with a fresco of *St Christopher* ascribed to Jacopo Bassano, and two 18th-century buildings, the Palazzo del Municipio and the church of San Giovanni Battista. Piazzetta Monte Vecchio, which was the main square of the city in the Middle Ages, is lined with fine old frescoed palaces, most notably the 15th-century **Palazzetto del Monte di Pietà**, with inscriptions and coats of arms on the façade. The square leads down to the famous **Ponte Coperto** (or Ponte degli Alpini), a covered wooden bridge over the Brenta documented as early as 1209 but destroyed and rebuilt many times, most recently in 1948. The present design, attributed to Andrea Palladio, dates from 1569. The adjacent Taverna al Ponte has a small **Museo degli Alpini** containing memorabilia and photographs regarding the two World Wars and the history of the bridge.

Around Bassano

In the environs of Bassano, to the southwest, is **Marostica**, famous for its cherries. The town is built to a square plan and surrounded by medieval towers and walls clambering up to the 14th-century **Castello Superiore**, now a restaurant, from which there is a fine view of the River Brenta, Vicenza, and the Colli Berici. The 15th-century **Castello Inferiore**, now the town hall, gives its name to the Piazza Castello, a large square surrounded by porticoes where a chess match with live human chessmen in Renaissance costume is held the second Saturday and Sunday in September, in even-numbered years. A few kilometres northeast of Bassano is **Possagno**, famous for its **Tempio di Canova**, designed by the sculptor in 1819 on the plan of the Pantheon in Rome and completed in 1830. Within are works by Luca Giordano, Moretto da Brescia, Palma Giovane, and Canova himself. The house of Canova and the adjacent *gipsoteca*, with a magnificent new wing of 1957 by Carlo Scarpa, display models by the artist and plaster casts of many of his works.

Castelfranco Veneto

Between Bassano and Treviso is **Castelfrance Veneto**. A medieval chronicle narrates that those who settled in this *castello* were freed (*affrancati*) of all fiscal obligations. The town was founded by the commune of Treviso in 1199 to defend its western frontier, and a rectangular fortification with five towers and brick walls and doorways, encircled by a moat (the **Castello** proper), still encloses its centre. Throughout the town are small porticoed palaces, some of them frescoed. The sky, the clouds and the green fields of the environs are those of Giorgione (1477/78–1510) who was born and began to paint here.

The **Cathedral** (San Liberale) was erected in 1723–45 to plans by Francesco Maria Preti, in a Palladian style. Inside, in the south apsidal chapel, is Giorgione's famous altarpiece of the *Madonna and Child with SS Francis and Liberale* (c 1505) and, in the sacristy, works by Palma Giovane, Jacopo Bassano and early frescoes by Paolo Veronese (*Allegorical Figures,* 1551) brought from the destroyed Villa Soranza; the campanile of the church is one of the towers of the defensive walls.

Adjoining the piazza, on the east, is the 15th-century **Casa di Giorgione** (or Casa Pellizzari), where Giorgione lived and worked (he painted the chiaroscuro deorative band, with symbols of the liberal and mechanical arts, in one room). Inside are reproductions of works by the painter, a small picture gallery, and collections of prehistoric and Roman antiquities, Venetian objects, minerals and medals. Also noteworthy is the **Teatro Accademico**, in

Ponte Coperto, Bassano del Grappa

the nearby Via Garibaldi. Designed by Francesco Maria Preti in 1754, it has a brick façade and four-tiered stuccoed interior.

Outside the walls are the old market square (now Piazza Giorgione), lined with 16th- to 18th-century townhouses, some with frescoed façades; the church of **Santa Maria della Pieve** (founded in the 11th century, but rebuilt 1821–25), with a Corinthian porch; and the **Villa Revedin-Bolasco** (built in 1607 by Vincenzo Scamozzi, but remodelled in the 19th century), surrounded by a large park with an open amphitheatre decorated with statues by Orazio Marinali.

Around Castelfranco

The area around Castelfranco abounds with magnificent villas. **Fanzolo di Vedelago**, a small farm town 8km (5 miles) northeast, is known for splendid **Villa Emo** (c 1564), one of Palladio's master-pieces. The central building, preceded by a wide, stepped ramp, has a monumental porch with seven Doric columns surmounted by a triangular pediment. At the sides are two long, symmetrical *barchesse* terminating in the little towers of dovecotes. The interior is frescoed with mythological scenes by G.B. Zelotti, possibly with the help of Paolo Veronese. Another villa by Palladio, the **Villa Cornaro** (1560–70), is at **Piombino Dese**, 10km (6¼ miles) southeast. At

Castelfranco Veneto, Castello

Sant'Andrea, 4km (2½ miles) southwest, the **Ca' Tiepolo** (now Chiminelli) is decorated with frescoes of the school of Paolo Veronese; it has two small museums illustrating methods of farming and tanning. At nearby **Treville** are remains of the **Villa Priuli Gran Can** (1530) and **Villa Priuli San Felice**, by Vincenzo Scamozzi. **Cittadella**, 13km (8 miles) west, is famous for its 13th- and 14th-century walls, with 32 towers and four gates, which form an irregular circuit around the old town centre. Built in 1220 by the Paduans as a defence against Treviso, it has an elliptical plan cut by two intersecting streets. The **Torre di Malta** was erected in 1251, and the neoclassical parish church (1775) contains a canvas by Jacopo Bassano.

Practical Information

Getting There

The **road** network in Treviso and Belluno provinces is both extensive and well maintained. Treviso is located on Autostrada A27, which runs from Mestre to Belluno, closely followed by Highways 13 and 51. Highway 50 connects Belluno with Feltre; Highway 47, Feltre with Bassano del Grappa and Padua via Cittadella; Highway 248, Bassano with Asolo; and Highway 53, Cittadella with Castelfranco and Treviso.

Treviso is on the main **rail** line from Venice to Udine and Tarvisio (with through service to Vienna and Prague); from here secondary lines connect with Castelfranco, Bassano, Feltre and Belluno. There are also direct trains from Vicenza to Castelfranco and Treviso; from Padua to Castelfranco, Fanzolo, Feltre and Belluno (continuing on to Cortina d'Ampezzo); and country buses from Venice and Padua to most points mentioned in the text.

To reach the Parco Naturale delle Dolomiti Bellunesi take Autostrada A27 and Highways 51 and 50 from Venice and Treviso to Belluno (north area); or Highways 348 and 50 from Treviso to Feltre (southern area). Frequent trains run to Feltre and Belluno from Padua. Maps: Tabacco 1:25,000, sheets 023 Alpi Feltrine and 024 Prealpi e Dolomiti Bellunesi; Kompass 1:50,000, sheets 76 and 77, available at tobacconists, news stands, and bookshops in the park area.

Tourist Information

ASOLO 258 Via Santa Caterina (tel. 0423 529 046/524 192, fax 524 137).

BASSANO DEL GRAPPA 35 Largo Corona d'Italia (tel. 0424 524 351, fax 525 301).

BELLUNO 21 Via Psaro (tel. 0437 940 083, fax 940073); Information Office,

27e Piazza dei Martiri (tel. 0437 941 746).

CASTELFRANCO VENETO 39 Via Francesco Maria Preti (tel. 0423 495 000).

FELTRE 9 Piazza Trento e Trieste (tel. 0439 2540, fax 2839).

PARCO NATURALE DELLE DOLOMITI BELLUNES Azienda Promomozione Turismo del Feltrino, 9 Piazza Trento e Trieste, 32032 Feltre (tel. 0439 2540, fax 2839); Azienda Promozione Turistica Prealpi e Dolomiti Bellunesi, 21 Via Psaro, 32100 Belluno (tel. 0437 940 083/084).

TREVISO 41 Via Toniolo (tel. 0422 547 632, fax 541 397).

Hotels

ASOLO
The **Villa Cipriani**, 298 Via Canova (tel. 0423 952 166, fax 952 166) is surely one of the most charming (and restful) hotels in the region, occupying a 16th-century villa with splendid views over the hills of Asolo. It's also expensive. The **Duse**, 190 Via Robert Browning (tel. 0423 55241, fax 950 404), is a small (12 rooms), comfortable and centrally located hotel; it is relatively inexpensive.

BASSANO DEL GRAPPA
There are at least two moderately priced and two inexpensive places to stay here. The **Belvedere**, 14 Piazzale Generale Giardino (tel. 0424 529 845, fax 529 849), is pleasant, with a renowned restaurant; the **Palladio**, 2 Via Gramsci (tel. 0424 523 777, fax 524 050), is modern and efficient. The inexpensive places are the **Brennero**, 7 Via Torino (tel. 0424 228 544, fax 227 021), and the **Victoria**, 33 Viale Diaz (tel. 0424 503 620, fax 503 130.) Both are comfortable.

BELLUNO
Hotel Delle Alpi, 13 Via Jacopo Tasso (tel. 0437 940 545, fax 940 565), is a comfortable place with a good restaurant, in a house midway between the train station and the cathedral. **Villa Carpenada**, 158 Via Mier (tel. 0437 948 343, fax 948 345), is a calm, relaxing hotel in an 18th-century villa with park, 2km (1¼miles) west of the city centre. Both are moderate. Somewhat less expensive are **Alle Dolomiti**, 46 Via Carrera (tel. 0437 941 660, fax 941 436), modern and comfortable; and **Astor**, 26e Piazza dei Martiri (tel. 0437 942 094, fax 942 493) on a lovely square. Both are centrally located.

CASTELFRANCO VENETO
Alla Torre, 7 Piazzetta Trento e Trieste (tel. 0423 498 707, fax 498 737), is a moderately priced hotel in a tastefully renovated old home conveniently located in the heart of the historic city centre. **Al Moretto**, 10 Via San Pio X (tel. 0423 721 313, fax 721 066), occupies another renovated old house, this time dating from the 17th century; it has been managed by the same family

for three generations; inexpensive. The **Roma**, 39 Via F. Filzi (tel. 0423 721 616, fax 721 515), overlooking Piazza Giorgione and the town walls, is a comfortable hotel with private parking; inexpensive. At Salvarosa, 3km (2 miles) northeast, are **Fior**, 18 Via dei Carpani (tel. 0423 721 212, fax 498 771), a very comfortable, moderately priced place, in an old patrician home with garden; and **Ca' delle Rose**, 33a Circonvallazione Est (tel. 0423 490 232, fax 490 261), yet another tastefully restored old building, with warm, comfortable rooms and modern facilities; inexpensive.

FELTRE
The **Doriguzzi**, 2 Viale Piave (tel. 0439 2902, fax 83660), is centrally located and moderately priced; the **Nuovo**, 5 Vicolo Fornere Pazze (tel. 0439 2110, fax 89241), is modern, efficient, and inexpensive.

TREVISO
Al Foghèr, 10 Viale della Repubblica (tel. 0422 432 950, fax 430 391), is a moderately priced hotel in a nicely renovated building with a renowned restaurant, outside the city centre on the road to Padua. There are also two inexpensive places to stay: **Campeol**, 11 Piazza Ancilotto (tel. 0422 56601, fax 540 871), a small (14 rooms), family-run establishment in the heart of the historic city centre, a stone's-throw from Piazza dei Signori (the restaurant, **Beccherie**, is excellent and also inexpensive); and **Scala**, 1 Viale Felissent (tel. 0422 307 600, fax 305 048), another small hotel (20 rooms) in a patrician home next to the gardens of Villa Manfrin, on the road to Conegliano.

Restaurants

ASOLO
Here you'll find two very satisfactory inexpensive restaurants: **Charley's One**, 55 Via Roma (tel. 0423 952 201; closed Wed evening and Thu, and mid-Jan–mid-Feb), with wholesome, straightforward regional cuisine in a warm atmosphere with wood panelling and antique furniture; and **Tavernetta**, 45 Via Schiavonesca (tel. 0423 952 273; closed Tue and a few days in Jul), an old tavern at once rustic and refined.

At **PAGNANO**, 2km (1¼ miles) west, is the somewhat pricier **Bacco e Tabacco**, 3 Via Ponte Pagnano (tel. 0423 529 475; closed Mon, Tue morning and Aug), dedicated – as the name suggests – to wine and tobacco and offering a limited but delicious menu.

BASSANO DEL GRAPPA
The best restaurant in town, and the most expensive, is **San Bassiano**, 36 Viale dei Martiri (tel. 0424 521 453, fax 525111; closed Sun and Aug). This fairly recent establishment (1984) has gained an excellent reputation for its good selection of regional dishes, prepared with skill and care, for its fine local cheeses (Asiago, Vezzena, Morlacco), and for its extensive list of regional, Italian and imported wines. Try the *moscardini affogati caldi, risotto con*

asparagi di Bassano, filetto di bue al radicchio rosso, funghi misti di bosco con polenta and *pera all'arancia con gelato di cannella*. More good local cuisine is to be found at the more moderate **Al Ponte da Renzo**, 60 Via Volpato (tel. 0424 503 055; closed Mon evening, Tue and Jan), and **Bauto**, 27 Via Trozzetti (tel. 0424 34696 (closed Sun and Aug), an inexpensive place with a great deal of rustic charm, run by the same family since 1917.

BELLUNO
Al Borgo, 8 Via Anconetta (tel. 0437 926 755, fax 926 411; closed Mon evening, Tue, and for one week in Jan and Jul), offers traditional fare (*minestrone di orzo e fagioli, agnello al forno, funghi e polenta*) and regional, Italian and imported wines, in an 18th-century villa with gardens; inexpensive.

At **SAN GREGORIO NELLE ALPI**, 16km (10 miles) southwest near the road to Feltre, is the **Locanda a l'Arte**, 43 Via Belvedere (tel. 0437 800 124; closed Mon and Tue morning), an inexpensive family-run establishment with garden (and fine views), serving personalised versions of traditional regional cuisine (try the *foglie e fiori fritti*, s*formati con erbe rustiche, coniglio farcito*, and *sfogliata di mele*).

At **PIEVE D'ALPAGO,** 17km (10½ miles) east, near the road to Treviso, is the Dolada, a restaurant with rooms (tel. 0437 479 141, fax 478 068; closed Feb and Mon and Tue morning except Jul–Aug), a more elegant (and somewhat more expensive) garden restaurant showing an innovative approach to such traditional regional recipes as *broet de scioss, casunzei, bocconcini di agnello*, and *lumache alla bellunese*. There is also a good *tortino di ricotta*.

CASTELFRANCO VENETO
There are two good, moderately priced restaurants: **Alle Mura**, 69 Via Preti (tel./fax 0423 498098; closed Thu, Jan and Aug), an elegant place set against the medieval town walls and specialising in seafood (try the *ostriche, tartufi e scampi; spaghetti con scampi, aragoste e radicchio* and *seppie al nero*); and **Osteria ai Due Mori**, 24 Vicolo Montebelluna (tel. 0423 497 174; closed Wed, Thu morning and three weeks in Sep), offering a small but excellent selection of refined, innovative dishes, specialising in game and mushrooms. **Al Teatro**, 17 Via Garibaldi (tel. 0423 721 425; closed Mon and Aug), situated across from the Teatro Accademico, is more traditional and less expensive.

At **SALVAROSA** (3km, 2 miles), in the Cà delle Rose hotel, is **Barbesin** (tel. 0423 490 446; closed Wed evening and Thu, Dec–Jan and Aug), offering a menu especially rich in vegetables (*punte di asparagi con morchelle alla crema, insalatina tiepida di manzo*) and regional and Italian wines; and at **FANZOLO** (8km, 5 miles) is the **Villa Emo** (tel. 0423 476 413; closed Mon and Tue morning), situated in a wing of Palladio's villa with fireplace, original paintings, and summer seating beneath the arcades. Both are inexpensive.

FELTRE
Although just about any place in town will be satisfactory, there are a couple of real musts out in the hills.

At **MIANE**, c. 32km (20 miles) southeast, is the area's finest (and most expensive) restaurant, **Da Gigetto** (tel. 0438 960 020, fax 960 111; closed Mon evening, Tue, and two weeks in Jan and Aug), where regional dishes (*fiori di zucca con funghi e tartufo, sformato di radicchio, sopa coada, petto d'anatra con tortelli e fagioli*) are served with an original twist, the wine list is endless, and there is summer service in the garden.

At **CAVASO DEL TOMBA**, c. 25km (16 miles) south, is **Al Ringraziamento**, 107 Via San Pio X (tel. 0423 543 271; closed Mon, Tue morning and Aug), a considerably more economical place where traditional regional specialities (*tagliatelle gratinate* and *lumache alle erbe*) are prepared with skill and imagination.

TREVISO

Alfredo - Relais el Toulà, 26 Via Collalto (tel./fax 0422 540 275; closed Sun evening, Mon, and a few days in Aug) is an elegant restaurant in a historic building, serving regional specialities and classic Italian dishes, with a wide selection of regional, Italian, and imported wines. It is known for its *blinis al Brie* and *ravioli di anatra con morchelle; filetto di bue in crosta di pane* and *rognoncini alla Savini*. **All'Antico Torre**, 55 Via Inferiore (tel. 0422 53694; closed Sun and Aug), also in a historical building in the old city, specialises in regional and seafood dishes, such as *gamberetti di laguna* and *granseola; tagliatelle all'aragosta* and *risotto alla marinara; branzino* and *rombo al vapore*, with regional and Italian wines. Both are moderate. A good inexpensive place is **Al Bersagliere**, 21 Via Barberia (tel. 0422 541 988, fax 51706; closed Sat morning, Sun, and a few days in Jan and Aug), offering traditional Trevisan dishes with a personal twist – *gnocchetti alla Bersagliere, scampi al curry, cervella dorata*. The building dates from the 13th century.

At **CONEGLIANO**, about 20km (12 miles) north of Treviso are two interesting places, both offering excellent fare at moderate prices. **Al Salisà**, 2 Via XX Settembre (tel. 0438 24288; closed Tue evening, Wed and Aug), an elegant restaurant in an old building with garden, was awarded the Accademia Italiana della Cucina's Diploma Cucina Eccellente in 1995. Here you'll find regional specialities served with a special flair (if you like snails, you'll enjoy the *lumache alla corsa*; otherwise *timballi vegetali, anatra muta al forno* or *baccalà alla vecia*, and for dessert, *gratin frutta di bosco*). **Tre Panoce**, 50 Via Vecchia Trevigiana (tel. 0438 60071, fax 62230; closed Sunday evening, Mon, and two weeks in Jan and Aug), also offers impeccably prepared regional dishes, plus extraordinary ambience in an 18th-century villa with gardens. Try the *risotto alla sbiraglia, faraona con salsa peverada e polenta*, and *torta degli angeli*, and don't overlook the fine selection of local cheeses. Both places have good wine lists.

Special Events

TREVISO

Treviso in Fiore (flower show, May–Sep); **Concorso Internazionale Cantanti Lirici** (opera competition, Jun); **Autunno Musicale Trevigiano** (classical music,

Oct–Dec); **Concorso Nazionale Di Esecuzione Pianistica** (classical piano competition, Dec).

Museums and Monuments

ASOLO
Museo Civico: closed for restoration at the time of writing.
Villa Barbaro, at Maser (7km/4¼ miles): Mar–Oct, Tue; Sat, Sun and hols 15.00–18.00; Nov–Feb Sat Sun and hols 14.30–17.00.

BASSANO DEL GRAPPA
Museo Civico: Mon–Sat 10.00–12.30, 14.00–18.30, Sun 10.00–12.30.
Museo degli Alpini: Tue–Sun 8.00–20.00.

BELLUNO
Museo Civico: daily except Mon, mid-Apr–mid-Oct 10.00–12.00, 15.00–18.00; Sun 10.00–12.00; mid-Oct–mid-Apr also closed Sat afternoon and Sun; there is a plan to move the museum to Palazzo Fulcis-De Bertoldi, soon to be renovated.

CASTELFRANCO VENETO
Casa del Giorgione: Tue–Sun 9.00–12.00, 15.00–18.00.
Teatro Accademico: Mon–Fri 9.00–12.30; hols on request (tel. 0423 494 5007).
Villa Revedin-Bolasco: by request (tel. 491 841).
Villa Emo, at Fanzolo di Vedelago (8km/5 miles): Nov–Apr, Sat, Sun and hols, 14.00–18.00; May–Oct, Mon, Wed, Thu, Fri, Sat 14.30–18.00; Tue 15.00–18.00, Sun 10.00–12.30, 14.30–18.00.
Villa Cornaro, at Piombino Dese (10km/6¼ miles): May–Sep, Sat 15.00–18.00 by request (tel. 049 936 5017).
Ca' Tiepolo, now **Chiminelli**, at Sant'Andrea (4km/2½ miles): Apr–Oct (tel. 0423 482 072).
Villa Priuli Gran Can and **Villa Priuli San Felice**, at Treville (tel. 0423 795000)

FELTRE
Museo Civico: closed for restoration at the time of writing.
Galleria d'Arte Moderna Carlo Rizzarda: Jun–Oct, Tue–Sun 10.00–13.00, 16.00–19.00; Nov–Apr on request (tel. 0439 89736).

TREVISO
Capitolo dei Domenicani (Chapter House of San Nicolò): daily 8.00–12.30, 15.30–17.30; summer until 19.00.
Museo Civico Luigi Bailo: Tue–Sat 9.00–12.00, 14.00–17.00, Sun 9.00–12.00.
Museo della Casa Trevigiana: by request (tel. 658 442).
Museo Diocesano di Arte Sacra: Mon–Thu 9.00–12.00, Sat 9.00–12.00, 15.00–18.00; closed Fri and hols.

8. SOUTH OF VENICE

This chapter centres around Padua. Big, busy and dirty, foggy in winter and unbearably muggy in summer, it is a tough town to deal with, especially if you're coming from Venice. But once you have got over its disastrous first impression, it grows on you, for culturally it is an extremely active, rich, and stimulating city.

Padua's cultural leadership dates back half a millennium and is closely tied to the presence, in the city, of one of Europe's oldest and most prestigious universities. Even after the rise of Venice, Padua remained a leading centre of humanist thought, and the best Renaissance artists were called here from Florence and elsewhere to work on important commissions for the city's enlightened patricians. Dante, Petrarch and Galileo all lived in Padua at some point of their respective lives. Here, too, is one of the key monuments of proto-Renaissance art, Giotto's magnificent fresco cycle in the Scrovegni Chapel.

Padua's environs are every bit as beautiful as the city is ugly. Between here and Venice flow the languid waters of the Brenta Canal, to whose green shores the best Venetian society moved *en masse* in summer. The luxurious villas here and in the hills to the north attest to the tenor of life that was enjoyed during the twilight of the republic. In the gentle southern landscape of the Euganean Hills an earlier aristocracy built its seigniories, and the great religious orders constructed vast retreats. All these areas invite leisurely exploration.

Padua

A legend tells that **Padua** (in Italian, *Padova*) was founded in the 12th century BC by Antenor, the Trojan hero. In reality the city was established later – not before the 8th or 7th century BC, probably by palaeo-Venetic tribes. In 89BC it became a Roman colony, called *Patavium,* and in 45BC it obtained the status of *municipium*. It has been the seat of a bishop since the 4th century. During the Middle Ages its factional struggles were pacified by the Portuguese Franciscan who would be canonised as St Anthony, and to whom the Paduans would erect a splendid basilica. Dante taught at the university (the oldest in

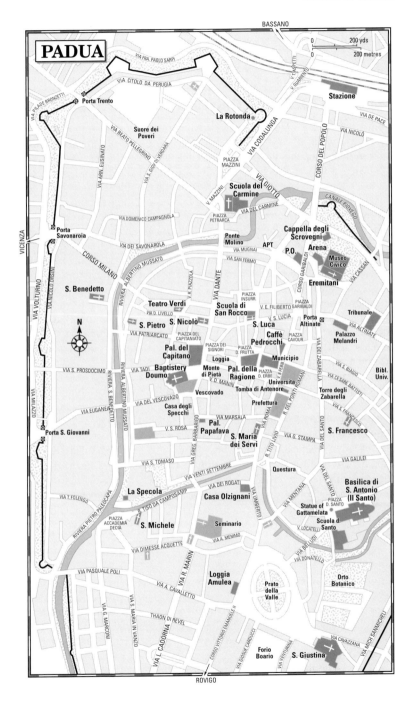

PADUA

BASSANO

0   200 yds
0   200 metres

VIA FRA. PAOLO SARPI

VIA CITOLO DA PERUGIA

VICENZA

VIA PILADE BRONZETTI

⊕ Porta Trento

Stazione

VIA DE PACE

VIA V. GASPETTI
VIA V. GUERRIERO

La Rotonda

Suore dei
Poveri

VIA BEATO PELLEGRINO

VIA ARN. EUSINATO

VIA S. GIOV DI VERGARA

VIA CODALUNGA

CORSO DEL POPOLO

VIA NICOLÒ

PIAZZA
MAZZINI

⊗ Porta
Savonaroia

V. MAZZINI

Scuola del
Carmine

VIA GIOTTO

CANALE PIOVEGO

VIA DOMENICO CAMPAGNOLA

PIAZZA
PETRARCA

VIA DEL CARMINE

Ponte
Molino

APT

Cappella degli
Scrovegni

Arena

VIA DEI SAVONAROLA

CORSO MILANO

RIVIERA ALBERTINO MUSSATO

VIA MUGNAI

VIA SAN FERMO

P.O.

CORSO GARIBALDI

Museo
Civico

VIA CASSAN

Eremitani

VICENZA

VIA VOLTURNO

VIA NICOLÒ ORSINI

S. Benedetto

VIA R. PIAZZOLA

VIA DANTE

PIAZZA
INSURR.

VIA S. PROSDOCIMO

Teatro Verdi

VIA D. LIVELLO

Scuola di
San Rocco

V. E. FILIBERTO GARIBALDI

PIAZZA
GARIBALDI

Tribunale

VIA ALTINATE

S. Pietro

S. Nicolò

VIA PATRIARCATO

PIAZZA DEL
CAPITANIATO

S. Luca

V. S. LUCIA

Caffè
Pedrocchi

Porta
Altinate

Palazzo
Melandri

VIA MILAZZO

⊗ Porta S. Giovanni

Pal. del
Capitano

PIAZZA DEI
SIGNORI

PIAZZA
D. FRUTTA

PIAZZA
CAVOUR

VIA CAVOUR

VIA DELLA ZABARELLA

Bibl.
Univ.

VIA S. BIAGIO

VIA S. PROSDOCIMO

VIA TADI

Baptistery
Duomo

Monte
di Pietà

Loggia

Pal. della
Ragione

V. D. MANIN

PIAZZA
D. ERBE

Municipio

V. IV FEBB

VIA CESARE BATTISTI

RIVIERA ALBERTINO MUSSATO

VIA DEL VESCOVADO

Vescovado

Tomba di Antenore

Università

R. DEL PONTI ROMANI

Torre degli
Zabarella

VIA S. FRANCESCO

Casa degli
Specchi

Prefettura

VIA EUGANEA

V. S. ROSA

Pal.
Papafava

VIA GREG. BARBARIGO

VIA MARSALA

S. Maria
dei Servi

VIA ROMA

R. TITO LIVIO

VIA G. STAMPA

S. Francesco

VIA DEL SANTO

VIA GALILEI

VIA S. TOMASO

VIA VENTI SETTEMBRE

Questura

VIA T. FOLENGO

La Specola

VIA DEI ROGATI

Casa Olzignani

VIA MENTANA

Basilica di
S. Antonio
(Il Santo)

PIAZZA
ACCADEMIA
DECIA

R. TISO DA CAMPOSAMP

S. Michele

Seminario

VIA DIMESSE ACQUETTE

VIA A. MEMMO

VIA UMBERTO I

Statue of
Gattamelata

PIAZZA
D. SANTO

V. LOCATELLI

Scuola d
Santo

VIA BELUDI

VIA DONATELLO

RIVIERA PIETRO PALEOCAPA

VIA PASQUALE POLI

VIA L. CADORNA

VIA A. CAVALLETTO

VIA R. MARIN

Loggia
Amulea

Prato
della
Valle

Orto
Botanico

VIA G. MARCONI

VIA S. MARIA IN VANZO

THAON DI REVEL

CORSO VITTORIO EMANUELE II

VIA GIOSUE CARDUCCI

Forio
Boario

S. Giustina

VIA VETTURIA

VIA CAVAZZANA

VIA MICO SANMICHELI

ROVIGO

Italy after that of Bologna), the city gave asylum to Petrarch, and Giotto, Donatello and Mantegna worked on important commissions here. In Shakespeare's *Taming of the Shrew* Lucentio speaks of 'faire *Padua,* nurserie of Arts'.

The Town Centre to the Carmine

Modern Padua is a large, busy city, and a full morning or afternoon is necessary if you want to do it justice. At the centre of the old town stands the **Palazzo della Ragione**, which Paduans call simply the Salone, after the large hall inside. It was built to house the law courts, in 1218–19, and enlarged in 1306–09. Set between two lively market squares, Piazza delle Erbe and Piazza della Frutta, it has two levels of arcades and a great ship's-keel roof reconstructed after a storm in 1756. The interior, reached by an external staircase, is occupied by a single large room 27m wide, 78m long and 27m high. Its original decoration, a cycle of more than 300 frescoes of religious and astrological subjects painted by Giotto, was destroyed by fire in 1420. The present paintings, executed around the middle of the 15th century, are very pale replacements.

Across the street to the east is the Palazzo Comunale or town hall. Its oldest part – the tower on the right flank, a remnant of the earlier Palazzo del Podestà – dates from the 13th century. In Piazza della Frutta are the fragmentary remains of two other 13th-century buildings, the Palazzo del Consiglio and Palazzo degli Anziani.

Via Manin leads west from Piazza delle Erbe to Piazza del Duomo and the **Cathedral**, dedicated to Santa Maria Assunta. This unusual church, which faces east instead of west, was founded in the 5th or 6th century but rebuilt in the 9th and 10th centuries and again before 1124. Its present appearance, with an unfinished façade, is the fruit of a reconstruction begun in 1551–52 to a design by Michelangelo. The interior follows a Latin-cross plan. Near the crossing are tomb monuments ranging in date from the 14th to the 16th centuries. The sacristy contains some small 14th-century paintings of Saints by Giorgio Schiavone, and canvases by Paris Bordone, Jacopo da Montagnana, and Gian Domenico Tiepolo. Here, too, is the cathedral treasury, highlights of which include illuminated manuscripts of the 12th and 13th centuries and a silver processional cross of 1228.

Far more interesting than the cathedral is the **Baptistery**, a Romanesque construction of 1171 rebuilt in 1260, whose interior is completely covered with frescoes by Giusto de' Menabuoi (1374-76). In the dome is *Christ Pantocrator,* surrounded by angels and the blessed; in the circular drum, scenes from the Book of Genesis; in the pendentives, the four Evangelists; on the walls, scenes from the lives of Christ and St John the Baptist; and in the apse, the *Apocalypse.* Giusto also made the polyptych above the altar. The baptismal font dates from 1260.

From the northeast corner of the square Via Dante leads past the 16th-century palazzo of the Monte di Pietà to Piazza dei Signori, which opens on the right. This square, named after the Carraresi (lords of Padua from 1318 to 1389), hosts several old buildings. On the east stands the 17th-century church of San Clemente; on the south, the elegant 16th-century Loggia del Consiglio or della Gran Guardia; and on the west, where the Carrarese castle once stood, the rusticated Palazzo del Capitanio (1599–1605). The **Arco dell'Orologio**, in the façade of the latter, was adapted in the 16th century to hold an astronomical clock of 1344, the first of its kind in Italy. You pass under this to reach the Corte Capitaniato, encircled by 16th-century buildings and the modern **Liviano**, the university Faculty of Letters. Designed in 1939 by Gio Ponti, one of the foremost Italian architects of the early 20th century, this unusual architectural 'liaison' ties together the older buildings that surround it. The atrium has frescoes by Massimo Campigli and a statue by Arturo Martini of the Roman historian Livy, a native of Padua.

At the north end of Via Dante rises the Romanesque church of **Santa Maria del Carmine**, sometimes more simply called the Carmini. It was completed – all but the façade – in 1494, and rebuilt in the early 16th century by Lorenzo da Bologna. The interior, a single, broad aisle, has a magnificent architectural decoration in the apse by Antonio Noale and a Renaissance sacristy designed by Lorenzo. The sacristan will show you the **Scuola del Carmine**, built in the 14th century and decorated with frescoes depicting stories of Christ and Mary attributed to the 16th-century painters Giulio and Domenico Campagnola.

A few blocks east, by Via del Carmine and Via Giotto, you come to the Giardino dell'Arena, with fragmentary remains of a Roman amphitheatre of the 1st century AD. Here stands Padua's loveliest attraction, which is not to be missed.

The Cappella degli Scrovegni

Also known as the Arena Chapel, the **Cappella degli Scrovegni** was commissioned by the merchant Enrico degli Scrovegni for his family palace, which was demolished in the 19th century. Inside are the magnificent frescoes executed around 1305 by Giotto and his pupils – the only cycle by the master to survive intact and one of the greatest achievements of Italian painting. The frescoes tell the story of Christian redemption through the lives of Mary and Christ – an important theme for Scrovegni, whose father had been a usurer. Their monumental composition, concise representation, and intense sense of drama were revolutionary in their time.

The chapel is small, intended for a congregation of the Scrovegni family and their retainers, and the frescoes themselves are about half life-size. They are arranged in three superimposed rows of scenes, enclosed in delicately ornamented frames that form a continuous structure, a sort of 'motion-picture' in which it is the viewer who moves from one dramatic incident to the next. The vault is painted the same bright blue as the background of the frescoes – quite naturally, as the vaults and domes of medieval churches were held to be symbolic of Heaven. This one is sprinkled with gold stars and with portraits of Christ and the four Evangelists set in circular medallions.

The wall surfaces are divided into 38 scenes. The narrative begins on the top band, to the right of the chancel arch. The frames trace the lives of Joachim and Anna, the Virgin's parents (*Expulsion of Joachim from the Temple, Joachim among the Shepherds, Annunciation to Anna, Sacrifice of Joachim, Vision of Joachim, Meeting of Joachim and Anna*) on the south wall, and the life of the Virgin (*Birth, Presentation in the Temple, Presentation of the Rods to Simeon, Watching of the Rods, Betrothal of the Virgin, The Virgin's Return Home*) on the north, ending with the *Annunciation* and (in a frame borrowed from the central order) *Visitation* on either side of the sanctuary and *God the Father Dispatching Gabriel* over the chancel arch. On the second level the Infancy of Christ (*Nativity, Adoration of the Magi, Presentation in the Temple, Flight into Egypt, Massacre of the Innocents*), on the south wall, leads into His adult life (*Dispute with the Elders, Baptism of Christ, Marriage at Cana, Raising of Lazarus, Entry into Jerusalem, Expulsion from the Temple*), on the north, ending in the *Pact of Judas,* by the arch. On the lowest tier, the Passion of Christ (*Last Supper, Washing of the Feet, Betrayal of Christ, Christ before Caiaphas, Mocking of Christ*) on the south is followed by His Death and Resurrection (*Way to Calvary, Crucifixion, Deposition, Angel at the Empty Tomb and Noli me tangere, Ascension, Pentecost*) on the north. A faux-marble dado below is punctuated by chiaroscuro images of the Seven Virtues (on the south side) and the Seven Deadly Sins (on the north). The drama of human salvation reaches its climax in the *Last Judgement* on the entrance wall. The stories of Mary in the apse were executed later by followers of Giotto; Giusto de' Menabuoi frescoed the two *Madonne del Latte* in the niches at the sides of the altar, and Giovanni Pisano carved the delicate statues of the Virgin and Angels. Behind the altar is the tomb of Enrico degli Scrovegni, who died in 1336.

Eremitani to the University and Piazza del Santo

The **Museo Civico** occupies the former Convento degli Eremitani, situated between the Cappella Scrovegni and the church of the Eremitani, on the south side of the park. It is worth a visit, and you can get in free on your ticket to the Scrovegni Chapel. The archaeological section has prehistoric, Roman, Egyptian, Etruscan and early Christian antiquities. The fabulous Emo Capodilista Collection has works by Venetian and Flemish painters, notably Giorgione's *Leda and the Swan* and *Country Idyll,* and a *Portrait of a Young Senator* by Giovanni Bellini. In the *pinacoteca* (picture gallery) are works by Giotto (the *Arena Chapel Crucifix*), Guariento (*Madonna with Angels*), Alvise Vivarini (*Male Portrait*), Jacopo Bellini (*Christ in Limbo*), Paolo Veronese (*Last Supper, Martyrdom of S Justina*), Jacopo Tintoretto (*Supper in the House of Simon*), G.B. Tiepolo, Francesco Guardi, Marco and Sebastiano Ricci, and others. There are also 19th-century paintings and sculptures, small bronzes by Italian and foreign sculptors of the 14th to the 17th centuries, ceramics and glass, and drawings and prints.

The adjacent church of the **Eremitani**, or Santi Filippo e Giacomo, was

Angels by Guariento, in the Museo Civico Eremitani, Padua

built in Romanesque-Gothic forms between 1276 and 1306 for the Augustinian monastic order. Damaged by bombs in 1944, it was rebuilt after the war. The lower part of the façade, added in 1360, has a broad doorway and tall, deep arches that continue on the south flank. Here, beneath an attached porch, is a remarkable Renaissance doorway with carvings representing the Months by the Florentine Niccolò Baroncellli.

The interior, a single broad aisle with a ship's-keel roof, contains tombs and sculptures of the 14th to 16th centuries and fragmentary frescoes. On the south side, the first chapel has remains of frescoes by Giusto de' Menabuoi; and the fourth chapel, a *Madonna and Child* and *Ecce Homo* by Guariento. At the end of the south aisle stands the **Cappella Ovetari**, once famous for its frescoes by Andrea Mantegna. Their destruction in 1944 was the greatest single loss of Italian art in the war. Of the remaining fragments, the best-preserved scenes are the *Martyrdom of St Christopher* (south wall), the *Assumption* (behind the altar), and the *Martyrdom of St James* (north wall). The terracotta altarpiece of the *Madonna and Child with Saints* was made by a follower of Donatello. There are more 14th-century frescoes in the sanctuary (*Stories of SS Augustine, James, and Philip,* by Guariento) and in the other apsidal chapels. In the north aisle is the tomb of Marco Mantova Benavides, a law professor, by Bartolomeo Ammannati, and that of Jacopo da Carrara, with Latin verses by Petrarch.

From the rear of the Eremitani Via Morgagni leads southeast to **Santa Sofia**, the oldest church in Padua. Possibly founded in the 9th century, it was rebuilt in the 11th and 12th centuries and remodelled in the 14th century and later. It has an interesting façade with five large niches, a fine apse recalling those of the early Christian churches of Ravenna, with blind arcading below and two rows of windows above, and a 14th-century campanile. The austere three-aisled Romanesque/Gothic interior has an unusual ambulatory around the sanctuary.

Via Altinate bears west from Santa Sofia to Piazza Garibaldi and Porta Altinate, a gateway of the 13th-century town wall. One block south is Piazza Cavour, another lively centre of city life. In the small adjoining square is Padua's most celebrated café, the neoclassical **Caffè Pedrocchi** (1831), where the city's intellectuals met in the 19th century. Its monumental façade, sumptuously furnished rooms, and Gothic-revival annex (the Pedrocchino, 1837), were designed by Giuseppe Japelli.

Via VIII Febbraio bears south from here, flanked on the west by the Palazzo Comunale and on the east by the **University**, nicknamed *Il Bo'* (The Ox) after an inn that previously stood on the same site. It was established in 1222, and its outstanding faculty (Galileo taught physics here from 1592 to 1610; Vesalius and Fallopius taught medicine) drew students from all parts of the continent. The 16th-century mannerist building, by Andrea Moroni, has a façade of 1757. It encloses a beautiful courtyard with portico and loggia, decorated with coats of arms. At the foot of the stairs is a statue of Elena Cornaro Piscopia, the first woman ever to receive a university degree – in 1678. On the upper floor – there are guided tours in summer – are the

Anatomical Theatre (Europe's oldest, 1594), the Sala dei Quaranta (with Galileo's chair), and the Aula Magna, with more coats of arms.

Behind the Bo' is the so-called Tomb of Antenor, an aedicule of 1283 with a marble sarcophagus once believed to hold the remains of Padua's mythical founder. Beyond, Via San Francesco and Via del Santo lead south to Piazza del Santo, a vast square developing around the city's most important religious monument, the church of St Anthony.

The square is dominated by the colossal bronze **Equestrian Statue of Gattamelata**, erected by family members to commemorate the Venetian mercenary general Erasmo da Narni (whose unlikely nickname translates as 'Honeyed Cat'). He was born in Padua around 1370, and his monument, executed ten years after his death in 1443, is a masterpiece of the Florentine sculptor Donatello, who also designed the tall pedestal. Although it is not the first equestrian statue of Renaissance Italy, it is the first free-standing public monument to an eminent citizen, and its placement here almost certainly required the authorisation of the Venetian senate. In defining his composition Donatello seems to have looked to ancient Roman examples, particularly the equestrian statue of Marcus Aurelius in Rome, then thought to represent Constantine.

Basilica of St Anthony

The Franciscan **Basilica di Sant'Antonio**, familiarly called 'Il Santo' by Paduans, was built between 1232 and the mid-14th century to enshrine the body of St Anthony of Padua. The single-gabled façade combines motifs of Romanesque and Gothic inspiration (the tall, blind ogival arches and central rose window belong to the Gothic tradition, the round-arched doorway and the general compositional scheme, to the Romanesque). The eight-domed roof – a medley of Byzantine, Venetian and French Romanesque elements – gives the building a distinctly Eastern appearance, which is further emphasised by the small towers and the two octagonal campanili.

Inside, the magnificent nave is separated from the lateral aisles by great piers and terminates, at the east end, in a profusely decorated ambulatory. The holy-water stoups against the first two piers bear statues of *St John the Baptist* (south) by Tullio Lombardo, and *Christ* (north) by Tiziano Aspetti. The second north pier holds the tomb of the Venetian general Alessandro Contarini (died 1553), designed by Michele Sanmicheli and incorporating sculptures by Danese Cattaneo and Alessandro Vittoria. On the opposite side is the tomb of Cardinal Bembo (died 1547), attributed to Palladio, with a bust by Cattaneo. The first chapel in the south aisle preserves the 15th-century tombs of Gattamelata, by Bartolomeo Bellano, and his son Giannantonio, by Pietro Lombardo. In the south transept, the 14th-century Cappella di San Felice, designed by Andriolo and Giovanni de Santi, has frescoes representing the *Legend of St James,* the *Crucifixion* and other scenes, by Altichiero.

Behind the bronze doors of the choir (the custodians will unlock these on request) is the **high altar**, the second major commission Donatello received during his ten-year sojourn among the 'fogs and frogs' of Padua, as he put it. The altar (1443–50) is decorated with splendid bronze statues and reliefs by the master and his pupils. Their original configuration is unknown, and their present arrangement, devised by Camillo Boito in 1895, has been a matter of controversy among art historians for a full century. Above the predella, with 12 small reliefs of *Angel Musicians* and a *Pietà*, are four larger reliefs (two on the front and two on the back) of *Miracles of St Anthony*, all showing a startlingly bold treatment of architectural space that would profoundly influence Venetian Renaissance painting from Mantegna onwards. Also on this level are a small *Christ in Pietà* and, at the ends, symbols of the Evangelists. At the top of the composition are an enthroned *Madonna* between life-size statues of the six patron saints of Padua (*St Louis of Anjou, St Justina, St Francis, St Anthony, St Daniel, and St Prosdocimus*), and a splendid bronze *Crucifix*, probably intended to be placed elsewhere in the church. The placement of the stone *Deposition,* behind the altar, is also questionable. North of the altar stands a magnificent bronze paschal candelabrum by Andrea Briosco, 'Il Riccio' (1507-15). Along the sanctuary walls are 12 bronze reliefs of Old Testament stories, by Bartolomeo Bellano and Andrea Briosco.

Around the sanctuary are the ambulatory and its radiating chapels; the fifth chapel, known as the **Cappella delle Reliquie** or del Tesoro, built to a central plan by Filippo Parodi (who also made the statues, in 1689) holds a rich treasury, with remarkable reliquaries (including one for St Anthony's tongue), incense boats, and the wood boxes that once held the remains of the saint. At the north end of the ambulatory is the Chapel of the Madonna Mora, a vestige of the earlier (12th-century) church of Santa Maria Mater Domini.

The **Cappella dell'Arca del Santo**, in the north transept, was designed in 1499 by Tullio Lombardo and executed by his assistant, Antonio Minello. The stuccoed ceiling was done by G.M. Falconetto in 1533. On the walls are nine large reliefs with stories of St Anthony, by 16th-century sculptors including Jacopo Sansovino (4th and 5th from the left), Tullio Lombardo (6th and 7th) and Antonio Lombardo (last). At the centre stands the magnificent altar, designed by Tiziano Aspetti (1593), behind which is St Anthony's tomb. This is still visited by hundred of pilgrims every year, many of whom leave votive offerings. The adjacent Cappella Conti, with the tomb of the Blessed Luca Belludi, St Anthony's companion, is frescoed by Giusto de' Menabuoi.

On the wall of the north aisle of the basilica are the 17th-century tomb of General Catrino Cornaro, by Juste le Court, and that of Antonio Roselli (died 1466), by Pietro Lombardo.

To the south of the church are four **cloisters**, built between the 13th and 15th centuries. In the second, with a Romanesque doorway, a Renaissance loggia and a well of 1492, is a monument to Cornelio Musso by Andrea Briosco. From the fourth, steps climb past the original stone reliefs from the Gattamelata monument to the Biblioteca Antoniana, with 85,000 books, manuscripts, and incunabula, including a manuscript of sermons with notes in the hand of St Anthony. The **Museo Antoniano** preserves paintings, sculpture, and votive offerings from the basilica, notably the fresco of *SS Anthony* *and Bernard Adoring the Monogram of Christ,* by Andrea Mantegna, formerly in the lunette of the main doorway.

Adjoining the basilica on the southwest are the **Scuola di Sant'Antonio** and the **Oratory of San Giorgio**. The *scuola* was begun in 1427, with an upper storey added in 1504. A handsdome 18th-century staircase ascends to the main hall, decorated with frescoes of the life of the saint by Venetian artists, including Bartolomeo Montagna, Domenico Campagnola, Girolamo del Santo and Titian, who painted the scenes of the *Miracle of the Irascible Son* (considered his first important independent works). The coloured terracotta *Madonna* is by Andrea Briosco. The oratory, once a chapel of the Soranzo family, is entirely covered with frescoes by Altichiero and his assistants (1379–84). The paintings represent the lives of Christ and SS George, Catherine, and Lucy, and their arrangement in horizontal bands clearly calls to mind Giotto's decoration for the Scrovegni Chapel.

South and West of the Basilica

On the south side of Piazza del Santo stands the eclectic building designed in the 1870s by Camillo Boito for the Museo Civico, today used for temporary exhibitions. Continuing southwards you come (left) to the **Orto Botanico** (Botanic Garden), established in 1544 and substantially unaltered since. It is the oldest botanic garden in Europe and one of Italy's most beautiful and complete. It has a circular walled garden with native and exotic plants arranged, in keeping with the original scheme, in four sections. In one of the hothouses is a palm-tree planted in 1585 and called *la palma di Goethe* after the German poet, who visited the garden in 1786.

Via Beato Luca Belludi leads west from the garden to **Prato della Valle**, an immense square laid out in 1775 to a design by Domenico Cerato. At the centre is a wooded garden with walkways known as the Isola Memmia, adorned with 78 statues of eminent Paduans and encircled by a canal. Set back from the southern end of the piazza is Padua's most important 16th-century monument, the majestic brick basilica of **Santa Giustina** (1532–60), designed by Andrea Briosco and Andrea Moroni. Its bare façade and eight domes, some with metal statues of saints, make explicit reference to the design of Sant'Antonio.

The large three-aisled interior is a masterpiece of Venetian Baroque architecture, with elaborate detailing and exuberant paintings. In the south transept, the Sacello di San Prosdocimo (burial place of St Prosdocimus, the first bishop of Padua) is a remnant of the original, early Christian basilica. It contains an unusual 6th-century marble screen and an altar made from a Roman sarcophagus. The 15th-century Coro Vecchio (Old Choir), reached from the ninth chapel (not always open) has fine inlaid stalls and a statue of St Justina; in the adjoining rooms are a contemporary terracotta of the Madonna and Child and the lunette and lintel of a Romanesque doorway, dating from the 11th century. The sanctuary contains walnut stalls carved in 1566; the large altarpiece of the *Martyrdom of St Justina* was painted by Paolo

Veronese in 1575. In the north transept is the so-called *Arca di San Luca,* with alabaster reliefs by a Pisan sculptor (1316). The second north chapel holds a painting of *St Gregory the Great Liberating Rome from the Plague,* by Sebastiano Ricci. On the south of the church stands the Benedictine monastery, founded in the 8th century, suppressed in the 19th century, and now shared by monks and soldiers. From the Prato della Valle, Via Umberto I and Via Roma lead back to the city centre.

Around Padua

The territory around Padua abounds with magnificent villas. At **Piazzola sul Brenta**, 18km (11 miles) northwest of the city, is the **Villa Contarini degli Scrigni** (open for concerts of classical music), in a fine park. Begun in 1546 and several times enlarged, it is preceded by a spectacular staircase and flanked by two long Baroque wings with balustrades and statues. Many of the rooms have frescoes and stuccoes ranging in date from the 16th to the early 20th century. Nearby is the small **Villa Da Ponte Camerini**, attributed to Palladio. Other villas in the area include the 15th-century **Villa Spessa**, at **Carmignano di Brenta**; **Villa dei Vescovi**, at **Luvigliano di Torreglia**; and the 17th-century **Villa Emo Capodilista** at **Battaglia Terme,** with frescoes by Luca Ferrari (1650). At **Noventa Padovana** are the 16th-century **Villa Cappello**, the 17th-century **Villa Giustianiani** (now De Chantal) and the 18th-century **Villa Giovanelli** (now De Benedetti).

If you're looking for more villas, take the short drive between **Noventa Vicentina**, 11km (7 miles) northeast of Montagnana, and **Poiana Maggiore**, 7km (4¼ miles) further. Here you will find, one after the other, three villas that belonged to the Pojana family: the first, on the south, is by Andrea Palladio (1550–63). At Noventa Vicentina itself the **Villa Barbarigo** (1588) is now the town hall, and the parish church has a painting by Giovanni Battista Tiepolo. Near **Finale** is the **Villa Saraceno**, also by Palladio (1549–68).

The Riviera del Brenta

The Venetians built the canal known as the **Naviglio di Brenta** or **Brenta Vecchia** to facilitate navigation between their city and Padua, diverting the river itself to the north in order to reduce the amount of silt pouring into the lagoon. The magnificent villas for which the area is famous first appeared in the 16th century when, in the face of Turkish expansion in the Eastern Mediterranean, Venetian patricians shifted their investments from foreign trade to real estate. The great farms that grew up here were intended both to generate income and to provide a pleasant escape from the heat and humidity of the lagoon in summer. The principal façades of the houses faced the water, like the palaces on the Grand Canal – and not by chance, for the same festive lifestyle that graced the latter in winter continued in summer in the villas of the Riviera. With the approach of the 18th century, the idyllic pleasures of country life merged with a taste for the exotic, and the architecture of the noble manors assumed connotations of luxury and extravagance, with spectacular parks, gardens, aviaries, greenhouses and private zoos stocked with exotic animals. Meanwhile patricians of limited means (of which there were quite a few), adventurers (even more) and the *nouveaux riches* rented lodgings in the towns, in order not to miss the great social events of the Venetian summer.

Those who, for one reason or another, chose not to make the trip up the canal in the family gondola took the *burchiello*, a large riverboat rowed by slaves or pulled by horses – a 'marvellous and comfortable craft' as Goldoni recalls, 'in which one glides along the Brenta sheltered from winter's cold and summer's ardour'. Today a motorised *burchiello* lazily winds its way from Padua to Venice or vice versa for a handsome fee, stopping to visit several several of the 50-odd extant villas. The trip can also be made by bicycle (there are marked cycling routes), or by car. Here the villas are listed in the order in which they appear if you depart from Padua.

At **Strà** is the largest villa on the Riviera, the 18th-century **Villa Pisani**, or Villa Nazionale, named after its original owner, the Venetian doge Alvise Pisani. Purchased by Napoleon in 1807, it was the site of the first meeting between Mussolini and Hitler in 1934. The interior is decorated by 18th-century Venetian artists, including Giovanni Battista Tiepolo, who frescoed the *Triumph of the Pisani Family* on the ceiling of the ballroom (1762). In the vast park is the labyrinth described by poet Gabriele D'Annunzio in '*Fire*'. A little beyond, on the opposite bank of the canal, rises the long front of the **Villa Lazara Pisani**, also called 'la Barbariga', with a Baroque central structure and symmetrical 18th-century wings.

At **Dolo**, the principal town of the Riviera in the 18th century, you can see a mill, a *squero* (or boatyard) and one of the old locks. The **Palazzo Faletti-Mocenigo** (now a school) was designed in 1596 by Vincenzo Scamozzi. In the environs are the **Villa Ferretti Angeli** (1598), also by Scamozzi; the Baroque **Villa Grimani Migliorini**, with a Doric porch; and the **Villas Andreuzzi Bon** and **Mocenigo Spiga**, both of the 18th century.

Next comes the fragmented town of **Mira**, still one of the more pleasant towns on the canal. Here Byron wrote the fourth canto of *Childe Harold* and first met Margherita Cogni, 'la bella Fornarina'. On the outskirts are the **Villas Pisani Contarini** (or 'dei Leoni'), **Querini-Stampalia** and **Valier** (or 'la Chitarra'). A little further, at **Riscossa,** is the **Villa Seriman**, and at **Oriago**, the **Villa Widmann-Rezzonico-Foscari**, built in 1719 but remodelled in the French Rococo manner after the middle of the 18th century. The most famous of the villas of Mira, it has a two-storey façade with curved tympanum, and frescoed rooms.

Ballroom at the Villa Pisani, Strà, with ceiling frescoes by Tiepolo

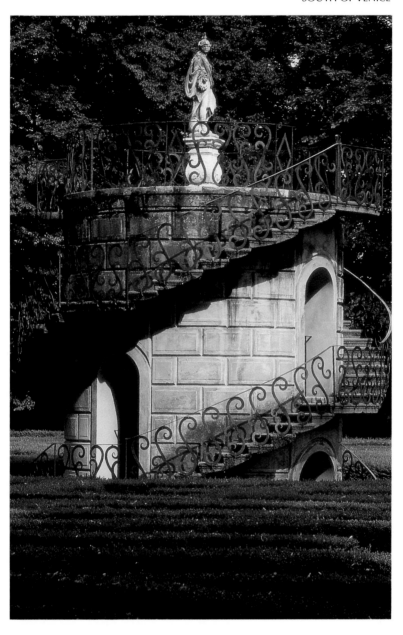

Villa Pisani, Strà, the labyrinth

After Oriago, on a shady bend of the river, stands the **Villa Foscari** (also known as La Malcontenta), which legend would have the home of a Dame Foscari (the 'malcontent' of the name), exiled here for betraying her husband. It was constructed around 1555–60 for the brothers Nicola and Alvisa Foscari by Andrea Palladio. The exterior is very slightly rusticated; the side towards the river is characterised by a noble seven-columned Ionic porch, which projects outward and is raised on a tall basement with lateral ramps. Within, the rooms are arranged around a large, central Greek-cross salone frescoed by Battista Franco and Giovan Battista Zelotti. Further on, at Fusina, the canal enters the lagoon and you glimpse Venice, 4km (2½ miles) away.

The Euganean Hills

Although the area to the southwest of Padua offers nothing as magnificent as the Brenta villas, the several small towns huddled in and around the Euganean Hills – a volcanic formation that rises unexpectedly in the midst of the Po River Basin – nevertheless provide a number of sights of considerable interest.

Abano Terme

Abano Terme is one of the leading spas in Europe. Known since Roman times for its hot springs, today it is famous for its mud therapy, which uses special thermophile algae and is especially helpful in the treatment of rheumatism and arthritis. Abano is an elegant town with a distinctive 19th-century atmosphere. Though it is virtually deserted in winter, during the season (March to October) it is thronged with visitors, many of whom return year after year. The main street is the shady Viale delle Terme, where the fancier hotels are located. The most notable of these is the neoclassical **Hotel Orologio**, designed in 1825 by Giuseppe Japelli, author of the Caffè Pedrocchi in Padua. The **Montirone**, a knoll at centre of the town planted as a park and the site of Abano's warmest spring (80°C), is adorned with an early 20th-century Corinthian colonnade and a Doric column of 1825 (also by Jappelli) commemorating a visit of Emperor Francis I of Austria. The Cathedral of San Lorenzo is undistinguished.

Perhaps the best thing about Abano is its proximity to the two major religious complexes of the Euganean Hills: the Santuario della Vergine at Monteortone, 3km (1¾ miles) west, and the Abbazia di Praglia, nestled in a pleasant valley about 12km (7½ miles) further in the same direction. The **Santuario della Vergine** was begun in 1435 on the site where a miraculous image of the Virgin Mary was reputedly found. It has a simple façade with a Baroque doorway of 1667, and a 15th-century brick campanile with pointed spire. The three-aisled interior is built in a hybrid Gothic-Renaissance style; it contains frescoes by Jacopo da Montagnana and a fine Renaissance altar in the sanctuary, and a *Crucifixion and Saints* by Palma Giovane in an adjoining chapel. The former Salesian convent, with a lovely Renaissance cloister, is now a hotel. The **Abbazia di Praglia**, approached by a beautiful, tree-lined driveway, is a Benedictine foundation of 1080 rebuilt in the 15th and 16th centuries. The church (Santa Maria Assunta) was built between 1490 and 1548, probably to a design by Tullio Lombardo; the Romanesque campanile is a remnant of the original building. The vaulted Latin-cross interior has 16th-century Venetian paintings, a 14th-century wooden crucifix over the high altar, and frescoes in the apse by Domenico Campagnola. The abbey is still active, and parts of it are closed to the public. However, you can see a 15th-century *chiostro botanico* or herb-garden cloister (a reminder that the most expert pharmacists, here as elswhere in Europe, were once monks); a *chiostro pensile,* or porch cloister, of the late 15th century; and a large refectory with ceiling paintings by Giovanni Battista Zelotti, 18th-century carved woodwork and a famous *Crucifixion* frescoed by Bartolomeo Montagna (1490–1500).

Monsélice

Rising on the southeast slopes of the Euganean Hills, **Monsélice** was a Roman settlement, a Lombard *gastaldato* (a sort of county), a free commune, a seigniory, and finally a Venetian dominion. Today it is an active industrial and agricultural centre. It takes its name (literally, 'mountain of flint') from the small mound of debris dug from the quarry that twice served to pave Piazza San Marco in Venice. The castle stands at the top of the hill, the town at the bottom, the monuments along a road and walkway that wind along the slopes.

In the lower town, on the east side of Piazza Mazzini, is the medieval **Torre Civica**, with a fine loggia and crenellated parapet. From the square, Via del Santuario climbs past the 16th-century Monte di Pietà, with a small loggia, to the **Castello**, a remarkable complex of buildings with an 11th- or 12th-century core, enlarged between the 13th and 16th centuries. The interior houses a collection of paintings, sculpture, weapons, Renaissance furniture, tapestries and, in the Sala del Camino Vecchio, a monumental fireplace shaped like a tower.

Continuing along Via del Santuario you soon come to the 16th- and 17th-century **Villa Nani-Mocenigo**, with a wall decorated with curious 18th-century statues of dwarfs and a spectacular terraced staircase. Just a little further on is the **Duomo Vecchio**, dedicated to St Justina, a Romanesque-Gothic church of 1256 with a 12th-century campanile and a three-part façade with a rose window, smaller mullioned windows, and a 15th-century porch. Within are frescoes and altarpieces by minor 15th-century Venetian painters. At the end of the avenue stands the **Villa Duodo**, by Vincenzo Scamozzi (1593), enlarged in the 18th century when the monumental staircase to the formal garden was added. It now belongs to the University of Padua. Its grounds include the cypress-shaded **Santuario delle Sette Chiese**, entered from the 18th-century Piazzale della Rotonda, a scenic viewpoint behind the Duomo Vecchio. The sanctuary comprises six chapels designed by

Castello, Monsélice

Villa Nani-Mocenigo, Monsélice, exterior detail

Scamozzi after 1605, containing paintings by Palma Giovane, and the church of San Giorgio, octagonal outside and elliptical within.

In a panoramic position at the top of the hill stands the ruined **Rocca**, built by the Holy Roman Emperor Frederick II and enlarged by the Carraresi. Today little more than the keep remains, but there is a fine view. On the east slope of the hill is the old church of San Tommaso, which conserves some 13th-century frescoes. At Valsanzibio di Galzignano, 8km (5 miles) north, is the Villa Barbarigo, now Pizzoni Ardemagni, with a 17th-century formal garden and fountains.

Este

Este is an ancient city just south of the Euganean Hills. In the Iron Age, it was the principal city of the Veneti. Its necropolises, sanctuaries, and certain areas of the town have yielded abundant vases and decorated bronzes. Remains of two bridges, an aqueduct, and some houses with mosaics survive from Roman times, when the settlement was called *Ateste*. Rebuilt in the Middle Ages, it was for two centuries a dominion of the powerful Este family before being joined to Venice, in 1405.

The town is overlooked by its **Castle** (1339–40). Built on the site of an 11th-century fortress, it has a trapezoidal enceinte (fortified enclosure) with 12 towers, running in part over the hill on which the keep stands. Today it encloses a pleasant park. The castle is home to the **Museo Nazionale Atestino**, situated in the 16th-century Palazzo Mocenigo north of the entrance to the park. One of the most important archaeological museums of Northern Italy, it displays pre-Roman and Roman antiquities, and architectural fragments and ceramics of the 11th through the 19th centuries. The Roman section, on the ground floor, contains inscriptions, mosaics, architectural fragments, sculpture, glass and medals. The pre-Roman section, on the first floor, has prehistoric collections that offer a glimpse of ancient Venetic civilisation, notably material of the Aeneolithic and Bronze Ages, and burial artefacts from the early Iron Age.

Este has developed on a rectangular plan, with its centre in Piazza Maggiore. The **Cathedral of St Tecla**, a medieval church rebuilt in 1690–1708 by Antonio Francesco Gaspari, has an 18th-century campanile built on an 8th-century base. The elliptical interior abounds with sculptures and paintings, among which the large *St Tecla Freeing Este from the Plague*, by Giovan Battista Tiepolo (1759), is certainly the most striking.

From here Via Garibaldi and Via Alessi bear southwest to the church of **Santa Maria delle Consolazioni** (or Santa Maria degli Zoccoli, 1504–10), with a campanile of 1598 and a single-aisled interior with a later addition. At the end of this is the Cappella della Vergine, containing a magnificent Roman mosaic pavement excavated nearby. The church possesses a fine Madonna by Cima da Conegliano, on temporary loan to the museum; and the adjoining cloister has 15th-century capitals.

On the other side of town (about 500m away) are the Romanesque church of **San Martino**, with a campanile of 1293 (leaning since 1618), 18th-century sculptures and two altarpieces by Antonio Zanchi; and the 15th-century basilica of **Santa Maria delle Grazie**, rebuilt in the 18th century, in the Latin-cross interior of which are marble altars, statues, frescoes from the earlier church and a Byzantine Madonna of the early 15th century, venerated as miraculous.

Other interesting monuments are the 16th-century Palazzo del Principe, by Vincenzo Scamozzi, who also designed the façade of the church of San Michele; Villa Cornaro (now Benvenuti), with a 19th-century park designed by G. Japelli; the 18th-century Villa Contarini, known also as the 'Vigna Contarena'; the Palazzo del Municipio, also dating from the 18th century; and the octagonal church of the Beata Vergine della Salute (1639), with two octagonal campanili flanking the apse. Ten kilometres (6¼ miles) south of Este is the **Abbazia di Càrceri**, dedicated to the Virgin Mary. Founded in the 11th century, it includes an octagonal church of 1643 with 15th- to 18th-century paintings, remains of a 12th-century Romanesque cloister, and a 16th-century Renaissance Chiostro Grande and library.

Montagnana

Of prehistoric origin, **Montagnana** was a Roman *vicus* (village) and a medieval Lombard centre. The old town – with porticoed streets, a large square, and the lazy atmosphere of the quintessential Venetian farm town – lies within a well-preserved complex of turreted walls built between the 12th and the 14th centuries. The walls are pierced by four gates and surrounded by a moat, now a park. During the Venetian period (after 1405) hemp was grown here for use in ships' rigging.

The **walls** surround the entire town, enclosing an area of 24 hectares within a perimeter of almost 2km. The most impressive of the gates are the Rocca degli Alberi or Porta Legnano, dating from 1362, with a bridge and tower fortified with parapets, and the Porta Padova, adjoining the Castello di San Zeno, with the tall Torre Ezzelina. The **Castello di San Zeno** was built in 1242; the Venetian wing (and temporarily also the small church of San Giovanni) holds the **Museo Civico**, with Bronze and Iron Age finds (9th to 8th century BC) from a local prehistoric complex, Roman burial treasures of the 1st century, Roman inscriptions, and medieval ceramics.

Inside the town, on the southwest side of the central Via Carrarese, rises the **Palazzo del Municipio**, an austere building with rusticated portico laid out in 1538 by Michele Sanmichele and remodelled in the 17th and 18th centuries. Within, the Sala del Consiglio has a coffered ceiling of 1555 by Marcantonio Vannini.

The **Cathedral** of Santa Maria, in the large, central Piazza Vittorio Emanuele, was built in a transitional Gothic-Renaissance style between 1431 and 1502 on the site of an 11th-century structure of which a few traces remain. The brick façade, with three bell niches, has a doorway shaped like a triumphal arch, attributed to Jacopo Sansovino. Notice also the south flank and large polygonal apse of the south transept. The tall, early Renaissance interior, a single aisle with barrel vaulting, contains a Venetian School gold-ground painting of the *Annunciation*, dating from the 14th century; 15th- and 16th-century frescoes; a *Transfiguration* by Paolo Veronese over the high altar; and a large fresco of the *Assumption of the Virgin* in the apse, attributed to Giovanni Buonconsiglio, an early 16th-century painter, author also of several altarpieces. Other frescoes possibly by his hand are on the west wall of the north transept and on the inside of the façade.

Up against the wall to the south is the church of **San Francesco**, a 14th- and 15th-century edifice altered in the 17th century, with a tall campanile of 1429 or 1468. Within are a *Transfiguration* by the School of Paolo Veronese, in the sanctuary, and a Madonna by Palma Giovane in the apse.

Just outside the walls, accross the moat from the Porta Padova, stands the **Palazzo Pisani** (now Placco), the central part of which was designed by Andrea Palladio. It was built around 1560. The two main elevations have a double central order of Ionic and Corinthian columns terminating in a pediment. Also noteworthy are the splendid frieze with bucranic metopes and the harmonious ground-floor atrium, with statues representing the Seasons by Alessandro Vittorio (1577).

Practical Information

Getting There

Roads in the Venice-Padua area are well kept and well marked. Padua stands at the junction of Autostrade A4 (Milan–Venice) and A13 (Bologna–Venice) and is the hub from which radiate many of the region's major highways. Highway 11 runs along the north bank of the Brenta from Padua to Mestre, and Highway 16 skirts the eastern slopes of the Euganean Hills to Monsélice. From Monsélice Highway 10 runs west to Este and Montagnana.

Padua is situated on the main **rail** lines from Milan and Rome to Venice. There are through services to Slovenia, Croatia, Hungary, Ukraine, and Russia (via Villa Opicina), to Vienna and Prague (via Tarvisio), and to Paris, Geneva and Munich. **Boat** trips along the Brenta may be arranged through the Azienda Promozione Turistica in Venice or Padua. The Euganean Hills are served by the main rail line from Padua to Bologna and Rome (change at Monsélice for Este and Montagnana). Country **buses** abound throughout the area.

Tourist Information

EUGANEAN HILLS 18 Via Pietro d'Abano, Abano Terme (tel. 049 866 9055, fax 866 905.

PADUA 8 Riviera dei Mugnai (tel. 049 875 0655, fax 650 794); at the train station (tel. 875 2077).

RIVIERA DEL BRENTA See Venice and Padua; also, there is an information office at 26 Via Don Minzoni, Mira Porte (tel. 04 424 973).

Hotels

EUGANEAN HILLS
The best place to stay in this area is without a doubt **ABANO TERME**. Hospitality is the only game in town here, and all the hotels are comfortable, modern, and restful, though there is not one that is downright luxurious. The moderately priced establishments are the **Ariston Molino Terme**, **Bristol Buja**, **Due Torri**, **Grand Hotel Trieste & Victoria**, **La Residence**, **Metropole**, **President Terme**, **Quisisana Terme**, **Ritz Terme**, **Terme Astoria**, **Terme Mioni Pezzato**, **Terme Savoia**; the less expensive places, **Harry's Terme**, **Terme Milano**, **Principe**, **Salus Terme**, **Smeraldo**, **Terme Bologna**, **Terme Columbia** and **Terme Patria**.

PADUA
The **Donatello**, 102 Via del Santo (tel. 049 875 0634, fax 875 0829; closed mid–Dec–mid–Jan), is a comfortable hotel overlooking the Santo; its **Sant'Antonio** restaurant has a pleasant summer terrace. The **Majestic Toscanelli,** 2 Via dell'Arco (tel. 049 663 244, fax 876 0025), is an elegant, distinctive establishment situated in a little square near Piazza delle Erbe. The **Leon Bianco**, 12 Piazzetta Pedrocchi (tel. 049 875 0814, fax 875 6184), is a small, quiet place in the heart of the old city, next door to the Caffè Pedrocchi. All the above are moderately priced. **Al Fagiano**, 45 Via Locatelli (tel./fax 049 875 3396), is a simple establishment just off Piazza del Santo; and **Igea**, 87 Via Ospedale Civile (tel. 049) 875 0577, fax 660 865, is a warm, homely inn near the Santo. These two are inexpensive.

Restaurants

EUGANEAN HILLS
At **MONSÉLICE**, **La Torre**, 14 Piazza Mazzini (tel. 0429 73752; closed Sun evening, Mon, mid-July–mid-Aug, and late Dec–early Jan), is an inexpensive place serving traditional dishes prepared with considerable skill. The *pasta fresca con piselli e oca* and *involtini di vitello e verdure* are especially good.

At **MONTAGNANA**, **Aldo Moro** (with rooms), 27 Via Marconi (tel. 0429 81351, fax 82842; closed Mon and a few days in Jan and Aug), offers local specialities – *risotto di zucca, bigoli con ragù d'anatra, lumache al Madera* – cooked with care and a good selection of regional and Italian wines. It is moderately priced.

PADUA

Eating well is an essential component of civilised existence in Padua, and the town is full of good restaurants as a result. **San Clemente**, 142 Corso Vittorio Emanule II (tel. 049 880 3180, fax 880 3015; closed Sun evening, Mon morning, Aug and a few days around Christmas), is probably the city's best. It is located a few blocks south of the Prato della Valle, in a historic building with a lovely garden. Try the *fettuccine nere al tonno e finocchio selvatico* and *risotto speziato; storione in crosta di patate* and *piccione con le pere;* and don't miss the *gratin al Calvados.* There's a wide selection of cheeses. **Antico Brolo**, 22 Corso Milano (tel. 049 664 555, fax 656 860; closed Sun morning, Mon and two weeks in Aug), is a small, traditional restaurant in a historic building in the city centre. Specialities include *fiori di zucca farciti, trenette al pesto con frutti di mare, guancia di manzo con salsa verde* and an excellent house dessert. Regional, Italian and imported wines. Moderately priced; excellent value. **Belle Parti**, 11 Via Belle Parti (tel./fax 049 875 1822; closed Sun and two weeks in Aug), situated near Piazza dei Signori, is another good place, serving innovative cuisine. Strong points: *bigoli con ragù di anatra, branzino al sale, tegame di orte e di corte, spuma al limone con salsa all'arancia.* **Trattoria Ai Porteghi**, 105 Via Battisti (tel. 049 660 746, fax 876 1720; closed Sun, Mon morning and Aug), is a traditional trattoria, located halfway between the Cappella Scrovegni and the Basilica del Santo, serving Paduan specialities such as *fesa di cavallo affumicata, risotti con ortaggi, carpaccio di pesce spada, costata al sale grosso e aceto balsamico,* and various fruit tarts. All of these restaurants are moderately priced. A good, inexpensive place located right on Piazza delle Erbe is **Cavalca**, 8 Via Manin (tel. 049 876 0061; closed Tue evening, Wed and three weeks in Jul). The menu offers traditional fare, notably home-made pasta, *bollito alla padovana* and *capretto al forno, zaletti* and *pazientina,* accompanied by regional and Italian wines.

At **RUBANO**, 8km (5 miles) west on the road to Vicenza, is moderately priced **Le Calandre**, 1 Via Liguria, Località Sarmeola (tel. 049 630 303, fax 603 3000; closed Mon and two weeks in Aug). A favourite haunt of local gourmets, it serves original variations on traditional recipes. Try the *lumache alle erbe aromatiche, gnocchi di rape rosse, rombo ai vapori di verbena, piccione disossato con porcini,* and home-made pastries and ice-cream.

RIVIERA DEL BRENTA

MIRA has two very good places, both moderately priced. Venetian specialities and grilled meat and fish are the strong points of **Da Nalin**, 29 Via Nuovissimo Argine Sinistro (tel. 041 420 083, fax 560 037; closed Sun evening, Mon, Aug, and late Dec–early Jan), a fine country restaurant established in 1914. Try the *risotto di ostriche, seppie alla veneziana con polenta bianca, anguille ai ferri barboni e moeche fritti* and *sorbetto al limone.* **Margherita** (with rooms), 312 Via Nazionale (tel. 041 420 879, fax 426 5838; closed Tue evening, Wed and three weeks in Jan), is an elegant restaurant in a garden along the Brenta likewise offering Venetian cuisine, especially grilled meat and fish. Specialities include *granceola al naturale, grigliate* *miste alla brace, branzino al sale, tortino di pere,* and a wide assortment of local cheeses.

Special Events

EUGANEAN HILLS
MONSÉLICE: **Giostra della Rocca** (popular feast in costume, Sep); **ESTE: Settembre Euganeo** (folk and cultural events) and **Mostra della Ceramica Estense** (ceramics show, Sep); MONTAGNANA: **Palio dei 10 Comuni** (popular festival, first Sun in Sep).

PADUA
Teatro Estate (theatre festival, Aug); **Stagione Concertistica** (classical music, Oct–Mar); **Rassegna del Jazz Italiano** (jazz festival, Nov–Dec).

Museums and Monuments

EUGANEAN HILLS
Abbazia di Praglia: guided tours Tue–Sun, winter 14.30–16.30, summer 15.30–17.30.
MONSÉLICE, Castello: for guided tours, Apr–Nov, Tue, Thu and Sat 10.30, 15.30 and 17.00, Sun 10.30; winter by request (tel. 72014).
ESTE, Museo Nazionale Atestino: Tue–Sun 9.00–13.00, 15.00–18.00; Apr–Sep and hols until 19.00.
MONTAGNANA, Museo Civico: by request – enquire at the Municipio.

PADUA
Palazzo della Ragione: Tue–Sun, Nov–Jan 9.00–18.00; Feb–Oct 9.00–19.00.
Liviano: Wed 9.30–12.30 and 15.00–18.00 during the academic year; other times by request.
Cappella degli Scrovegni: daily 9.00–19.00.
Museo Civico: Tue–Sun 9.00–19.00.
Eremitani: Mon–Sat 8.15–12.00, 15.30–17.30.
Sant'Antonio: 7.00–19.00; **Cloisters and Museum**: Tue and Thu 10.00–12.00.
Scuola di Sant'Antonio: daily, Apr–Sep 9.00–12.30, 14.30–19.00; Oct–Mar 9.00–12.30, 14.30–17.00.
Oratorio di San Giorgio: closed for restoration at the time of writing.
Orto Botanico: Mon–Sat 9.00–13.00; summer also 15.00–18.00.

RIVIERA DEL BRENTA
STRÀ, Villa Pisani: Tue–Sat 9.00–16.00, Sun and hols 9.00–13.00.
DOLO, Park of Villa Ferretti Angeli: Thu–Fri, 13.00–18.00, Sat–Sun, 9.00–18.00. **Villa Grimani Migliorini**: by request (tel. 625 2991).
RISCOSSA, Villa Seriman: Tue–Sun 9.00–19.00.
ORIAGO, Villa Foscari: Mar–Nov, Tue and Sat 9.00–12.00; other times by request (tel. 041 520 3966).

9. WEST OF VENICE

The region west of Venice – which includes Vicenza, Verona and Lake Garda – is one of Italy's most beautiful and artistically one of its richest. The cities need no introduction: Vicenza is an incomparable showcase of Renaissance architecture and town planning, while Verona's medieval monuments and atmosphere have charmed visitors for centuries.

It is the countryside here that deserves special mention, for no province of Italy could be better suited to the rediscovery of nature than this. Certainly, the Alpine wilderness, like the sea-swept coasts of Sicily or Sardinia, are more primeval, more 'natural'. But this is precisely the point: this region is more than a 'cradle' of civilisation, it is its womb; for the relations between man and nature have developed so continuously and so intensely over the millennia here, that to isolate a natural object from its context is impossible. The landscape of the region is a mirror in which we ourselves are reflected: suffice it to recall that every tree, every vine that graces these hills and plains was planted by human hands. As Pliny and Catullus knew, the archetypes of our human heritage are here deposited in every stone, plant and animal, and they return, periodically and forcefully, to make their presence felt.

Vicenza

Vicenza stands in a pleasant geographical position at the confluence of two mountain torrents, the Retrone and the Bacchiglione, at the foot of the Colli Berici. It was a palaeo-Venetic settlement and a Roman *municipium*. After the barbarian invasions and a period of relative independence, it flourished under Venetian rule, which began in 1404. Although it did not achieve the greatness of its neighbours, Verona and Padua, during the 16th century it experienced a period of splendour that was reflected in a vast building programme. The many fine buildings by the town's favourite son, architect Andrea Palladio, have given the city centre a noble, classical aspect. The high standard of life is reflected today in the constant maintenance of the old palaces and monuments, which contributes to the unusual stylistic coherence and unmistakable elegance of the historic city centre. The ancient Roman street plan is clearly recognisable, structured along the monumental Corso Palladio (the Roman *decumanus maximus*) and around Piazza dei Signori (probably the ancient forum), both of which are now distinguished by the 16th-century classical creations of Palladio. Downtown Vicenza is really quite small, and can be visited comfortably in a couple of hours.

Corso Palladio, the Cathedral and Piazza dei Signori

The 11th-century Porta Castello, the west gate of the city, is the most conspicuous remainder of the town walls. It is adjoined by a shady garden, with a 16th-century loggia on a small canal. Just inside the gate, in Piazza Castello, stand the **Palazzo Piovini** (1656-58) and **Palazzo Porto Breganze**, begun by Vicenzo Scamozzi to a design by Palladio (c 1600) and never finished.

Here begins the magnificent **Corso Andrea Palladio**, the main street of the city centre, lined with monumental palaces and churches dating from the 14th to the 18th centuries. The corner house, **Palazzo Bonin Thiene** (No. 13), was designed by Palladio, continued by Vincenzo Scamozzi and, like the Palazzo Porto Breganze, left incomplete; the Renaissance **Palazzo Capra-Clementi** (No. 45) dates from the late 15th century. Nos. 47 and 67 are 15th-century Venetian Gothic houses.

The first important cross street, Corso Fogazzaro, is flanked by more fine palaces: on the right, (No. 16), the splendid **Palazzo Valmarana-Braga** (1566), a remodelling by Palladio of an earlier building; and further on, the **Palazzo Repeta**, now the Banca d'Italia, by Francesco Muttoni (1711). The latter fronts on Piazza **San Lorenzo**, which takes its name from the simple Franciscan church erected in the 13th century. The single-gabled façade has an elaborately carved doorway of 1344 set against a tall blind arcade and flanked by

---

Palladio and the Music of Architecture

The 16th-century architect Andrea di Pietro della Gondola, better known as Palladio, designed villas, palaces and churches throughout the Veneto in a classical style that would profoundly change the face of the region and inspire numerous imitations. His *Quattro Libri,* or *Four Books on Architecture,* became a manual for later architects, especially in England and the United States. In the engraved illustrations for this treatise, Palladio noted the significant dimensions of his buildings, linking together their plan, section and elevation in a series of proportional relationships. The seemingly easy elegance that distinguishes Palladio's designs was, in fact, the result of his careful calculation of such proportional relationships. In applying these systems of numerical progression, which were often associated with contemporary musical harmonic theory, to the spatial relationships of a building, Palladio succeeded in creating the pleasing visual harmonies that characterise his architecture.

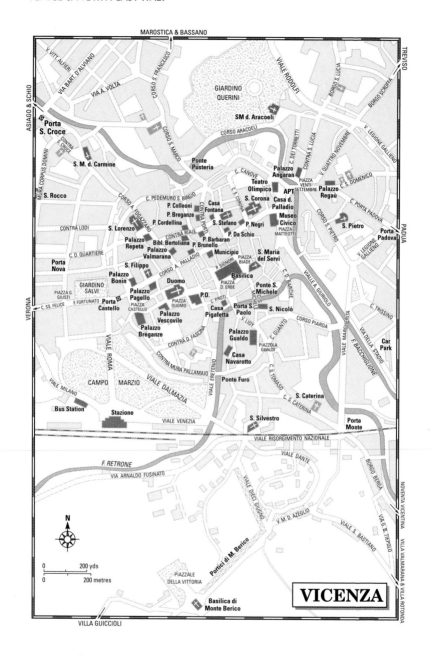

VICENZA

monumental tombs. The three-aisled interior with polygonal apses is entirely Gothic in flavor and contains the *Poiana Altar*, with a delicate relief (1474), a detached fresco of the *Beheading of St Paul* by Bartolomeo Montagna, and the cenotaph of architect Vincenzo Scamozzi (died 1616). In the north aisle is the door to the cloister (1492), where some sculptural fragments are displayed.

Retracing your steps and crossing over Corso Palladio, you soon come to the **Cathedral**, dating from the 14th, 15th and 16th centuries. It has a coloured-marble façade designed in 1467 by Domenico da Venezia, a stout Romanesque campanile on a Roman foundation, a Gothic lateral doorway, another attributed to Palladio, and a large Renaissance tribune begun in 1482 and finished nearly a century later. The interior, a single broad aisle with tall lancet arches and high, vaulted ceiling, contains a number of fine artworks, notably Lorenzo Veneziano's polyptych of the *Dormitio Virginis* (fifth south altar, 1356), a gold-ground altarpiece of considerable primitive charm showing the sleeping Virgin. There are also an *Adoration of the Magi* by Francesco Maffei (third south altar), and a *Madonna* by Bartolomeo Montagna (fourth north altar). The adjoining neoclassical Bishop's Palace has a splendid Renaissance portico, known as the **Loggia Zeno**, in the courtyard. On the south side of the square, beside the APT, is the entrance to the **Criptoportico Romano**, probably part of a Roman house of the 1st century AD.

Back in Corso Palladio, the **Galleria d'Arte Municipale**, displaying canvases by local painters of the 16th and 17th centuries, occupies the restored 16th-century church of Santi Giacomo e Filippo, set back somewhat from the street. Vincenzo Scamozzi's masterpiece is No. 98, the **Palazzo del Commune**, originally a private palace (designed 1592, completed 1662), with a doorway flanked by Ionic columns and a large arched window at the centre of the middle floor. Four symmetrical atria lead into the rectangular courtyard; within are rooms with 17th- and 18th-century decorations. Turning right at the corner, you immediately reach Piazza dei Signori, the centre of civic life. The south side of the square is occupied by the **Basilica**, or **Palazzo della Ragione**, Vicenza's most important monument and one of the finest buildings of the Venetian Renaissance, created by Palladio after 1549. What he made here is in fact a transparent involucre that encircles a pre-existent Gothic construction designed by Domenico da Venezia and built in the latter half of the 15th century. A double order of porticoes and loggias, carried by Tuscan Doric columns on the ground floor and Ionic columns on the floor above, frames rounded arches and is crowned by a balustrade with statues. The huge interior hall (today used for temporary exhibitions) is covered by a ship's-keel vault and lighted by 24 ogival windows opening onto the loggias.

Across the square stands the **Loggia del Capitaniato** (or Loggia Bernarda), which Palladio designed, in 1571, when construction on the Basilica was well underway. Once the residence of the military commander, it has immense, engaged Corinthian columns rising from the pavement to the attic level and framing the tall arches of the ground-floor portico as well as the windows and balconies of the floor above. The roof-line is marked by a

Vicenza, Loggia del Capitano

Vicenza, street view

trabeation and balcony, behind which the discreetly low, set-back attic can be glimpsed. On the same side of the square, across the street from the Loggia, is the Renaissance **Monte di Pietà** (1499). It incorporates the church of San Vincenzo, which was built a century and a quarter later than the palace proper and shows a lively Baroque face with two tiers of arcades and locally-made sculptures. The complex stands in the shadow of the **Torre di Piazza**, a slender campanile begun in the 12th and completed in the 14th century, rising 82m above the pavement and ending in a fine Gothic belfry with mullioned windows and dome. Below, two columns, surmounted by the Lion of St Mark and Christ the Redeemer, and respectively dating from 1520 and 1640, separate Piazza dei Signori from the adjoining Piazza delle Biade, where the 15th-century church of **Santa Maria dei Servi** presents a curious façade of 1710 incorporating the original Renaissance doorway. Inside is an *Enthroned Madonna* by Benedetto Montagna.

South to the Retrone, then North to Santa Corona

The square on the south side of the Basilica, the narrow Piazza delle Erbe, is considerably less monumental than Piazza dei Signori and, as its name suggests, less noble in function. It is a marketplace, packed with colourful stalls and thronged with shoppers on weekday mornings. As though to make sure that the difference in symbolic value of the two squares is understood, the humble Piazza delle Erbe lies on a lower level than its ostentatious counterpart. The outstanding buildings here are the medieval Torre del Girone or ('del Tormento'), and the late 15th-century Arco del Registro.

Continuing southwards, just before the bridge over the River Retrone you come to the birthplace (9 Via Pigafetta) of Antonio Pigafetta, the navigator, who accompanied Magellan on his first trip around the world (1519–22). It is a graceful Gothic mansion with a small façade delicately adorned with spiral columns. On the other side of the Retrone, here little more than a creek, stands **San Nicola da Tolentino**, a 17th-century oratory interesting for its elaborate stuccoes framing canvases by Francesco Maffei (who also did the *Trinity* over the altar), Giulio Carpioni, Antonio Zanchi, and others. The **Ponte di San Michele**, of 1623, offers a good view over the city centre.

You return to Piazza dei Signori, walk north between the Loggia del Capitaniato and the Monte di Pietà, and continue across Corso Palladio to reach Contrà Porti, another street flanked by superb palaces. Here are: at No. 6–10, **Palazzo Cavalloni-Thiene**, a 15th-century Venetian Gothic building; at No. 11, the majestic **Palazzo Barbaran-Porto**, by Palladio (1571), awaiting a new 'Museo Palladiano'; at No. 12 **Palazzo Thiene**, with a main façade and terracotta doorway attributed to Lorenzo da Bologna (1489), and a courtyard and rear façade (1550–58) designed by Palladio; at No. 14 the Gothic **Palazzo Trissino-Sperotti** (1450–60); at No. 16 the Renaissance **Palazzo Porto-Fontana**; at No. 17 the **Palazzo Porto-Breganze**, a Venetian Gothic building of 1481 with a fine Renaissance doorway and porticoed courtyard; at No. 19 the magnificent, early 14th-century **Palazzo Porto-Colleoni**, the oldest Venetian Gothic house on the street; and at No. 21 the unfinished **Palazzo Iseppo da Porto**, by Palladio (1552).

Now go around the block to the east and return by Contrà Zanella. No. 2 is the **Casa Fontana** (formerly Secco-Zen); its large, mullioned windows are unusual in Vicentine Gothic architecture. No. 1, at the corner of Piazzetta Santo Stefano, is the crenellated **Palazzo Negri De Salvi**, a 15th-century Renaissance mansion. Beyond the Baroque church of **Santo Stefano** (where there is a *Madonna and Child with Saints* by Palma Vecchio in the north transept), is Palladio's rear façade of Palazzo Thiene.

Back in Corso Palladio you soon reach the **Palazzo Caldogno da Schio** (No. 147), also called Ca' d'Oro, a gem of Venetian Gothic architecture with fine mullioned windows and a round-arched Renaissance doorway. Its design is attributed to Lorenzo da Bologna, author of the Casa Valmarana Bertolini; in the atrium are architectural fragments and antique inscriptions. No. 165–7 is the **Casa Cogollo**, a house once attributed to Palladio, with late Renaissance façade of 1559–62 possibly by Giovanni Antonio Fasolo.

The most magnificent religious building in town is the Dominican monastic church of **Santa Corona**, built in the 13th century, given a new transept and apse in the 15th century, and fine-tuned over the following centuries. The single-gabled façade has Gothic windows, including a large rose window. Inside, the sense of space is Romanesque, while the verticality is Gothic and the harmony of the easternmost areas, Renaissance. The deep, raised Renaissance sanctuary was laid out in 1489 by Lorenzo da Bologna. The crypt is entered through the Cappella Valmarana, designed by Palladio. Above, the 17th-century high altar and 15th-century choir stalls bear beautiful inlay work. Among the many altarpieces are two genuine masterpieces: Paolo Veronese's *Adoration of the Magi* (1573; third south altar) and Giovanni Bellini's magnificent *Baptism of Christ* (c 1502; fifth north altar), the latter set in a monumental architectural frame of 1501. The third altar on this side has a *St Anthony* by Leandro Bassano; the second, a *Magdalen and Saints* by Bartolomeo Montagna. The church takes its name from a thorn of the Crown of Christ, donated by St Louis of France and shown on Good Friday.

The adjoining cloister has a small **Museo Naturalistico** illustrating the geology, vegetation, and zoology of the Colli Bèrici, and a **Museo Archeologico**, with prehistoric, Roman, and Lombard antiquities. Particularly interesting are the square-mouthed Neolithic vases and the Palaeo-Venetic figured votive plates of the 4th and 3rd centuries BC. Both museums are open same times as the church.

Piazza Matteotti: Palladian Highlights

Corso Palladio ends in Piazza Matteotti, a broad open space planted as a garden, at the northeastern end of the pedestrian zone. On the north side of the square, in a garden surmounted by a crenellated medieval tower, stands the **Teatro Olimpico**, Palladio's last work (1580, completed in 1584 by

Interior of the Teatro Olimpico, Vicenza

Scamozzi). A corridor leads from the entrance to the Odeon, the meeting place of the literary circle known as the Accademia degli Olimpici, realised by Scamozzi in 1608, with a magnificent wooden ceiling and walls frescoed by Francesco Maffei. There follows the Antiodeon, also with a wooden ceiling; from here you enter the theatre proper. The latter, made of wood and stucco, takes up the forms of the theatres of classical antiquity described by Vitruvius: it has a cavea of 13 semi-elliptical tiers ending in a Corinthian colonnade crowned by an attic with statues, and a magnificent, two-storied fixed backdrop (designed by Scamozzi), populated by statues (95 altogether) and presenting spectacular architectural views of seven streets, supposedly of the ancient city of Thebes.

The majestic **Palazzo Chiericati**, designed by Palladio in 1550–57, stands alone on the west side of the square, without the spatial limitations of adjoining buildings – which left the architect free to design a double portico, Doric below and Ionic above, closed in the central part of the upper level by a wall with rectangular windows. The luminous, elegant solution of the façade finds an ideal complement in the spatial definition of the courtyard and of the ground floor rooms, decorated with frescoes by Domenico Brusasorci and Giovan Battista Zelotti and with stuccoes by Bartolomeo Ridolfi.

The building is home to the **Museo Civico**, established in 1855. The ground floor hosts the contemporary paintings of the Raccolta Neri Pozza, recently donated to the museum. In the courtyard is a small but valuable selection of Renaissance sculptures. On the first floor is the picture gallery, displaying mainly Venetian painting of the 16th to the 18th century, by Cima da Conegliano, Bartolomeo Montagna (*Madonna and Child with Saints*), Paolo Veronese (*Madonna and Child with Saints*), Jacopo Tintoretto, Jacopo Bassano, Francesco Maffei, Sebastiano and Marco Ricci, Pietro della Vecchia, Giuseppe Zais, Giovan Battista Tiepolo (*Time Revealing Truth*), and G.B. Piazzetta. Among the artists of other schools are Memling (*Crucifixion*), Van Dyck (*The Three Ages of Man*) and Sansovino. The museum also possesses a precious collection of drawings by Andrea Palladio.

Out of Town

In the immediate environs of Vicenza are two or three outstanding sights easily reached on foot. A point of pilgrimage is the **Sanctuary of Monte Berico**, in a panoramic position south of the city centre, to which it is connected by a long portico (Viale X Giugno) designed by the 18th-century architect Francesco Muttoni. The church (1668–1703), the work of Carlo Borella, has three symmetrical Baroque façades with 42 statues by Orazio Marinali; the stout campanile dates from the early 19th century. The Greek-cross interior conserves, in its eastern part, the primitive sanctuary of 1428, which legend holds was traced out by the Virgin Mary who appeared to a woman of the people. Among the votive decorations are a venerated statue of the Virgin, of 1430, and a splendid painting of the *Pietà* by Bartolomeo Montagna. A 15th-century cloister precedes the refectory, in which is set the large painting of the *Supper of St Gregory the Great,* by Veronese (1572). From the square in front of the basilica there is a splendid view of Vicenza and the mountains; further on, the 18th-century Villa Ambellicopoli-Guiccioli hosts the **Museo del Risorgimento e della Resistenza**.

From the great bend in Viale X Giugno, Viale d'Azeglio and Via San Bastiano wind southeast to two spectacular villas. The **Villa Valmarana ai Nani**, attributed to Antonio Muttoni, has a panoramic terrace overlooking the sanctuary of Monte Berico. Five rooms of the villa are decorated with frescoes by Giovanni Battista Tiepolo (1757), inspired by epic poems (*Iliad, Aeneid, Orlando Furioso, Gerusalemme Liberata*); the guest house is frescoed with scenes of country life by Giandomenico Tiepolo, Giovanni Battista's son. A brief walk leads to the equally famous Villa Almerico, better known as **La Rotonda**, the masterpiece of Palladio, designed in 1550 and completed by Scamozzi in 1606. The building, splendidly isolated on a hill, appears as an almost cubic volume from which four hexastyle porches surmounted by pediments and preceded by broad steps project in the four cardinal directions. The focal point of the interior is the circular central hall, covered by a dome and decorated with 17th-century frescoes and stuccoes, but the complex is well worth admiring from the street or gardens if you don't happen to be there during the rather tight visiting hours.

Around Vicenza

The gently rolling landscape of the Colli Bèrici abounds in vineyards and woodlands, amid which the villas seem to grow like mushrooms. **Costozza**, an old town at the eastern edge of this hilly district, is famous for the 18th-century **Villa Da Schio**, framed by a terraced garden, and the **Villa Trento-Carli** (1645), also in a remarkable park. Next to the latter is the **Villa Eolia**, now a restaurant. At **Lugo di Vicenza** are the **Villa Godi** (now Valmarana) and the **Villa Piovene Porto Godi**, both by Palladio. At **Villaverla** are the **Palazzo Verlato** (now Dalla Negra Dianin), by Vincenzo Scamozzi (1576, enlarged in the 17th century), and the 17th-century **Palazzo Ghellini** (now Dall'Olmo), by A. Pizzocaro.

Verona

Verona is one of the most beautiful and fascinating cities of north east Italy, and the richest artistic centre after Venice. It is also a wealthy manufacturing town, strategically positioned along the main road and rail routes from Germany to Central Italy.

Archaeologists have found evidence of lake dwellings on this site dating back to the Bronze Age. From the 7th century BC there was a centre of Atestine culture here, and the Goths seem to have entered the area in the 4th century BC. Contacts with Rome began in the 3rd century, and Verona became a Roman colony in 89BC. The seat of various medieval monarchies (Ostrogoths, Lombards and Franks), in the 11th century it became an independent commune. In the 13th and 14th centuries it was a seigniory, first of Ezzelino da Romano, then of the Della Scala (or Scaliger) family, and finally of the Milanese Visconti. It came under the rule of Venice in 1405 and thereafter shared the fate of the Venetian Republic.

Piazza Brà and Piazza delle Erbe

Our visit begins on the outskirts of the old city centre, amid the shady gardens and swanky pavement cafés of **Piazza Brà**. Once a suburban meadow (*braida*), this huge square is the undisputed centre of modern Verona. Corso Porta Nuova, from the station, enters it by a double archway known as the **Portoni della Brà** (1389), which once carried a covered passage joining the Scaliger fortress of Castelvecchio to the Visconti citadel. A pentagonal tower of the latter can still be seen as you arrive, to the right of the arches.

The south side of the square is dominated by the immense Doric façade of the **Gran Guardia**, begun in 1609 by Domenico Curtoni (using stones taken from the Arena) and completed some two centuries later. Originally built as a military parade ground, it is now used as a venue for exhibitions. Further along on this side stands the neoclassical **Gran Guardia Nuova** , or Palazzo Municipale (1838). On the other side of the Portoni della Brà is the Accademia Filarmonica, a concert hall with a majestic Ionic porch designed by Curtoni (1604) in the courtyard. Here is the **Museo Lapidario Maffeiano**, one of the oldest public museums in Italy (established 1716), with a collection that includes some 100 Greek inscriptions ranging in date from the 5th century BC to the 5th century AD, as well as Etruscan, Roman, early Christian and medieval material from sites throughout the Veneto. Steps ascend to the walkway over the Portoni del Brà, from which there is a fine view. On the northwest side of the square extends the lively promenade known as the *Listón*, lined with fashionable cafés and restaurants and backed by patrician palaces.

By far the most remarkable monument on the piazza is the great elliptical **Arena**. This is one of the largest extant Roman amphitheatres, third in order of size after the Colosseum in Rome and the amphitheatre of Capua. It was built in the 1st century AD using limestone quarried in the nearby Valpolicella. The most famous of Verona's ancient buildings, it retains only four of the triple archways of its outer walls, but the second circuit of 74 double arcades is intact. The interior, 139m long, 110m wide, and 30m high, has a cavea of 44 tiers (restored), capable of holding 22,000 spectators, surrounding the platea. The Arena hosts a famous opera festival in July and August, and if you are in town at this time be sure to ask your hotel concierge to obtain tickets. The performances are truly spectacular.

Via Mazzini (commonly called Via Nuova), Verona's elegant shopping street, leads from the northwest corner of Piazza Brà towards Piazza delle Erbe, to which we'll come in a minute. First, though, turn right at the end of Via Mazzini to reach what is billed as the **House of Juliet** (Nos 21–23), a 13th-century Gothic townhouse with a balcony of questionable authenticity and a bronze statue of Shakespeare's fictional heroine. Legend has it that you'll have a new lover if you rub her breast. Although there is nothing here that relates concretely to Juliet (the famous feud between the Montagues and the Capulets is probably an invention of the Bard), the painted walls and finely crafted ceilings of the interior merit a glance.

If you continue to walk to the end of Via Cappello you come to the Roman **Porta dei Leoni**, built in the 1st century AD, with a great arch, fluted columns, pedimented windows, loggia, and niches. Just outside the gate is one of Verona's great medieval monuments, **San Fermo Maggiore**, a complex of two superimposed churches, the lower one of 1065–1143, the upper of 1313–20. It has a fine façade featuring a broad Romanesque doorway with deep splay, a gallery of small arches, tall ogival windows, and a central mullioned window. On the north side is another doorway (the usual entrance) of 1363, beneath an attached porch.

The interior, a single vast aisle covered by a wooden ship's-keel roof of 1314, holds a number of important artworks. In the lunette over the doorway is a *Crucifixion* attributed to Turone; on the south side, next to the ambo with its baldachin and pointed spire, a fragment of a detached fresco of *Angels* by

Arena, Verona, with props for Aida

Stefano da Verona. Half-way along the north side is the Baroque Cappella della Madonna, with unimpressive 17th-century paintings and a *Madonna and Saints* by Gianfrancesco Caroto (1528). Over the first north altar is a *St Nicholas with Saints* by Battista dal Moro and, in the corner, the Brenzoni Tomb, by the Florentine Nanni di Bartolo (1427–39). This is framed by a famous fresco of the *Annunciation* by Pisanello. From the right transept you can enter the old Romanesque cloister and from here descend to to the lower church, with fragmentary frescoes of the 11th to 13th centuries and, behind the high altar, a 14th-century wooden crucifix.

Retrace your steps to the end of Via Mazzini. The long, rectangular **Piazza**

Verona, street view

delle Erbe stands over the ancient Roman forum. Today, as in the Middle Ages, it is the site of a colourful market, in the midst of whose hustle and bustle you can make out some medieval sculptures: the 15th-century Colonna del Mercato (with a Gothic stone lion), the 16th-century Berlina or Capitello (where the city's rulers took office), the 14th-century Fontana di Madonna Verona (incorporating a Roman statue) and the 16th-century Colonna di San Marco (with a Venetian lion).

The square is bounded on the southwest by the 14th-century **Casa dei Mercanti**, or merchants' hall, now the chamber of commerce; its mullioned windows and crenellated roof are all that remains of the original building,

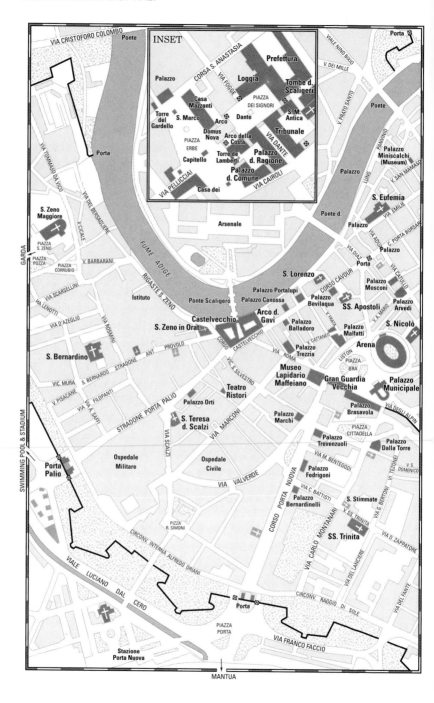

INSET

VIA CRISTOFORO COLOMBO
Ponte
Porta
VIALE NINO BIXIO
V. DEI MILLE
Porta

Palazzo
CORSA S. ANASTASIA
VIA FOGGE
Loggia
Prefettura
Tombe d.
Scaligeri
VIALE NINO BIXIO
V. DEI MILLE
V. DEI PRATO SANTO
Ponte

Casa
Mazzanti
PIAZZA
DEI SIGNORI
Dante
S. M.
Antica

Torre
del
Gardello
S. Marco
Arco
Domus
Nova
Arco della
Costa
Tribunale
VIA DANTE

PIAZZA
ERBE
Torre de
Lamberti
Palazzo
d. Ragione
PANVINIO
Palazzo
Miniscalchi
(Museum)
V. SAN MAMASO

Capitello
Palazzo
d. Comune
VIA CAIROLI
Palazzo
LUNG

VIA PELLICCIAI
Casa dei
S. Eufemia
VIA EMILIE

Porta
VIA TOMMASO DA VICO
VIA DEL BERSAGLIERE
Porta
Arsenale
Ponte d.
Palazzo
Palazzo
C. PORTA BORSAR

V. CICALE
S. Zeno
Maggiore
VIA DIAZ
Porta
VIA CATULO

PIAZZA
S. ZENO
PIAZZA
POZZA
PIAZZA
CORRUBIO
V. BARBARANI
S. Lorenzo
CORSO CAVOUR
Palazzo
Mosconi
Palazzo
Arvedi

GARDA
VIA SCARSELLINI
FIUME ADIGE
RIGASTE S. ZENO
Istituto
Ponte Scaligero
Palazzo Portalupi
Palazzo Canossa
Palazzo
Bevilaqua
SS. Apostoli
S. Nicolò

VIA LENOTTI
VIA D'AZEGLIO
Castelvecchio
Arco d.
Gavi
Palazzo
Balladoro
V. FRATA
V. A. MARIO
Palazzo
Malfatti
Arena

S. Zeno in Orat.
CORSO CASTELVECCHIO
V. CATTANEO
VIA
ROMA
Palazzo
Trezzia
LISTON
PIAZZA
BRA

S. Bernardino
VIA ROSMINI
VIC. S. SILVESTRO
Museo
Lapidario
Maffeiano
Gran Guardia
Vecchia
Palazzo
Municipale

VIC. MURA
S. BERNARDO
STRADONE
ANT
PROVOLO
Teatro
Ristori
Palazzo
Brasavola
VIA DEGLI ALPIN

V. PISACANE
VIA A. SAFFI
S. BERNARDO
V. FILOPANTI
STRADONE PORTA PALIO
Palazzo Orti
VIA MARCONI
Palazzo
Marchi
PIAZZA
CITTADELLA

SWIMMING POOL & STADIUM
S. Teresa
d. Scalzi
VIA SCALZI
Palazzo
Trevenzuoli
Palazzo
Dalla Torre
V. S.
DOMENICO

Ospedale
Militare
Ospedale
Civile
VIA M. BENTEGODI
Palazzo
Fedrigoni
VI. TEZONEI

Porta
Palio
VIA VALVERDE
CORSO PORTA NUOVA
VIA C. BATTISTI
Palazzo
Bernardinelli
S. Stimmate
V. SS. TRINITA
V. G. BERTONI

PIZZA
R. SIMONI
CIRCONV. INTERNA ALFREDO ORIANI
SS. Trinita
VIA D. ZAPPATORE

VIALE LUCIANO DAL CERO
Porta
CIRCONV. RAGGIO DI SOLE
VIA CARLO MONTANARI
VIA DEL LANCIERE
VIA DEL FANTE

PIAZZA
PORTA
VIA FRANCO FACCIO

Stazione
Porta Nuova
MANTUA

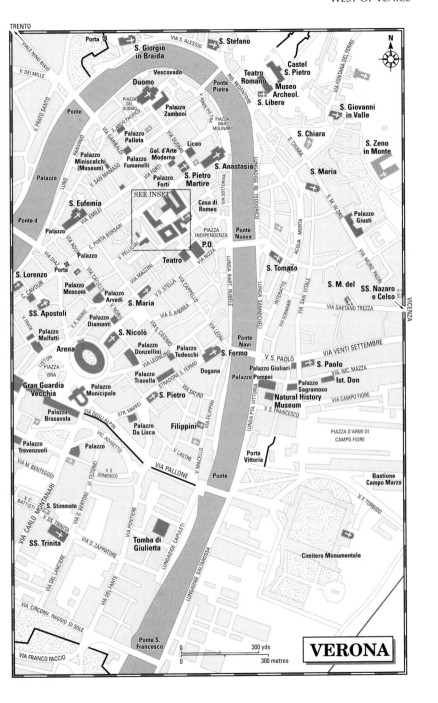

VERONA

extensively altered in the 17th century. The monument in the small piazzetta here commemorates the victims of an Austrian bomb which fell nearby during World War I. At the narrow northwest end of the piazza are the 14th-century Torre del Gardello (or Torre delle Ore) and the **Palazzo Maffei**, a Baroque building of 1668 crowned by statues. The northeast side is bounded by the frescoed **Case Mazzanti**, begun in the 14th century as a residence of the Scaligers but radically altered in the 16th; the **Domus Nova** (or Palazzo dei Giudici), a 17th-century reconstruction of the 14th-century residence of the *podestà* or mayor; and the Palazzo della Ragione (or Palazzo del Comune), begun in the late 12th century but modified in the 16th century and again in the 19th, when the neoclassical façade on this side was added.

Piazza dei Signori and the Scaliger Tombs

By the 15th-century Arco della Costa – which takes its name from a whale's rib hung beneath the vault, ready to fall, the legend says, on the first honest person to walk beneath it – you enter **Piazza dei Signori**, a small, handsome square with monumental buildings surrounding a central monument to Dante. This was the seat of city government in the Middle Ages. The **Palazzo della Ragione**, here seen in its earlier form, has a splendid Romanesque courtyard encircled by a portico on piers and occupied in part by a fine external Gothic-Renaissance staircase. Above it rises the symbol of civic power, the 84m **Torre dei Lamberti**, begun in 1172 and completed in the mid-15th century. Stairs and a lift go to the top, from which there is a splendid view over the city and its surroundings.

The **Palazzo del Capitanio**, now the courthouse, stands on the other side of the narrow Via Dante. It is a 14th-century building with a crenellated tower and a doorway by Michele Sanmichele (1531). It has another, rather unusual doorway by Giuseppe Miglioranzi (1687) in the courtyard. The **Palazzo della Prefettura** (formerly Palazzo del Governo) rises at the end of the square. Built in the 14th century, it was restored to its original appearance in 1929–30; the doorway of 1533 is by Sanmicheli. Here Dante and Giotto stayed as guests of the Scaligers.

The adjoining **Loggia del Consiglio**, built in the late 15th century as the seat of the city council, is the first significant expression of the Veronese Renaissance. It consists of an elegant portico and an order of mullioned windows flanked by small pilasters; the coloured-marble facing and the sculptural decoration (by Alberto da Milano, 1493) give it a sense both of vivacity and of delicate harmony. An arch surmounted by a 16th-century statue joins the loggia to the Casa della Pietà, built in 1490. On the side facing Piazza delle Erbe the square terminates in the ornate façade of the Domus Nova.

The passage on the right of the Palazzo della Prefettura leads into the little Piazzaletto delle Arche, which takes its name from the monumental **Arche Scaligere** or tombs of the Scaligers, executed in the 14th century by Bonino da Campione and his followers. At the centre of a stone-and-iron enclosure

Giardini di Palazzo Giusti, Verona

bearing the family emblem, the ladder (in Italian, *scala*), stands the graceful Romanesque church of **Santa Maria Antica** (1185, several times restored), its doorway surmounted by the tomb of Cangrande I (died 1329), with a copy of the equestrian statue now in the Museo del Castelvecchio. Inside the enclosure are, against the wall of the church, the simple tomb of Mastino I, the first of the dynasty, assassinated in 1277 in Piazza dei Signori; on the left of the entrance, the tomb of the Mastino II (died 1351); in the opposite corner, that of Cansignorio (died 1375); and at the rear, the tomb of Giovanni della Scala (died 1359) – all in the form of aedicules surmounted by rich Gothic baldachins and adorned with statues. Also part of the complex are the profusely carved sarcophagi of Bartolomeo (1304), Alboino (1311), Cangrande II (1359) and Alberto (1301) della Scala. The Gothic house at the corner of Via delle Arche Scaligere is thought to be the home of Romeo, though on what grounds nobody seems to know.

Across the River

Now walk back to Piazza dei Signori, through the courtyard of Palazzo del Capitanio, and along the wooded left flank of the post office. You'll come out at the foot of the Ponte Nuovo, which crosses the River Adige with good views (left) of the Roman Theatre and the hill of San Pietro (see below).

On the other side of the river Via Carducci leads past the 15th-century church of San Tommaso Cantuariense to the **Giardini di Palazzo Giusti**, a famous and beautiful formal garden with terraces, a boxwood labyrinth, and a *belvedere,* or scenic viewpoint. This green hillside oasis, laid out in the 16th century with the contemporary Palazzo Giusti, was one of Goethe's favourite spots in Italy.

One block northwest is **Santa Maria in Organo**, founded on this site in the 7th century but dating in its present form from 1481. Michele Sanmicheli is probably the author of the white marble façade (1546) on the otherwise Gothic west front. The elegant interior is entirely covered with frescoes, by Nicolò Giolfino (south side), Gian Francesco Caroto (north side), Domenico Brusasorci (north transept and sacristy) and Francesco Morone (sacristy), among others. The choir and sacristy have extraordinary inlaid woodwork executed in the late 15th century by Fra' Giovanni da Verona. In the three-aisled crypt are traces of the primitive church (7th or 8th century) and remains of the Roman walls. A large Renaissance cloister of the Olivetan convent adjoins the church on the north.

To the northwest, in a lovely position on the hill of San Pietro, is the **Roman Theatre**. This extraordinary complex, of which the scena, the semicircular cavea and the two entrances survive, was built in the early 1st century AD and later enlarged. It was brought to light in the 18th century, in one of the first archaeological excavations conducted to modern scientific standards. The ruins of the cavea end on one side in the small church of Santi Siro e Libera, founded in the 9th century and altered in the 14th, and on the other in the arcades that once marked the perimeter of the edifice. Plays and ballet are staged in the theatre in summer. Above the theatre (lift), the Renaissance cloister of the former convent of San Girolamo houses a **Museo Archeologico** with glass, sculpture and mosaics from Roman Verona, and Greek and Etruscan material. The views from the windows and terraces over the theatre, the river, and the city are themselves worth the climb. The church has a fine ceiling and frescoes by Gian Francesco Caroto and others; over the altar is a Renaissance triptych by an anonymous Veronese artist. High up on the hill is the Castel San Pietro, built by the Visconti, destroyed by the French and rebuilt by the Austrians.

At the foot of the hill the **Ponte della Pietra**, part Roman and part medieval, leads back across the Adige. Its five arches were destroyed in World War II and rebuilt, in 1957–59, after dredging the original stones from the river. The bridge enjoys a superb view over the city and the San Pietro hill.

Sant Anastasia and the Cathedral

Turn left as soon as you set foot on the right bank to reach the Gothic church of **Sant'Anastasia**, whose polygonal apses and spired campanile have been visible from the river. The largest church in Verona, it was erected by the Dominicans between 1291 and 1323 and reworked in 1423–81. The unfinished façade has a superb 14th-century doorway with coloured marbles and carvings. Inside, the 16th-century *Acquasantiere dei Gobbi* take their name from the crouching figures (*gobbi* means 'hunchbacks') in their bases. The first altar on the south side, incorporating the Fregoso Tomb, was designed by Sanmicheli in 1565. The third altar on this side is surrounded by frescoes attributed to Liberale and Benaglio da Verona. Over the altar in the south transept is a painting of the *Madonna and SS Thomas Aquinas and Augustine* by Girolamo dai Libri. The first south apsidal chapel has a large fresco depicting the *Cavalli Family Presented to the Virgin,* by Altichiero (1390–95); and the second south apsidal chapel, two Gothic tombs and 24 terracotta reliefs with stories from the life of Christ by Michele da Firenze (1435). In the sanctuary are a large, 14th-century fresco of the *Last Judgement* by a painter called the Master of the Last Judgement, and the Tomb of General Cortesia Serego, attributed to the Florentine Nanni di Bartolo (1424–29). From the north transept, with an altarpiece by Francesco Morone, a Gothic doorway leads into the sacristy, with a delightful detached fresco of *St George and the Dragon* by Pisanello, the church's chief claim to fame. Here too are 15th-century stalls and stained glass, and the banner of the Millers' and Bakers' Guild.

Via Duomo leads northwest. The **Cathedral of Santa Maria Matricolare,** dominating the secluded Piazza del Duomo, is a 12th-century Romanesque building with Gothic and Renaissance additions. The front has a monumental two-storeyed porch adorned with column-bearing lions and reliefs by Maestro Nicolò (1139); another Romanesque porch is on the south side. The campanile, Romanesque at the base and 16th century above, was completed in the 20th century. The overall design is by Sanmicheli. The 12th-century

Impressions of Verona

Verona is a place that has left its mark on literary minds. Here are a few of the results.

Romeo:
There is no world without *Verona* walles,
But Purgatorie, Torture, hell it selfe:
Hence banished, is banisht from the world,
And worlds exile in death.
William Shakespeare, *Romeo and Juliet,* ca. 1594–95

This most faire City is built in the forme of a Lute.... It hath a pure aire, and is ennobled by the civility and auncient Nobility of the Citizens, who are inbued with a chearfull countenance, magnificent mindes, and much inclined to all good literature.
Fynes Moryson, *An Itinerary,* 1617.

Certainly this Citty deserv'd all those Elogies Scaliger has honour'd it with, for in my opinion, tis situated in one of the most delightfullst places that ever I came in, so sweetly mixed with risings, & Vallies, so Elegantly planted with Trees, on which Bacchus seems riding as it were in Triumph every Autumn, for the Vines reach from tree to tree; & here of all places I have travell'd in *Italy* would I fix preferable to any other, so as well has that learned Man given it the name of the very Eye of the World.
John Evelyn, *Diary,* May 1646.

I have been over Verone.... Of the truth of Juliet's story, they seem tenacious to a degree, insisting on the fact – giving a date (1303), and showing a tomb. It is a plain, open, and partly decayed sarcophagus, with withered leaves in it, in a wild and desolate conventual garden, once a cemetery, now ruined to the very graves. The situation struck me as being very appropriate to the legent, being blighted as their love. I have brought away a few pieces of the granite, to give to my daughter and my nieces.
Lord Byron, Letter to Augusta Leigh, 7 November 1816

It was natural enough to go straight from the Market-place, to the House of the Capulets, now degenerated into a most miserable little inn. Noisy vetturini and muddy market-carts were disputing possession of the yard, which was ankle-deep in dirt, with a brook of splashed and bespattered geese; and there was a grim-visaged dog,

viciously panting in a doorway, who would certainly have had Romeo by the leg, the moment he put it over the wall, if he had existed, and been at large in these times.... The house is a distrustful jealous-looking house as one would desire to see, though of a very moderate size.
Charles Dickens, *Pictures from Italy*, 1846.

I must not say more of Verona, than that, though truly Rouen, Geneva and Pisa have been the centres of thought and teaching to me, Verona has given the colouring to all they taught. She has virtually repre-sented the fate and beauty of Italy to me; and whatever concerning Italy I have felt, or been able with any charm or force to say, has been dealt with more deeply, and said more earnestly for her sake.
John Ruskin, *Praeterita*, 1885-9

Juliet's home-town, I suppose some would call it. The phrase takes the edge off romance, and I designed it to do so, determined as I am somehow to vent my rage at being shown Juliet's house, a picturesque and untidy tenement, with balconies certainly too high for love, unless Juliet was a trapeze acrobat, accustomed to hanging downwards by her toes.
This was not Juliet's house, for the sufficient reason that so far as authentic history knows, there never was any Juliet.
Arnold Bennett, *Journal 1929*, 1930.

At Verona, an American in Auden's compartment said to his companion, 'Hey, didn't Shakespeare live here?' at which Auden observed loudly, 'Surely it was Bacon.'
Charles Osborne, *W.H. Auden, 1980* – of 5 September 1951.

semicircular tufa apse, a pure expression of the Veronese Romanesque style, is adorned with pilasters and a fine classical frieze. The entrance is by a door in the south flank, also with a good porch.

The Gothic interior has broad arches on tall compound piers. The walls of the west bays are decorated with architectural frescoes by Gian Maria Falconetto (c 1503). More frescoes, by Francesco Torbido after cartoons by Giulio Romano, adorn the sanctuary, which is enclosed by a fine curved choir screen by Sanmicheli, incorporating a *Crucifixion with the Virgin and St John* by Giambattista da Verona (1534). The second south chapel has a painting of the *Adoration of the Magi* by Liberale da Verona, and the first north chapel an *Assumption* by Titian, in a frame by Jacopo Sansovino. The Nichesola tomb here is also by Sansovino.

From the north side entrance is gained to the church of **San Giovanni in Fonte** (1123), the former Romanesque baptistery, a three-aisled apsidal

The cathedral, Verona

building with fine 9th-century capitals and an octagonal baptismal font decorated with reliefs (c 1200); and to the little church of **Sant'Elena**, also of the 9th century, rebuilt in the 12th century and preserving part of its early Christian structures. Excavations here have revealed 6th-century mosaic pavements and the tombs of two early bishops.

To the Castelvecchio

Return to Piazza delle Erbe. From the southwest corner of the square Corso di Porta Bórsari follows the straight line of the Roman *decumanus maximus* to the 1st-century **Porta dei Bórsari**, which takes its name from the episcopal tax collectors, or *bursari*, whose offices were located here. Outside the gate Corso Cavour continues along the path of the *decumanus*. Set back from the street on the south are the campanile and flank of the Romanesque church of the **Santissimi Apostoli**, from the sacristy of which you can enter the small, partially underground church of Santi Tosca e Teuteria, which supposedly dates back to the 5th century. Across the street is the beautiful Romanesque church of **San Lorenzo** (1110), in alternating bands of tufa and brick, with a narrow façade flanked by towers. No. 19 (left) is the spectacular **Palazzo Bevilacqua**, Sanmicheli's masterpiece, with rusticated ground floor, balcony, loggia with spiral columns, and a fine cornice. Sanmichele also designed the **Palazzo Canossa** (No. 44), with a splendid atrium and courtyard. At the end of the street, in a little garden on the right, is the **Arco dei Gavi**, a Roman arch erected in the 1st century AD in honour of the family of the Gavii, demolished in 1805, and reconstructed from the fragments in 1932

The **Castelvecchio**, the main monument of medieval civil architecture in Verona, dominates the busy square here. It was built by Cangrande II Della Scala as his home and fortress in 1354–57 and completed with the addition of the keep in 1375. It has been restored many times, most recently between 1958 and 1964 by Carlo Scarpa. The imposing brick fortress consists of two main blocks divided by the crenellated **Ponte Scaligero**, which extends to the left bank of the Adige, and the tall tower of the keep. The rectangular east block surrounds a large courtyard, formerly a parade ground; the trapezoidal west block (the original fortified residence of Cangrande) has a double circuit of walls with two courtyards and drawbridges.

Inside the castle is the **Civico Museo d'Arte**, famous for its Veronese art from the 14th to the 18th century. Here are works by the primitives Turone (*Trinity*), Altichiero, Stefano da Verona (*Madonna del Roseto)* and Pisanello (*Madonna della Quaglia*); the 15th-century painters Francesco Morone, Liberale da Verona, Paolo Cavazzola and Gian Francesco Caroto (*Boy with Drawing*); and the 16th-century masters Paolo Veronese (*Bevilacqua-Lazise Altarpiece, Deposition*) and Paolo Farinati. Among the Venetian artists are Andrea Mantegna (*Holy Family*), Jacopo Bellini (*St Jerome, Crucifix*), Giovanni Bellini (two *Madonnas*), Carlo Crivelli (*Madonna della Passione*), Bartolomeo Montagna, Alvise Vivarini (*Madonna*), Bernardo Strozzi (*Male Portrait*), Jacopo Tintoretto (*Concert of the Muses* and *Adoration of the*

Shepherds) Gian Battista Tiepolo (*Heliodorus and the Treasure of the Temple;* sketch for a ceiling painting), and Francesco Guardi (two *Capricci*). Also present are Tomaso da Modena and several Flemish artists. The museum contains some important antiquities and artefacts – notably early Christian glass, 7th-century gold, the so-called *Tesoretto di Isola Razza,* including 4th-century devotional spoons – fabrics and silks from the Arca di Cangrande I and miniatures by Liberale and by Girolamo dai Libri. An outstanding collection of arms and armour ranges from the Lombard period to the 17th century. The focal point of the collection of 14th-century Veronese sculpture is the dramatically displayed *Equestrian Statue of Cangrande I,* from the Arche Scaligere.

San Zeno Maggiore

Regaste San Zeno runs along the Adige, offering good views back over the Castelvecchio and its bridge. At the end of the street and to the right is the basilica of **San Zeno Maggiore**, Verona's most distinctive religious building and one of the most important Romanesque churches of Northern Italy. Buy a ticket on the left, as you enter the square, if you plan to go in.

Erected in the 5th century and rebuilt in the 9th century as the church of the Benedictine monastery of which one stout battlemented tower remains (to the north of the façade as you face the church), San Zeno was reconstructed in 1120–38 and completed in the 13th century. The polygonal apse, with Gothic ogival windows and engaged buttresses, dates from 1385–98. The warm-hued tufa façade is divided horizontally by pilaster strips and vertically by a gallery with mullioned windows, and pierced by a large rose window (representing the Wheel of Fortune) and a fine doorway of 1138. The latter, with an attached porch, carved arch, lunette, column-bearing lions and two splendid bands of reliefs representings biblical and allegorical scenes, was executed by Maestro Nicolò and his pupil Guglielmo, around 1135. Equally splendid are the 12th-century doors, with bronze relief panels depicting Old and New Testament stories and the lives of SS Zeno and Michael. The south flank presents the red and white marble bands typical of Veronese churches. The tall, detached campanile (1045–1140) terminates in a two-tiered belfry with mullioned windows.

From the north side you enter the noble interior, with three aisles on piers and columns, wooden ship's-keel roof and split-level east end – sanctuary above, crypt below. Fine 13th-century statues decorate the choir screen. On the west wall is a *Crucifixion* by Lorenzo Veneziano, painted around 1360; at the beginning of the south aisle, an octagonal **baptistery** of the late 12th century. The walls of the nave and sanctuary are decorated with fragments of Romanesque-Gothic frescoes; over the high altar is the splendid triptych of the *Madonna and Saints* by Andrea Mantegna (1457–59), one of the key works of Renaissance painting in Verona. The wooden choir stalls date from the 15th century. The 13th-century crypt, with antique columns, holds a modern sarcophagus containing the remains of Saint Zeno, Verona's first bishop (died 380), and the tombs of other saints and bishops. In the north apse is a curious 13th- or 14th-century polychrome statue of St Zeno laughing. From the north aisle you go out into the fine Romanesque cloister (with small double columns of red marble, dating from the 12th, 13th, and 14th centuries), left over from the abbey. Beneath the portico are tombs and sepulchral monuments. A doorway on the left leads to the **Oratorio di San Benedetto**, a 13th-century chapel displaying columns and piers with 'recycled' capitals, some dating as far back as the 6th century.

Walking southwards through streets with a distinctly suburban atmosphere, you come to the **Porta del Palio** (1552–57), through which the *palio* horse race passed. Mentioned by Dante, it is the most harmonious of the four city gates designed by Sanmicheli – the others are the Porta San Giorgio, 1525; Porta Nuova, 1533–46; and Porta San Zeno, 1541–42. Skirting the outside of the walls, the design and construction of which were probably Sanmicheli's greatest single commission, you soon reach the Porta Nuova, from which Corso Porta Nuova returns to Piazza Brà.

Around Verona

The area north of Verona, a lovely region of long hills separating the valleys of the rivers Fumane, Merano and Negrar, is known as **Lessinia** and is a favourite weekend retreat of the Veronese. Several roads run up along the valleys to the 'Tredici Comuni', a constellation of little hill towns occupied by the descendants of Germanic settlers who migrated here in the Middle Ages. At **Pedemonte** is the **Villa Boccoli**, in a park, partly built to a design by Andrea Palladio (1565–69). Outside the wine-growing centre of **Fumane** is the **Villa della Torre** (1562), attributed to Sanmicheli or to Giulio Romano, interesting for the distribution of the ground-floor rooms around a peristyle, as in ancient Roman villas. Some 10km (6 miles) further, in the Valle del Progno, is the **Parco Naturale delle Cascate di Molina**, with waterfalls and unusual rock formations; and near **Sant'Anna di Alfaédo**, is a famous natural arch, the **Ponte di Vela**, which Mantegna painted and Dante supposedly took as his inspiration for the Malebolge of the *Inferno*. The town has a small museum of prehistoric finds and fossils. **San Giorgio di Valpolicella** stands in a fine position overlooking Lake Garda. Here the **Pieve,** a very old church rebuilt in Romanesque forms in the 13th century, has fragmentary frescoes, an octagonal baptistery, a baldachin over the high altar made with remains of an 8th-century ciborium, and a fine cloister. Nearby **Santa Maria in Stelle** has a curious Roman nympheum of the 3rd century, originally meant to carry to the surface the waters of an underground spring, converted to

Christian use in the 5th or 6th century. Today called the **Pantheon di Santa Maria in Stelle**, it is reached by steps from the square of the church. The road up the Val Pantena to via Grezzana and Stallavena (near which is the Riparo Tagliente, a shelter used by Palaeolithic hunters) to **Bosco Chiesanuova**, the chief resort of the region (skiing).

Lake Garda

An early 20th-century traveller remarked: 'The Italian lakes play at being little seas. They have little ports, little lighthouses, little fleets for war, and little customs-houses, and little storms and little lines of steamers. Indeed, if one wanted to give a rich child a perfect model or toy, one could not give him anything better than an Italian lake.' The largest of the Italian lakes, **Lake Garda** (*Lago di Garda,* sometimes called *Lago di Benaco*), is indeed a world unto itself. It is one of the more romantic spots in Italy, and even in the height of summer, when car- and bus-loads of Germans and Austrians descend via the Brennero pass to bask on its sun-baked shores, it amply repays a day or two of leisurely exploration.

Lake Garda occupies a glacial valley about 50km long and little over 15km across at its widest point. The broad southern basin lies between low hills and is divided into two bays by the long, narrow peninsula of Sirmione. The narrow north part is locked on the west by rocky cliffs and on the east by Monte Baldo, which rises to a towering 2218m. The vegetation is highly varied, sometimes quite wild and always very beautiful. The mass of water is such as to have created a distinctly Mediterranean microclimate (today cooled somewhat by the affluence, in a tunnel, of flood waters from the Adige). The variety of the scenery and its historical stratifications are surprising: here are olives, cypresses, citrus groves and vineyards; gentle morainic hills and a harsh, narrow fjord carved out of the rock; and a variety of old towns, villages and farms to which the centuries have given the tones of their respective origins – Venetian on one shore, Lombard on the other.

The lake has a long, intense history as a resort. The Roman poet Gaius Valerius Catullus (84?–54BC) is known to have had a villa near Sirmione. He devoted a brief poem to the headland on which the city stood – and still stands today – which he called the 'flower of peninsulas and islands' ('Paene insularum, Sirmio, insularumque ocelle...'). The French essayist Montaigne, on a visit to the lake in the 16th century, observed that the mountains were 'more desolate and arid than I have ever seen'; and that the temperament of the lake was 'subject to terrible and furious storms'. Today, Sirmione is still a favourite resort of Italians and foreigners alike. On the Lombard (western) shore – which includes Salò, Gardone Riviera, Maderno, and Gargnano – are innumerable villas, hotels, gardens and lakeside promenades. On the Veronese (eastern) shore the most popular localities are Lazise, Bardolino,

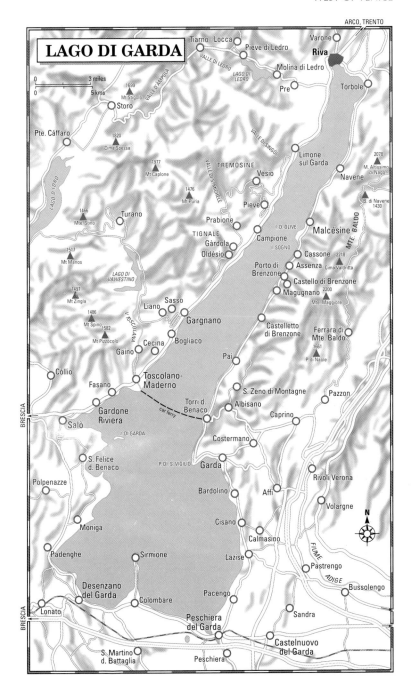

ARCO, TRENTO

LAGO DI GARDA

0 — 3 miles
0 — 5 kms

1699 Mt Stigolo
Storo

Tiarno Locca
Pieve di Ledro
VALLE DI LEDRO
LAGO DI LEDRO
Pre
Molina di Ledro
Varone
Riva
Tórbole

Pte. Cáffaro

1820 Cima Spessa

1977 Mt Caplone

TREMÓSINE
Vesio

VALLE DI SINGOL
Limone sul Garda
Navene

2078 M. Altissimo di Nago

B. di Navene 1430

1466 Mte Stino
Turano

VALLE DI S.MICHELE
1476 Mt Puria
Pieve

Prabione

I D. OLIVE
Malcésine

1517 Mt Manos

TIGNALE
Gàrdola
Oldésio

Campione
I SOGNO

Cassone 2218

MTE. BALDO

LAGO DI VALVESTINO

1497 Mt Zingla

Porto di Brenzone
Assenza
Castello di Brenzone
Magugnano

Cima Valdritta

2200 Mte. Maggiore

Liano
Sasso

Gargnano

1486 Mt Spino
1582 Mt Pizzócolo
Gaino
Cecina
Bogliaco

Pai

Castelletto di Brenzone

Ferrara di Mte. Baldo
1661 P. di Naole

Cóllio

Fasano

Toscolano-Maderno

Torri d. Benaco
Albisano

S. Zeno di Montagne

Pazzon

car ferry

Gardone Riviera
Saló

I DI GARDA

Caprino

Costermano

S. Felice d. Benaco

P. DI S.VIGILIO
Garda

Rivoli Verona

Polpenazze

Bardolino
Affi

Volargne

Moniga

Cisano

Calmasino

N

Padenghe

Sirmione

Lazise

FIUME

Pastrengo

Desenzano del Garda
Colombare

Pacengo

ADIGE

Bussolengo

Lonáto

Sandra

S. Martino d. Battaglia

Peschiera del Garda

Peschiera

Castelnuovo del Garda

Garda, the San Vigilio headland, Torri del Benaco, and Malcesine. Riva del Garda and Torbole are well-known resorts on the Trentine (northern) shore.

There are frequent ferries and hydrofoils between most towns on the lake – including a paddle-wheeled steamer built in 1901 – and the round-trip boat tour is undoubtedly a unique experience, although a circuit of the lake by car or bus (about 150km), along the panoramic road known as the 'Gardesana', is much faster. The itinerary proposed below may be followed by either means. It begins in the wide, sunny bay of Desenzano; lingers on the Lombard side among the villas and gardens frequented by Italian and foreign literati (Gabriele D'Annunzio, D.H. Lawrence, Nietzsche, Kafka and Mann); then crosses the beautiful little Valtènesi, ending amid the vineyards and olive groves of the Venetian shore.

Sirmione to Riva del Garda

The most interesting town on the southern shore, **Sirmione**, stands near the end of the long, narrow peninsula to which it gives its name. It is a well-known spa, with warm sulphur springs ('La Boiola') that bubble up just off shore. It has a very special atmosphere, a combination of the spectacular medieval walls of the **Rocca Scaligera**, originally a stronghold of Verona's ruling Della Scala family, the narrow lanes of the old town, and the striking views of the lake. There are some antique columns in the 15th-century church of **Santa Maria Maggiore**, and fragmentary 8th-century frescoes in the Romanesque church of **San Pietro**, on the outskirts of the town. Romantically set among olive groves at the northern end of the peninsula are the extensive remains of a Roman villa of the early imperial period (complete with anti-quarium), commonly called the **Grotte di Catullo** but in fact unrelated to the poet. The view alone justifies the walk out.

Desenzano del Garda, the largest town on the lake, is a busy transportation hub and the best starting point for boat excursions. It has a fine old harbour and a handsome, arcaded main square; a **Parish Church** with a Last Supper by Tiepolo; and an excavated **Roman villa** with 4th-century mosaics.

Beyond Desanzano the highway runs almost due north. To the east is the **Rocca di Manerba,** a panoramic headland high above the lake reached by a narrow, steep road. Here are **Pieve Vecchia,** a village which takes its name from its small Romanesque church; and **San Fermo,** another little church standing on the site of a Roman villa. The promontory stretches towards the islet (private) known as Isola di Garda, with a 19th-century Venetian-Gothic villa.

Salò, the Roman *Salodium,* lies huddled amid green hills on a little bay. The beauty of the site explains its fame, today somewhat marred by the town's association with Mussolini's Repubblica Sociale Italiana (or Repubblica di Salò), established after the armistice of 1943 which brought an end to hostilities between Italy and the Allies. The Repubblica Sociale was a puppet republic set up under Nazi control by the Fascist hard-core, led by Mussolini, who took up residence with his mistress Clara Petacci at nearby Gargnano.

The 'republic' lasted until the war's end, 25 April 1945; three days later Mussolini and Clara were captured and summarily executed while trying to escape to Switzerland. The Gothic **Cathedral** has a Renaissance doorway of 1509, paintings by Paolo Veneziano (west end of the north aisle) and Romanino (in the baptistery), and a carved wooden tabernacle. Villa Fiordaliso (132 Via Zanardelli) was a favourite watering hole of the Fascist élite.

Beyond Salò stretches the Riviera Bresciana, where groves of pine, cedar and olive frame small villages and immense villas, many of which are now hotels. The chief town on this shore is **Gardone Riviera**, with a tranquil lake-front promenade. Its unusually mild climate has made it a popular winter resort, and its parks and gardens are planted with exotic trees. On the north-eastern edge of the town is **Il Vittoriale,** the extravagant villa of Italy's contro-versial poet and militant nationalist, Gabriele d'Annunzio (1863–1938), who is buried here. The villa, which takes its name from the Italian victory over Austria in 1918, is now a museum, and a walk through its uncanny interior and even weirder park are edifying, for lack of a better word. At the northern end of the Riviera Bresciana is **Gargnano**, a lovely town of 19th-century villas with a square opening onto the little harbour. In the country near here D.H. Lawrence wrote *Twilight in Italy*. From Campione del Garda, a few kilome-tres beyond, a mountain road with plenty of curves climbs to **Pieve di Tremòsine**, a village on a steep cliff from which there are spectacular views over the lake, returning to the lakeshore at Limone sul Garda.

Limone sul Garda, amid olive groves and terraced plantations of lemons and limes (whence the name) has some fine houses in the old town centre. It is the last port of call before the main centre of the northern part of the lake, **Riva del Garda**. This, the Roman *Ripa,* has long been admired by Germans: it belonged to Habsburg Austria until it was incorporated into Italy after World War I, and together with the rest of the Trentino, it was briefly annexed by Nazi Germany in the last years of World War II. The highlight of its long, complicated history is the daring endeavour of Stafano Contarini, the Venetian general who, in April 1440, with 2000 oxen and a few hundred men, brought six galleys and 25 smaller boats over the mountains from the River Adige to take the town from Filippo Maria Visconti, Duke of Milan. Riva's villas, avenues, and parks, where the German writers Friedrich Nietzsche and Thomas Mann, and the Czech Franz Kafka once dwelled, extend harmoniously to the River Sarca. In high season the town draws wall-to-wall crowds, due to its singular landscape and ambience, and to its strong, constant breezes, which make it a favourite spot for windsurfing.

Old Riva combines Alpine, Trentine, and Venetian influences. The centre of town life is Piazza III Novembre, on the waterfront, flanked by porticoes. Here rise the 14th-century **Torre Apponale** and, across the square, the complex formed by the **Municipio** (1482) and the 14th-century **Palazzo Pretorio**, where walls beneath the arcades are adorned with Roman and medieval inscriptions. From the foot of the tower Via Gazzoletti leads east to the **Rocca**, a rectangular fortress with corner bastions and a massive keep,

Sirmione, Grotte di Catullo

surrounded by water. Built in the 12th century, it was altered by the Scaligers, the Venetians, and the Austrians. It now houses the town library and the **Museo Civico,** the chief attraction of which is a picture gallery with works by Giuseppe Craffonara (1790–1837), a native and the foremost neoclassical artist of the Trentino. There are also interesting finds from the Bronze Age pile dwellings of Lake Ledro, fossil and naturalistic collections, local memorabilia, a small ethnographic collection, and old weapons and prints.

Beyond the Rocca, in a garden, is the entrance to the **Spiagga degli Olivi**, the town bathing beach. North of the old town, at the end of Viale Roma, is the **Inviolata**, an octagonal church begun in 1603 by an unknown Portuguese architect and displaying an elegant interior decorated with stuccowork and altarpieces, and an 18th-century cloister. **Il Bastione**, a cylindrical tower of 1508 beneath Monte Rocchetta, offers good views over the town and lake and can be reached by foot in about half an hour. Another fascinating spot in the environs, 4km (2½ miles) north on the road for Tenno, is the **Cascata del Varone**, a waterfall that plummets some 87m into a deep, misty gorge.

Torbole to Peschiera del Garda

Tórbole is an elegant resort just east of Riva, with an enchanting view of the lake. On the road to Nago and Arco are the so-called **Marmitte dei Giganti**, a unique formation of pothole-like depressions caused by glacial erosion.

Malcésine, the seat of the Veronese Captains (or governors) of the Lake in the 16th and 17th centuries, is protected by a **Castello** erected on a cliff over-

Street view of Torri del Benaco

looking lake. The fortress, founded by the Scaligers in the 12th century and enlarged by the Venetians in the 17th, has a tall keep and crenellated walls. Goethe drew it in his album and was suspected of being a spy by the guards of the declining Serene Republic. Inside is the small **Museo Ariani** with archaeological material, arms, memorabilia of the Risorgimento and local history. In the adjoining guards' quarters is a natural history collection dealing with Garda and Monte Baldo and, in the former powder magazine, a room devoted to Goethe.

A maze of narrow lanes makes up the old town, the high points of which are the 16th-century **Palazzo dei Capitani del Lago**, its Sala delle Sedute frescoed with coats of arms; and the churches of the **Madonna del Lago** (or del Rosario, 1600–34), and **Santo Stefano** (1729–49), the latter containing a *Deposition* by Girolamo dai Libri. A cableway will take you in roughly 15 minutes up to 1780m where, from the crest of **Monte Baldo**, there is an incomparable 360° view over Garda and the Val d'Adige. For hearty climbers only, a footpath entailing a sustained seven- to eight-hour ascent through the 2000-hectare wilderness of the **Riserva naturale integrale di Selva Pezzi** terminates at the same point. It might be prudent to ride up and walk down.

Torri del Benaco was the Roman *Castrum Turrium* and an important Lombard stronghold. Today it is a quaint little town, with fine old houses around a harbour. Its architectural highlights include the 15th-century Gothic church of the **Santissima Trinità** and the formidable 14th-century **Castello Scaligero**. From the outskirts a mountain road climbs through endless switchbacks to **San Zeno di Montagna** (581m) with a good view over the lake, continuing through forests to **Prada** (1005m), a ski centre and starting point for walks.

Perhaps the most romantic spot on the east shore of the lake is the **Punta di San Vigilio,** the headland that separates Torri del Benaco from the pleasant little bay of Garda. Should you tire of the view from this lovely cypress-lined promontory, take a stroll past the old church of **San Vigilio** or through the beautiful formal gardens of the 16th-century **Villa Guarienti**, attributed to Sanmicheli.

It was **Garda** that gave the lake its name (a corruption of the German *Warte*, 'fortress') in the early Middle Ages, though archaeological evidence suggests that the first settlement on this site dates from Roman or even pre-Roman times. Later a Venetian dominion, today it is a resort with a fine lakeside promenade and environs dotted with dark cypresses and lovely villas. Its chief attractions are the 18th-century **Palazzo del Capitano**, the contemporary church of **Santa Maria Maggiore** (preserving fragments of an earlier, 15th-century edifice) and the **Villa Albertini**, a neo-Gothic folly surrounded by an English garden. Just outside the town rises the **Eremo dei Camaldolesi** (1664–73), a monastery with a painting by Palma Giovane in the church.

The hills become lower and more civilised as you approach **Bardolino**, nestled among the vineyards where pale, light Bardolino wine is made. Here are a couple of very important monuments – the small Latin-cross church of **San Zeno**, one of the few monuments in Italy from the Carolingian period (9th century), with fine pink marble columns; and the Romanesque church of **San Severo** (documented in 893, enlarged in the 12th century and subsequently restored), with a fine porch, a 9th-century crypt and 12th- to 14th-century frescoes. Also interesting are the remains of a **Castle** of the Scaligers (crenellated tower and two gates).

Lazise, with an almost intact circuit of medieval walls, lies amid gentle countryside. Its small harbour, which is all that remains of the *teza* or dock where the Scaligers and the Venetians moored their warships, is quite charming when it is not too crowded. Its main monuments are situated near the water. They are **San Nicolò**, a 12th-century church with 17th-century campanile and 13th-century frescoes by the school of Giotto; and the long, low, 16th-century **Dogana Vecchia**, or customs warehouse, with a portico on the lake. The walls connect to the 14th-century **Castle**, with five towers and a keep. All around the town are olive groves. At **Pastrengo**, about 30km (18 miles) southwest, the **Parco-zoo**, visited on foot (allow approximately two hours), has examples of European, Asiatic and American fauna and reproductions of prehistoric animals; in the **Parco Safari**, visited by car, other animals (mainly African) roam free. **Bussolengo**, a village above the River Adige, has a church (San Valentino) in Romanesque-Gothic style, with 15th- and 16th-century frescoes inside and out. On the other side of the Adige is **Pescantina**, where the Parish Church has 17th- and 18th-century paintings, and zoomorphic capitals from an earlier, Romanesque baslilica.

Peschiera del Garda was originally a Roman town, later a dominion of the Scaligers, then a fortified city of the Venetians, who between 1553 and 1556 built a fortress here to plans by Guidobaldo da Urbino and Michele Sanmicheli. Its historical role is suggested in the military fortifications that surround the Venetian centre, nestled between the lake and its outflow, the River Mincio. The eels of the Roman *Arilica Pischeriae* – from which the modern name of the city derives – are mentioned by Pliny the Elder and appear on the municipal coat of arms. From its history as a fortress comes Dante's definition, *'bello e forte arnese'* (beautiful, strong contrivance) – as well as the Venetian town walls and the Napoleonic and Austrian additions that made it one of the points of the Quadrilateral (a defensive complex that also included Verona, Mantua, and Legnano) during the Risorgimento. The main monument in town is the **Palazzina del Commando del Presidio**, celebrated for the meeting that took place here on 8 November 1917, after the Italian defeat at Caporetto, to organise the new line of defence on the Piave. The building faces the gardens of the **Parco Catullo**, surrounded by buildings housing a small military museum. The southern part of the town, with the regular street plan of a military camp and the fortified **Porta Brescia**, one of the old entrances to the fortress, is also interesting. Children of all ages will probably find Italy's largest amusement park, **Gardaland** – 4km (2½ miles) northwest on the lake shore – even more fascinating.

Torri del Benaco, panorama

Practical Information

Getting There

By **road**, Vicenza, Verona and Lake Garda are all on Italy's main east–west *autostrada*, the A4, from Venice to Milan. All exits for Lake Garda (Peschiera del Garda, Sirmione and Desenzano del Garda) are clearly marked. Verona and Lake Garda can also be reached from Innsbruck (Austria) and the Passo del Brennero via Autostrada A22 and State Highway 12; the *autostrada* continues south to Modena. A secondary road (Highway 240; exit the A22 at Rovereto Sud) connects Rovereto, on the latter route, to Riva del Garda, at the north end of the lake.

Verona stands at the junction of two of Italy's most important **rail** lines. The principal trains connect with Venice, Trieste, Milan, Turin and Genoa; Bologna, Florence and Rome; and Trent, Bolzano and Bressanone. There are direct through services to and from Basel, Berlin, Bern, Dortmund, Geneva, Lugano, Munich, Munster, Nice, Paris, Vienna, and Zurich. The Venice–Milan line also serves Vicenza, Peschiera del Garda and Desenzano del Garda, from which there are frequent country **bus** services to outlying points. Navigazione sul Lago di Garda, Piazza Matteotti, Desenzano (tel. 030 914 1321) operates **ferries and hydrofoils** on Lake Garda; ask the information offices listed below for timetables and fares.

Tourist Information

LAKE GARDA See **Verona**. There are information offices also at **Sirmione**, 2 Viale Marconi (tel. 030 916 114, fax 916 222); **Desenzano del Garda**, 27 Piazza Matteotti (tel. 030 914 1510, fax 914 4209); **Salò**, 39 Lungolago Zanardelli (tel. 0365 21423); **Gardone Riviera**, 35 Corso della Repubblica (tel./fax 0365 20347); **Riva del Garda**, 8 Giardini di Porta Orientale (tel. 0464 554 444, fax 520 308); **Malcésine**, 6 Via Capitanato (tel. 045 740 0044, fax 740 1633); **Garda**, Lungolago Regina Adelaide (tel. 045 725 5194, fax 725 6720); and **Lazise**, 14 Via Francesca Fontana (tel. 40457 758 0114, fax 758 1040).
VERONA 61 Via Leoncino (tel. 045 592 828, fax 800 3638) and 42 Piazza delle Erbe, (tel. 803 0086, summer only).
VICENZA 12 Piazza Matteotti (tel. 0444 320 854, fax 325001)

Hotels

LAKE GARDA
Needless to say, there is no lack of good hotels in this popular holiday spot. At **SIRMIONE**, the **Palace Hotel Villa Cortine**, 12 Via Grotte (tel. 030 990 5890, fax 916 390, offers luxury accommodation in a 19th–century villa with large park, on the lake shore. The moderately priced **Ideal**, 31 Via Catullo (tel./fax 990 4245), enjoys one of the finest settings on the peninsula, a tranquil olive grove overlooking the lake and the Grotte di Catullo.

A good, inexpensive choice at **SALÒ** (località Barbarano) is the Barbarano al Lago (tel. 0365 20324; closed Oct–May), a small (16 rooms), tranquil hotel with a pleasant garden. At **FASANO DEL GARDA**, near Gardone Riviera are two more up–market venues, the **Grand Hotel Fasano e Villa Principe** (tel. 0365 290 220, fax 290 221), a former hunting lodge of the emperors of Austria set in a lovely park with garden terrace overlooking the lake; and the **Villa del Sogno** (tel. 0365 290 181, fax 290 230), another villa in a romantic garden with an immense terrace on the lake. Just down the road are three inexpensive places, all with fine views of the lake and mountains: at **GARGNANO** (Roccolino), the **Roccolino** (tel. 0365 71443, fax 72059; closed Jan–mid-Feb), with just ten rooms; at **TREMOSINE** (Campi-Voltino), **Le Balze** (tel. 0365 917 179, fax 917 033; closed Nov–mid-March) and the **Pineta Campi** (tel. 0365 917 158, fax 917 015; closed Nov–mid-March).

The best hotel in **RIVA DEL GARDA** is the **Du Lac et du Parc**, 44 Viale Rovereto (tel. 0464 551500, fax 555 200), a luxurious establishment in a large park, offering peace and quiet, elegance, and refinement. It is followed closely by the more moderate **Grand Hotel di Riva**, 10 Piazza Garibaldi (tel. 0464 521 800, fax 552 293), another classic hotel with a quiet park, frequented also for its roof-garden restaurant. At **TORRI DEL BENACO** is the inexpensive **Europa** (tel. 045 722 5086, fax 722 5065; closed Nov–Mar), a small establishment (18 rooms) in a renovated villa with a pleasant garden, enjoying splendid views over the lake and mountains.

VERONA

Given its position – midway between Vicenza and Lake Garda – and its considerable architectural and artistic heritage, Verona is the best place to stay west of Venice. The variety of accommodation offered is immense. At the high end are the **Due Torri Baglioni**, 4 Piazza Sant'Anastasia (tel. 045 595 044, fax 800 4130, a 17th-century inn transformed into a luxurious hotel with rooms furnished in different styles using genuine antiques (the restaurant, **L'Aquila**, is also warm and refined) and the **Gabbia d'Oro**, 4a Corso Borsari (tel. 045 800 3060, fax 590 293), a small hotel (27 rooms) known for its genteel, cosy atmosphere, situated halfway down Corso Borsari, in the very centre of the old town.

The mid-range offers several fine choices, including the **Academia**, 12 Via Scala (tel./fax 045 596 222), occupying the former Academy of Fine Arts, not far from the Arena; the **Grand**, 105 Corso Porta Nuova (tel. 045 595 600, fax 596 385), near the train station, with antique furniture, old paintings, and a small garden with fountain; the **Montresor Giberti**, 7 Via Giberti (tel. 045 810 1444, fax 810 0523), in a quiet street, also not far from the station; the **Victoria**, 8 Via Adua (tel. 045 590 566, fax 590 155), occupying a tastefully restored historic building and hosting a small museum of Roman archaeology (near the Ponte della Vittoria, halfway between the cathedral and the Castelvecchio) and the **Giulietta e Romeo**, 3 Via Tre Marchetti (tel. 045 800 3554, fax 801 0862), a well–known establishment situated in the pedestrian area near the Arena.

Two inexpensive venues are the **Torcolo**, 3 Vicolo Listone (tel. 045 800 7512, fax 800 4058; closed in Jan), a warm, cosy hotel in a small square near the Arena but off the beaten track, with restaurant service outside during summer; and the **Cavour**, 4 Vicolo Chiodo (tel./fax 045 590 508, a small place (17 rooms) in a renovated old building near the Castelvecchio.

VICENZA

The **Campo Marzio**, 21 Viale Rome (tel. 0444 545 700, fax 329 495) is a quiet, moderately priced place in the large public garden between the train station and the Corso Palladio. The **Cristina**, 32 Corso Santi Felice e Fortunato (tel. 0444 323 751, fax 543 656; closed 25 Dec–2 Jan and a few days in Aug) is an inexpensive, family–run hotel at the edge of the historic city centre, just outside Porta Giusti.

Restaurants

LAKE GARDA

At **LUGANA**, 5km (3 miles) southeast of Sirmione, is the moderately priced **Vecchia Lugana** (tel. 030 919 012, fax 990 4045; closed Mon evening, Tue and Jan–mid-Feb), with summer seating on a terrace overlooking the lake. Here you'll find creative interpretations of local specialities, with special attention to seasonal dishes – *terrina di pesci gardesani e verdure con salsa alle erbe aromatiche*, fresh pastas with vegetables, and grilled Gardesan meats and fish. At **DESENZANO DEL GARDA** are two more middle-range restaurants: **Esplanade**, 10 Via Lario (tel./fax 030 9143361; closed Wed), with summer seating in a garden overlooking the lake – try the *cappesante in salsa di ostriche* (Oct–Jun), risotto con asparagi fiori di zucchine e zafferano (Apr–Jun), *medaglione di vitello con fiori di zucca, trancio di lucioperca con spinaci e crema di patate* (Mar–Sep), and *mousse al cioccolato con crema alla menta* – and **Cavallino**, 30 Via Gherla (tel. 030 912 0217, fax 991 2751; closed Mon, Tue morning, Jan and Aug mornings), known for its *tortino di coregone su mousseline di patate, faraona all'uva nera e porcini* (summer–autumn), *pescatrice e gamberi al nero di seppia*.

At **GARDONE RIVIERA** the **Ristorante Hotel Villa Fiordaliso**, with seven rooms (tel. 0365 20158, fax 290 010; closed Mon and Jan–Feb), occupying an old villa in a small park with summer seating on a terrace overlooking the lake, has been in business since 1890. Specialities include *piovretta all'alloro e fagiolini fini; tagliolini neri con calamari, piselli e bottarga di muggine; filetto di cavedano all'aceto di Groppello con polenta n'onsa; petto di faraona con melanzane; gelato di cannella con pere al vino rosso*. Prices are moderate. At **GARGNANO**, by the harbour, **La Tortuga** (tel. 0365 71251; closed Mon evening, except Jun–Sep, Tue, and a few days in Jan), is a more expensive place known for its *charlotte di melanzane, spaghettini di pasta fresca al pesce di lago, filetti di persico croccanti in battuta di rosmarino, sella di coniglio al profumo di timo* and *torte di pere con salsa di fragole* and its excellent selection of regional, Italian, and imported wines. At **TORRI DEL BENACO** you'll find moderately priced local cuisine and regional wines at **Al Calval**, a restaurant with rooms (tel. 045 722 5666, fax 629 6570; closed Mon, mid-Jan–Feb and mid-Nov–mid-Dec), and at **PESCHIERA DEL GARDA**, similar fare at somewhat lower prices at **Papa** (also with rooms), 40 Via Bella Italia (tel. 045 755 0476, fax 755 0589; closed Wed and Nov–early Dec).

ROVERETO, 21km (13 miles) east of Riva del Garda on the road to Trent, has one of the restaurants best loved by residents of the area: **Al Borgo**, 13 Via Garibaldi, (tel./fax 0464 436 300; closed Sun evening, Mon, and a few days in Feb and Jul). Try the *sformato di cappesante e zucchine con salsa allo zafferano* (spring–summer), *scaloppa di cernia gratinata su letto si spinaci* and *strudel di ciliegie tiepido con bavarese al Kirsch* (summer). There is a good selection of regional, Italian, and imported wines, and prices are moderate.

VERONA

The Veronese love good food, and consequently Verona has some of the finest restaurants in Italy; unfortunately, few are inexpensive. **Arche**, 6 Via Arche Scaligere (tel. 045 800 7415; closed Sun, Mon morning and Jan), a seafood restaurant near Sant'Anastasia, has been in business since 1879. Specialities are *chela di astice in foglia di zucchino* and *gamberone in foglia di melanzana; zuppa di capelonghe* and *risotto con pesce e basilico; branzino al Camembert* and *Sanpietro ai funghi porcini; plateau di formaggi Caprini sardi e della Valle d'Aosta serviti con miele di acacia* and *zuppa di mirtilli*. **Il Desco**, 7 Via Dietro San Sebastiano (tel. 045 595 358, fax 590 236; closed

Sun and a few days in Jan and Jun), near the Adige on the east side of the city centre, features innovative cuisine. Try the *tortino di patate con funghi pioppini e tartufo nero, zuppa di patate e tartufo bianco in crosta di pane, filetti di triglia impannati al rosmarino* and *filetto di manzo all'Amarone*. **Dodici Apostoli**, 3 Vicolo San Marco (tel. 045 596 999, fax 800 4827; closed Sun evening, Mon and a few days in Jan and Jun), an elegant restaurant located in a historic building in the heart of the city centre, has been serving traditional Veronese dishes since 1750. Strong points include the *crespelle di asparagi* and *zuppa scaligera; garberoni alla cardinale* and *patisada di caval*. All the above offer a wide selection of regional, Italian and imported wines, and all are expensive.

More moderately priced, but certainly not to be overlooked, is **Maffei**, 38 Piazza delle Erbe (tel. 045 801 0015, fax 800 5124; closed Sun; also Mon in Jul and Aug), with pavement seating in Verona's most colourful square in summer. Try the *tagliolini freschi alle capesante, spada al pomodoro fresco* (seasonal), *vitello alla fonduta e tartufi* and *crêpe al croccantino*. The same holds for the **Bottega del Vino**, 3 Via Scudo di Francia (tel. 045 800 4535, fax 595 291; closed Tue and Feb), a very traditional Veronese restaurant in a quiet lane off Via Mazzini. Sure bets are the *bogoli e fasoi, risotto* and *brasato all'Amarone, pastissada de caval* and *sbrisolona*. The vino is Italian, and there is a good variety.

VICENZA

Across the River Bacchiglione from the city centre is **Cinzia e Valerio**, 65/67 Piazzetta Porta Padova (tel. 0444 505 213, fax 512 796; closed Mon, early Jan and a few days in Aug), a seafood restaurant generally considered the best (and most expensive) place in town. The *brodetto di pesce con alghe marine, sogliole nostrane dell'Adriatico ai ferri* and home-made pastries and ice-cream come with a good selection of regional and Italian wines. Occupying tastefully furnished rooms in an aristocratic palace of the 15th century, one block north of Corso Palladio, is the more moderate A**ntica Trattoria Tre Visi**, 6 Contrà Porti (tel. 0444 324 868; closed Sun evening, Mon and Jul), serving Vicentine specialities with regional and Italian wines. The similarly priced **Scudo di Francia**, 4 Contrà Piancoli (tel. 0444 323 322; closed Sun evening, Mon, Christmas–Epiphany and a few days in Aug), just a few steps from the Basilica, also offers classical Vicentine cuisine: *risotti di verdure* (with asparagus, peas, *bruscandoli*, or mushrooms, depending on the season), *ravioli con radicchio trevisano, baccalà alla vicentina, fesa di vitello in salsa tartufata* and *zuppa di more* are house specialities.

Vicenza's best inexpensive restaurants lie on the outskirts of the town. **Da Remo**, 14 Via Caimpenta, Caimpenta (tel. 0444) 911007, fax 911856; closed Sun evening, Mon, Aug and late Dec–early Jan) is 2km (1¼ miles) east. It is a converted farmhouse with garden seating in summer, serving regional dishes such as *bigoli all'anatra, baccalà alla vicentina*, Asiago and Vezzena cheese and *torta di pere*. At **Tinello**, 181 Corso Padova (tel. 0444 500325; closed Sun evening, Mon and a few days in Aug), a renovated train station provides the setting for a popular restaurant serving local delicacies with regional and Italian wines.

Special Events

LAKE GARDA
RIVA DEL GARDA: **Intervela** (international sailing week, Jul); **Musica Riva** (international conference of young musicians, Jul); **Flicorno d'oro** (international band competition, Aug); **Mostra Internazionale di Musica Leggera Vela d'oro** (pop music festival, Sep).

VERONA
Stagione Sinfonica (classical music, at the Teatro Filarmonico, Feb–Apr); **Settimana Cinematografica Internazionale** (film festival, Apr); **Estate Teatrale** (drama at the Roman theatre, Jun–Aug); **Stagione Lirica** (opera at the Arena, Jul–Aug).

VICENZA
Stagione Concertistica al Teatro Olimpico (classical music at the Teatro Olimpico, May–Jun).

Museums and Monuments

LAKE GARDA
SIRMIONE, **Grotte di Catullo**: Tue–Sun, Apr–Sep 9.00–18.00; Oct–Mar 9.00–16.00.
DESENZANO DEL GARDA, **Villa Romana**: Tue–Sun, Apr–Sep 9.00–18.00; Nov–Feb 9.00–16.00; Oct and Mar 9.00–17.30; **Museo Archeologico**: Tue, Fri, Sat, Sun and hols 15.00–19.00.
GARDONE RIVIERA, **Vittoriale degli Italiani**: Apr–Sep 8.30–20.00; Oct–Mar 9.00–12.30, 14.00–17.30.
RIVA DEL GARDA, **Museo Civico**: 9.00–12.00,14.30–18.30; summer 16.00–22.00.
MALCÉSINE, **Museo Ariani**: Mar–Oct 9.30–19.00; Dec–Feb Sat and Sun 12.00–17.00, closed Nov; **Museo del Castello Scaligero**: Tue–Sun, Apr–Oct 9.30–19.00; Nov–Mar 11.00–17.00.
PESCHIERA DEL GARDA, **Parco Catullo**: Tue–Sun 10.00–12.00, 16.00–18.00; **Gardaland**: 9.00–dusk.
PASTRENGO, **Parco Zoo**: Nov–15 Mar, 9.00–16.00; 16 Mar–Oct, 9.00–18.00; closed Wed; **Parco Safari**: Apr–Sep 9.00–12.00, 13.00–17.00; Oct – afternoons only.

VERONA
Torre dei Lamberti: Wed–Sun 9.30–13.30, Sat 9.30–18.00; lift.
Giardini di Palazzo Giusto: daily 9.00–dusk; summer 9.00–20.00.
Archaeological area of the Roman Theatre: Tue–Sun 8.00–13.30.

Museo Archeologico: as the Theatre.
Museo Lapidario Maffeiano: Tue–Sun 8.00–13.30.
Arena: Tue–Sun 8.00–18.30, during opera season 8.00–13.00.
Casa di Giulietta: Tue–Sun 8.00–18.30.
Civico Museo d'Arte di Castelvecchio: Tue–Sun 8.00–18.30.
San Fermo Maggiore: Mon–Sat 9.00–18.00, Sun and hols 12.00–18.00.
Sant'Anastasia: Mon–Sat 9.00–18.30, Sun and hols 13.00–18.30.
Cathedral, San Giovanni in Fonte and Sant'Elena: Mon–Sat 9.30–18.00, Sun. 13.00–18.00.
San Lorenzo: Mon–Fri 9.00–18.30, Sun and hols 10.00–18.30.
San Zeno Maggiore: Mon–Sat 8.30–18.30, Sun and hols 13.00–18.30.

VICENZA
Criptoportico Romano: Sat 10.00–11.30.
Galleria d'Arte Municipale: Tue and Sat 10.00–12.30, 16.00–19.00, Sun 10.00–12.00.
Basilica: Tue–Sat 9.30–12.00, 14.30–17.00, Sun 10.00–12.00.
San Nicola da Tolentino: ring bell on left flank to open.
Santa Corona: Oct–May 9.30–12.30, 15.00–18.00; Jun–Sep 8.30–12.30, 15.00–18.30.
Teatro Olimpico: mid-Mar–mid-Oct 9.30–12.20, 15–17.30, Sun and hols 9.30–12.20; mid-Oct–mid-Mar 9.30–12.20, 14–16.30, closed Sun afternoon.
Museo Civico: 9.00–12.30, 14.30–17.30, closed Sun afternoon and Mon.
Museo del Risorgimento e della Resistenza: Tue–Sat 9.30–12.00, 14.30–17.30, Sun – morning only.
Villa Valmarana ai Nani: mid-Mar–Nov, Tue, Thu, Sat, Sun 10.00–12.00; Tue–Sun 15.00–18.00.
La Rotonda: mid-Mar–Oct Tue–Sun 10–12.00, 15.00–18.00; interior Wed only.

10. THE EASTERN ALPS

Strictly speaking, the Dolomites are the mountains of the Eastern Alps that lie between the Adige and Piave rivers. But anyone who has seen them knows that they are much more than that. 'The Dolomites ... recall quaint Eastern architecture, whose daring pinnacles derive their charm from a studied defiance of the sober principles of stability.... The Dolomites are strange adventurous experiments, which one can scarcely believe to be formed of ordinary rock. They would have been fit background for the garden of Kubla Khan,' wrote Leslie Stephen in *The Playground of Europe* (1871). This region, the 'Playground of Europe', has attracted visitors for centuries. Only recently (in the last ten years or so), large areas of its unique landscape have come under special tutelage. The major nature reserves of the Dolomites are dealt with at length in this chapter. So, too, are the region's three main cities, Trento, Bolzano and Bressanone – Germanic enclaves in the Latin Southern Alps – each of which has its own, distinctive charm.

Trento

A pre-Roman Raetian settlement in which traces of Celtic influence have been found, **Trento** was Romanised in the course of the 1st century BC and became a *municipium* and an honorary colony (called *Tridentum*) in the Antonine period. Laid out on a regular plan around the *Capitolium,* which stood on the Doss Trento, the lone hill that rises above the left bank of the Adige, it was later extended along the left bank of the Adige. During the Middle Ages Trento owed its importance to its position on the main road from the Germany to Italy. Invaded by the Goths, Lombards, and Franks, it became an episcopal fief in 1027, its bishops acquiring the temporal power that they held almost without interruption until 1802. The city reached its peak of splendour in the 16th century. This was the period of the extraordinary bishop-prince, Cardinal Bernardo Clesio, who gave the city the Renaissance appearance that still characterises its central streets. He and his successor, Bishop Cristoforo Madruzzo, prepared the famous Council of Trent, which met in several sessions, between 1545 and 1563, in the cathedral and in

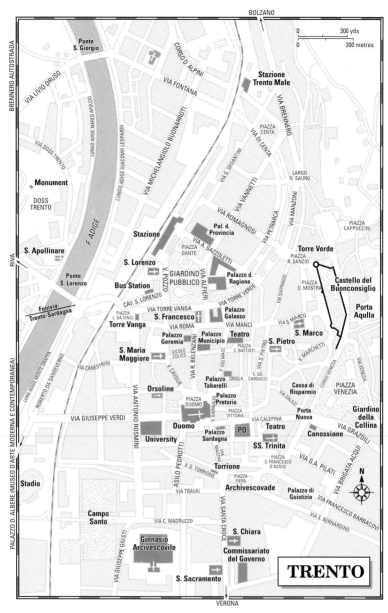

Santa Maria Maggiore, to redefine the course of the Catholic Church after the Reformation. The following periods are remembered only for the campaigns of the War of Spanish Succession, when Trento was unsuccessfully besieged by Marshal Vendôme (1703); the French occupations of 1796 and 1801 (the secularisation of the principality dates from 1802); the brief unions with

Palazzo Geremia, Trento

Bavaria (1806–09), and with Napoleon's Kingdom of Italy (1810–13); and the long Austrian occupation, which ended only in 1918.

Piazza del Duomo

Piazza del Duomo is the monumental centre of the city. It is an extraordinarily handsome square, with an 18th-century Neptune Fountain standing in the shadow of the 13th-century **Palazzo Pretorio** and **Torre Civica** (in front of which some Roman ruins have been excavated), and the 16th-century **Case Cazuffi**, adorned with frescoes by Fogolino and preceded by the small

Fontana dell'Aquila. On the south side of the square extends the austere left flank of the **Cathedral of San Vigilio**, a Romanesque-Gothic building of the 12th and 13th centuries with a powerful 16th-century campanile and a Romanesque-revival dome. Faced entirely in marble, it has magnificent decorative detailing and a beautiful apse against which stands the 13th-century Castelletto, with mullioned windows and crenellated roof.

The interior has three tall aisles with compound piers, a small clerestory in the nave, and cross vaults. Arcaded staircases ascend the west wall, amid 16th-century tomb monuments, to the galleries. The large Cappella del Crocifisso, in the south aisle, preserves a 16th-century wooden crucifix before which the decrees of the Council of Trent (1543–63) were promulgated. In the transepts are remains of 13th- and 15th-century frescoes, and at the end of the north aisle, a 13th-century stone statue known as the *Madonna degli Annegati* (Madonna of the Drowned), at the foot of which people drowned in the Adige were identified. It used to stand in a niche outside. The baldachin over the high altar makes deliberate reference to that of St Peter's in Rome. Beneath the church are some masonry, remains of a mosaic pavement, and sculptural fragments from the 6th-century early Christian basilica, which was rebuilt in the 11th century and replaced by the present building two centuries later.

The **Museo Diocesano**, in the Palazzo Pretorio, once the bishops' palace, has a wonderful collection of paintings and sculpture from local churches and the most valuable objects from the cathedral treasury. These include the 13th-century treasure of Bishop Federico Vanga, the 15th-century crosier of Bishop Giorgio Hack, and a fine series of 16th-century Flemish tapestries by Pieter van Aelst.

From Via Belenzani to the River

Via Belenzani, the city's elegant shopping street, is flanked by Renaissance palaces showing a strong Venetian influence, some – like the 16th-century **Palazzo Geremia** (No. 19) and Palazzo Alberti Colico (No. 32) – with frescoed façades. Across the street stands Palazzo Thun, today the town hall. At the corner here Vicolo Colico leads left to **Santa Maria Maggiore**, a Renaissance church of 1520–24 with a remarkable doorway and a fine campanile. Several sessions of the Council of Trent were held here, including the last one. The *Assumption* over the high altar is by Pietro Ricchi, a pupil of Guido Reni; the marble cantoria of 1534 is a masterpiece of the Vicentine sculptors Vincenzo and Gian Gerolamo Grandi.

Via Belanzani ends before the church of San Francesco Saverio, a fine example of local Baroque architecture; you take Via Manci to the right. Here, too, are some interesting 16th- and early 17th-century houses, notably No. 63, the Baroque Palazzo Galasso; No. 57, **Palazzo Pedrotti**, with a small museum of mountain-climbing; and, at the corner of Via del Suffragio, Palazzo del Monte, with a fine door and frescoes depicting the Labours of Hercules, executed around 1540.

Via San Marco, the continuation of Via Manci, ends at the foot of the **Castello del Buonconsiglio**, once the stronghold of the bishop-princes. The crenellated Castelvecchio, on the north, was built in the 13th century and altered in 1475. It has a pretty courtyard with porticoes and frescoes, some by Fogolino (1535). The Magno Palazzo, on the south, is a Renaissance edifice built in 1528–36 by Bernardo Clesio. Its great loggia overlooks the Cortile dei Leoni, frescoed by Girolamo Romanino (1531-32). Beyond the gardens – where you can see the cells of Damiano Chiesa, Cesare Battisti and Fabio Filzi, Austrian-born Italian patriots who were shot as traitors here in 1916 – is the **Museo del Castello del Buonconsiglio**, housing the municipal collections of antiquities, coins, manuscripts and incunabula, liturgical objects, paintings and ethnographical material. The museum occupies the rooms of the Magno Palazzo, some of which have carved wooden ceilings and 16th-century frescoes by Dosso Dossi, Romanino and Fogolino. The custodian will show you some more frescoes – a delightful 15th-century Gothic cycle representing the Months (March has been lost) in the adjacent Torre dell'Aquila. The castle complex also houses the **Museo Civico del Risorgimento e della Lotta per la Libertà** with memorabilia mainly of the 19th-century irredentist movement, of World War I, and of the Resistance.

On the right bank of the Adige is the 14th-century church of Sant'Apollinare, with a doorway and rose window in Veronese red porphyry, a distinctive pointed roof and polygonal apse. Behind it rises the hill known as the **Doss Trento**, crowned by the mausoleum of Cesare Battisti, from which there is a fine view over the city. Nearby are the remains of an early Christian basilica and, to the south, the **Museo Storico delle Truppe Alpine**, tracing the history of the famous Italian Alpine Corps.

Returning to the left bank and walking southwards, you eventually come to **Palazzo delle Albere**, a square suburban villa encircled by a moat, built around 1535 for Bishop-Prince Cristoforo Madruzzo. Decorated with frescoes of which only traces remain today, it is home to the Trentine section of the **Museo d'Arte Moderna e Contemporanea di Trento e Rovereto**, with works by Depero, Marinetti, Ballo, Cangiullo, Prampolini, and other artists of the Futurist area; and exhibitions of contemporary art.

The Paneveggio-Pale di San Martino Nature Park

The marvellous peaks of the Pale di San Martino and the vast national forest of Paneveggio comprise this spectacular nature reserve in the province of Trento, opened in 1987. It is an area of extraordinary beauty, marred only by the presence of ski slopes around the popular resort of **San Martino di Castrozza**, which though surrounded by the park does not fall under its protection.

The park covers an area of 190 square kilometres, geology of which varies considerably from place to place. The northwestern region is characterised by porphyritic rock of volcanic origin and by areas of sandstone and marl; the

Around Trento

Monte Bondone, cloaked in forests, overlooks the city from the southwest. It is known for its alpine flora (it produces herbs used in baths in special establishments) and as a ski resort. The Conca delle Viotte, set beneath the peaks of the massif (Palon, 2090m; Doss d'Abramo, 2140m; and Monte Cornetto, 2180m), hosts the **Giardino Botanico Alpino**, with over 2000 plant species from the Trentino and the principal mountains of the world. Sixteen kilometres (10 miles) west of the city, the **Lago di Toblino**, lying amid rocky mountains in the valley of the Sarca, is overlooked by a medieval castle. The lake is joined by an isthmus to the **Lago di Santa Massenza**, surrounded by olive trees. At **Mattarello**, near the airport, the modern **Museo Aeronautico Gianni Caproni** has 18 antique planes and various exhibits regarding the history of flight in Italy. The resort of **Vigolo Vattaro** has a 16th-century church and castle.

The most important town in the environs of Trent is **Rovereto**, a city possibly of Roman origin, spread out at the foot of a 14th-century castle. The castle is now home to the **Museo Storico Italiano della Guerra**, with some 30 rooms devoted to World War I. The 15th-century Palazzo del Municipio has remains of façade frescoes attributed to Fogolino, and the contemporary Palazzo della Cassa di Risparmio shows Venetian influence. The town is the birthplace of Fortunato Depero, the Futurist painter (1892–1960), whose works can be seen at the **Museo Fortunato Depero,** 53 via della Terra. Temporary exhibitions of early 20th-century art are held at the Archivio dell Novecento, 58 Corso Risimini.

southwest by Palaeozoic metamorphic rock, and the southeast (the Pale di San Martino area) by Triassic dolomite, of which the highest mountains – the Cima della Vezzana (3192m) and the Cimon de la Pala (3184m) – are made.

The great green mantle of the **Foresta di Paneveggio**, which occupies the upper valley of the Travignolo, includes 2690 hectares of conifers and 1300 hectares of active pastures. Although it suffered extensive damage during World War I, it remains an example (rare in Italy) of correct forest management, where a century-old tradition inaugurated during the Austro-Hungarian period has been carefully preserved. Here you'll find red and white firs, larches, cembra pines, yews, and various deciduous trees, including beeches, oaks, and aspens. At higher altitudes the ground is covered with scrub pine and rhododendron, whortleberry and heather.

The flora of the park presents a wide variety of alpine species, among which edelweiss, dwarf rhododenron, the indigenous bellflower *Campanula morettiana*, poppies, gentians and arnicae. The most interesting area is the Val Venegia, where you can find over 500 species, among them rare endemic plants such as *Saxifraga facchinii, Primula tyrolensis, Juncus arcticus* and *Dactilorhiza cruenta*.

The park's fauna includes hundreds of chamois and roe-deer, and numerous deer, which were extinct in the area until they were reintroduced in the 1960s. Present in good numbers also are marmot, squirrel, hare, ermine, weasel, marten and fox. Among the more interesting birds are the royal eagle, dwarf owl, white partridge and black woodpecker.

Walk: Val Venegia

Departure point: Passo Rolle (1980m), on State Highway 50. Time: 8 hours. Difficulty: easy (though long).

This walk, in addition to interesting fauna and flora (the Paneveggio Forest), offers a text-book tour of the Dolomites' chief geological formations, ranging from the crystalline calcium magnesium carbonate that gives the mountains their name, to magmatic porphyry, to sedimentary Werfen strata.

From the curve just east of the Passo Rolle you take a dirt road that climbs northwards to the **Capanna Cervino** (2082m) and, beyond the Passo Costazza, to the **Rifugio Segantini** (2174m), amid stunning scenery. From the shelter, a dirt track descends into the stupendous Val Venegia beneath the steep walls of the **Cimon della Pala** (3184m), the **Vezzana** (3192m) and the **Bureloni** (3130m). At an altitude of 1884m you turn right on Trail 749, which climbs through the vast pastures of the Buse dei Laibi to the **Forcella Venegia** (2217m), where it joins the Dolomite High Trail No. 2. Heading northwest, you soon reach the **Passo Vallès** (2032m), with its shelter (tel. 0437 50270). From here you descend on the dirt road to **Malga Vallazza** (1935m), where you pick up, heading south, an old military mule track that crosses the **Paneveggio Forest**, passes near the **Malga Juribrutto** (1912m) and descends to Paneveggio. From here you can return to the Passo Rolle on foot or by bus.

Bolzano

Mentioned for the first time (as *Bauzanum*) by Paulus Diaconus in his medieval history of the Lombards, **Bolzano** (in German, Bozen) formed part of the episcopal principality of Trento in the 11th century and was joined to the Tyrol in the 16th century. The oldest part of the city grew up around the little Romanesque church of San Giovanni in Villa (12th century), but the greatest building activity was in the Gothic period, when Bolzano became a major mercantile centre. Long a possession of the bishop-princes of Trento, it eventually passed to the Counts of the Tyrol, who were succeeded by the Dukes of Carinthia and, after 1363, the Dukes of Austria. The Habsburgs held the city until 1918, except during the Napoleonic period, when it was briefly united first with Bavaria and then with the Napoleonic Kingdom of Italy. In the late 19th century the old city, having remained substantially unchanged over the centuries, grew to include the elegant suburb of Gries. In the 1930s industrial development gave rise to a number of new factories and working-class neighbourhoods towards the west and south, which also changed the city's predominantly German ethnic composition by attracting large numbers of labourers from Southern Italy.

City Sights

Today the city centre is still **Piazza Walther**, which takes its name from a monument erected in the 19th century to the medieval German poet Walther von der Vogelweide, thought to have been a native of the region. Here stands the **Cathedral**, a Gothic church of the 14th and 15th centuries (damaged in World War II and restored after 1945) with an elegant apse, a steep tiled roof and a fretwork spire. Fine doorways and reliefs adorn the exterior; the three-aisled interior has frescoes of the 14th to the 16th century, a fine pulpit with reliefs, of 1514, and a great Baroque altar. The **Chiesa dei Domenicani,** one block west, is the old church of the Italian community in Bolzano. It too was damaged in the war and has subsequently been rebuilt. The interior preserves remains of 14th- and 15th-century frescoes. Over the last north altar is a restored altarpiece by Guercino (1655); and adjoining the apse, the Cappella di San Giovanni, with fine frescoes by followers of Giotto (c 1340). More frescoes, dating from the 14th to the 16th centuries, are in the Gothic cloister (entrance at No. 19A), the Chapter House and the Cappella di Santa Caterina. Piazza Domenicani ends on the west at the corner of Via Sernesi, where an obtrusive iron palisade marks the entrance to the **Museion-Museum für Moderne Kunst**, with a small permanent collection of modern and contemporary art and an excellent programme of temporary exhibitions.

Returning to the church, turn left at the east end of the square to reach Piazza delle Erbe, the site of a colourful fruit and vegetable market. This lively square, at the crossing of two major pedestrian streets, is flanked by fine old houses and adorned, on one side, by the 18th-century Fontana del Nettuno, with a bronze statue by Giorgio Mayr, a local artist. To the east stretches the straight, narrow Via dei Portici, the oldest thoroughfare in the city and now also its main shopping street. It is flanked by handsome porticoed houses dating from the 15th to the 18th century, with distinctive bay windows; at no. 39 (the main façade is in Via Argentieri) is the Baroque **Palazzo Mercantile** (1708), by the Veronese architect Francesco Pedrotti.

From Piazza delle Erbe Via dei Francescani winds northwards to the 14th-century Gothic **Chiesa dei Francescani**, with a richly carved high altar (1500) and a graceful 14th-century cloister with fragmentary frescoes. At the next corner Via Vinfler leads right to the **Museo Provinciale di Scienze Naturali**, devoted to the landscape and ecosystems of the upper valley of the Adige. Continuing along Via Hofer you take your first left, first right, and first left again to reach **San Giovanni in Villa**, the oldest church in Bolzano, built in the 13th century and enlarged in the early 14th. It has a powerful Romanesque-Gothic campanile and 14th-century frescoes.

Via del Museo, also with elegant shops (and cafés serving unforgettable cakes and pastries) leads west to the **Museo Civico**, in the former Hullach mansion at the corner of Via Cassa di Risparmio. It contains antiquities from Mesolithic times to the Roman age (such as the anthropomorphic *Menhir of Lungostagno* and the Bronze Age *Sword of Hauenstein*), ethnographic material (notably a collection of costumes, household articles and reconstructions of *stube* from old farmhouses), and a picture gallery with works by local artists of the 15th century (including numerous shuttered altars and wood sculptures).

The Ponte Tàlvera crosses the river to the **Monumento della Vittoria**, a huge triumphal arch erected to a design by the Roman architect Marcello Piacentini in 1928. The monument, seen as a provocation by ethnic Germans, has been the object of several terrorist attacks and is now inaccessible. On the river banks are parks with beautiful promenades. The promenade on the east bank leads northwards to join the Passeggiata Sant'Osvaldo, which climbs the slopes of the Renon hill, offering splendid views back over the town and valley. At the foot of the hill the promenade passes the medieval Castel Mareccio, now a convention centre.

East of the Tàlvera, Corso Libertà leads through the rationalist neighbourhoods of the early 20th-century extension of the city to the garden suburb of Gries. On the main square is the **Abbazia dei Benedittini**, whose late Baroque church (1771) has frescoes and altarpieces by the Tyrolean painter Martin Knoller. A little further on is the old Gothic **parish church**, with a carved and painted altarpiece by Michael Pacher (1475).

Walks out of Town

One of the characteristic features of Bolzano is the amazing number of walks you can take in the immediate environs of the city. The **Passeggiata del Guncina** winds up the hill behind the parish church in Gries to the Castel Guncina (476m), with great views over Bolzano and the Dolomites. The path, cut out of a porphyry wall, is planted with Mediterranean flora. The **Passeggiata Sant'Osvaldo-Santa Maddalena** ascends the hill of Santa Maddalena, with a Romanesque church of Mary Magdalen in a picturesque setting amid vineyards. It can be followed from Via Sant'Osvaldo to the Lungotàlvera and vice versa. A cableway (lower station in Via Sarentino) climbs the 1087m to **San Genesio Altesino**, a busy summer and winter resort on the Altopiano del Salto, with splendid views over the Val Sarentina and the Dolomites. Another cableway starts from Via Renon and mounts to **Soprabolzano** (Oberbozen), on the Renon highland north of the city. Near **Collalbo**, the main town of the plateau and an excellent starting point for walks and climbs, are the earth-pillars of Longomoso, the most dramatic of the many examples of this curious erosion phenomenon in the area; the path continues to the Rifugio Corno di Renon (2259m, a three-hour ascent), commanding a magnificent view.

You need a car to reach **Castel Ròncolo** (Schloss Runkelstein), a 13th-century castle on a cliff-top at the mouth of the Val Sarentina. Inside are fres-

Street in Bolzano

coes of late medieval court life and stories of Tristan and Isolde (in the Palazzo Occidentale, Stua da Bagno and Sala del Torneo), 16th-century scenes of chivalry (in the Casa d'Estate) and a *Martyrdom of St Catherine* (in the 13th-century chapel). **Terlano** (Terlan), 10km (6¼ miles) northwest on the road to Merano, is the centre of a wine-growing district. It has a Gothic parish church with a 15th-century fresco of St Christopher on the façade and two campanili.

The Sciliar Nature Reserve

Established in 1974, the **Parco Naturale dello Sciliar** combines the rocky walls, cliffs and ledges of the Sciliar massif with the verdant pastures of the Alpe di Siusi, where traditional human activities are allowed, but new building (including ski lifts) is strictly limited and the circulation of motor vehicles is forbidden.

The geological history of the Sciliar can be read clearly by following the succession of rock layers from the lowest altitudes (where the oldest formations are to be found) up. Above the dark-red quartz-bearing porphyry of the Adige valley are the sandstones of the Val Gardena which, because of their high iron content, colour the soil of the fields red. Higher up, covered by forests, are rocks that were formed just 65 million years ago, in the Permian and lower Triassic eras. There follow layers of sedimentary and volcanic rock – a clear sign that the coral reefs of the ancient Mediterranean (which over time would become the pink stone of the Sciliar) were periodically submerged beneath layers of lava and ash (to which the soil of the Alpe di Siusi, by the way, owes its fertility).

The fact that it was spared by the glaciers of the Pleistocene era and is constituted of a variety of rocks of diverse origin has allowed the Sciliar to accommodate an extraordinary variety of plant species. In addition to the common alpine flowers (gentians, primroses, crocuses, anemones) you'll find numerous saxifrages (*S. oppositifolia, S. caesia, S. squarrosa*), the so-called '*strega dello Sciliar*' (*Armeria alpina*), edelweiss, alpine poppies, streaked daphnae, and many more. In the forests, keep an eye out for chamois, roe-deer, hare and ermine; sparrowhawks and various owls; grouse, white partridge, alpine crows, black woodpeckers, and numerous sparrows.

The park is reached via **Siusi/Seis am Schlern**, a summer and winter resort with a pleasant main square, or **Castelrotto/Kastelruth,** a fairy-tale village huddled around a massive (and loud) 18th-century campanile and taking its name from the medieval castle, set on a wooded knoll a short way from the village square. **Tires** and **San Cipriano** are the gateways to the wild Val Ciamin and the adjacent Catinaccio/Rosengarten mountain group, the mythical lair of the dwarf-king Laurin.

Walk: To the Rifugio Alpe di Tires

Departure point: Malga Ciamin/ Tschaminschwaige (1184m), reached from Tires via San Cipriano and the road (left) for Bagni di Lavina Bianca. Time: 6-7 hours. Difficulty: moderate.

From the car park at the Rifugio Tschaminschwaige you cross the bridge over the Rio di Ciamin and follow the mule track (Trail 3) that climbs in switchbacks through fir woods to reach a forest road. By this road and another mule track (marked) you ascend the forested Valle di Ciamin and, beyond a malga, climb left to the base of the rocky walls of the gorge known as the Buco dell'Orso. After crossing the stream at an altitude of 1890m, you leave on your right Trail 3a, which leads to the Rifugio Bergamo, and climb left over stony ground dotted with scrub pine to the steep walls of the Buco dell'Orso. The trail, fitted with a steel cable that you'll want to grasp tightly in the narrower stretches, climbs the rocks on the right of the gorge and comes out on the pastures dominated by the Cima di Terrarossa (2655m) where you are joined by Trail 4 from the Rifugio Bolzano. Turning right, in just a few minutes you comfortably reach the **Rifugio Alpe di Tures** (*Tierser Alpe,* 2441m, tel. 0471 727 958), beneath the imposing bastions of the Denti di Terrarossa. The return can be made along the same route, or if you want to avoid the Buco dell'Orso, by taking the trail that, climbing southwards over the **Passo di Molignon** (2598m) and the **Passo Principe** (2400m), leads to the **Rifugio Bergamo** (2134m), from which it is easy to descend to the Val Ciamin. This route will take at least an hour longer.

Bressanone

Bressanone (in German, Brixen) stands at the meeting-point of two Alpine streams, the Isarco and the Rienza, and of two important old roads, from the Val Pusteria and the eastern Tyrol, and from Brennero and Austria. Situated in a lovely open landscape of cultivated hills between steep mountain peaks and green forests and meadows, the city conserves the austere mark of its history as a centre of a vast ecclesiastical principality. The power of its bishop-princes in fact lasted 800 years, from 1027 to 1803. The Germanic quality of its architecture, monuments, and artworks, which embody the full variety of styles from the Romanesque to the Baroque (it is the largest art centre of the Alto Adige), carries the peculiar inflections of a site on a cultural frontier.

The **Cathedral**, built in the 9th century, enlarged in the 13th century, and completely rebuilt in Baroque forms in 1745–90, dominates the shady Piazza del Duomo. The beautifully preserved interior is adorned with ceiling frescoes by the Austrian artist Paul Troger, and fine carvings. In the adjacent Romanesque **cloister** are 14th- and 15th-century frescoes of Old and New Testament scenes and the entrance to the 11th-century Baptistery, which hosted the famous council called in 1080 to depose Pope Gregory VII (Hildebrand) and elect the antipope Clement III.

The **Palazzo dei Principi Vescovi** is a fortified building, behind a moat, in the nearby Piazza del Palazzo. Built in the early 13th century by the bishop-prince Bruno de Kirchberg, it was several times enlarged and then rebuilt as a Renaissance château, after 1595, for Cardinal Andrea of Austria. Altered in Baroque style after 1710, it remained the residence of the bishop-princes and the administrative centre of their fief until 1803. It has an elegant façade and an imposing courtyard with 24 life-size terracotta statues representing members of the Habsburg family.

The interior hosts the **Museo Diocesano**, with one of the largest art collections in Northeastern Italy. It includes sculptures, paintings and medieval decorative arts from churches in the area; original furnishings of the bishop's residence; objects from the cathedral treasury dating from the 12th to the 16th century; manuscripts and incunabula, old fabrics, embroideries and vestments; diplomas and seals of the bishop-princes and of the aristocracy; and, last but not least, an extraordinary collection of *presepi*, or Christmas crêches, ranging in date from the 18th to the 20th century.

Adjoining Piazza del Duomo on the north, Piazza della Parrocchia takes its name from the 15th-century Gothic parish church of **San Michele**, with a spired campanile called the Torre Bianca. Inside are 18th-century frescoes by the Viennese painter Josef Hautzinger. To the north of the church stands the Renaissance **Casa Pfaundler** (1581), a medley of Nordic and Italian elements. From here Via dei Portici Maggiori, a lovely old street full of shops, leads westward, flanked by houses of the 16th and 17th centuries, many with crenellated roofs and bay windows. At No. 14, the old **Municipio** has a painting of the *Judgement of Solomon* in the courtyard.

The courtyard of the Palazza dei Principi Vescovi, Bressanone

221

Around Bressanone

To explore the lovely environs of Bressanone you don't necessarily need wheels. The **Rifugio Città di Bressanone/Plosehütte,** an alpine shelter in an incomparable setting at 2447m, can be reached by cableway, or by 23km of scenic highway in the Valle d'Eores. In the latter case you drive as far as Valcroce/Kreuztal, 2050m, then continue the ascent on foot (1.30hr) or by chairlift. The shelter is on the southern crest of the Cima della Plose, 2504m, a massif frequented for as much for its spectacular views over the Dolomites and the Alpi Aurine as for its excellent skiing.

Surrounded by meadows and vineyards 3km north on the main road to Brennero and the Val Pusteria (Highway 12) is the **Abbazia di Novacella/Neustift**, a vast complex of monastic buildings ranging in date from the 12th to the 18th century. Among the older structures are the circular chapel of San Michele (12th century, fortified in the 16th century); the campanile (12th to 13th century); the cloister, rebuilt at the end of the 14th century, with frescoes of the same period; the Romanesque chapel of San Vittore, with frescoes of the early 14th century; and the monastery church (Santa Maria Assunta), a Romanesque foundation rebuilt in Bavarian Baroque form in the 18th century and adorned with exuberant frescoes by Matthäus Gündter of Augsburg, a disciple of G.B. Tiepolo. Also noteworthy is the Biblioteca, by Antonio Giuseppe Sartori (1773), with stoccoes by Hans Mussack. It preserves some 75,000 volumns and 14th- and 15th-century paintings by local artists. On a steep rock nearby is the **Monastero di Sabiona**, an episcopal seat under the patriarch of Aquileia from the 6th to the 10th century. Destroyed in the 16th century and rebuilt in the 17th, it preserves parts of its ancient walls.

Interesting castles in the area include the **Castello di Rodengo/Schloss Rodeneck** (868m), a 12th-century fortress over-looking the valley of the Rienza near the ski resort of Rio di Pusterìa/Mühlback; and **Castello di Velturno/Schloss Ziernberg,** 3km southwest, the Renaissance summer residence of the bishops of Bressanone. Both have frescoes inside.

The Vedrette di Ries Nature Reserve

Established in 1989, the **Parco Naturale Vedrette di Ries** covers a surface of 21,850 hectares between the Val Pusteria and the Valle di Anterselva on the south, the Val di Tures on the west, the Valle Aurina on the north and the Austrian border on the east. In addition to the crystalline Riesenferner group, the park includes the southwest slopes of the Durreck massif. These mountains constitute a small subgroup of the chain of the Alti Tauri (Hohen Tauren);

nevertheless they include a dozen peaks over 3000m and some fine glaciers on the northern slopes – the Vedrette di Ries and the Schneebiger Nock, Gelttal and Althaus.

The rocks that form much of the Riesenferner group are gneiss and schists extant in the Palaeozoic era, which were subjected to metamorphosis during the formation of the Alps. On the wooded northern slopes of the Durreck massif you find schists belonging to the so-called *finestra dei Tauri,* while the main chain of the Riesenferner, which includes the **Collalto** (Hochgall, 3436m), the highest peak, is composed of a powerful mass of solid tonalite inserted among more fragile schists and gneiss.

The glaciers of the Pleistocene have deeply moulded these mountains, transforming the heads of the valleys into glacial cirques, carving grooves in the mountain walls, accumulating moraines along their path and hollowing in the rock the niches now occupied by numerous **high-mountain lakes,** found mainly between 2200 and 2500m. Lower down, the streams have formed spectacular gorges and **cascades** like the Cascate di Riva, near Campo Tures. Among the geological peculiarities of the park are the **erosion pyramids** (*Platten*) on the right orographic side of the Val Pusteria. At the head of the Valle di Anterselva is one of the larger lakes of the Alto Adige, the **Lago di Anterselva,** formed by the alluvial cones that descend the southern slope of the Collalto and the Rotwand. At the entrance to the same valley, but outside the borders of the park, is the **biotope of Rasun,** a wetland frequented by migratory birds.

A continental climate and the siliceous nature of the soil are the main influences that have shaped plant life in the Riesenferner group. The most common tree in the forests is the red fir, in the shadow of which rhododendron and whortleberry form a sort of underwood. On the sunnier slopes, larches also grow. Deciduous trees are few and far between, with the notable exception of a local variety of sorb (or service tree). The tree line reaches a maximum of 2200m, but a few isolated cembra pines can be found as high up as 2465m on the Tristennöckl, at the foot of the Vedretta di Tristen (Tristenkees). The most beautiful flowers in the park – which include arnica, bellflowers, anemones, dwarf primrose, edelweiss, dwarf gentian, saxifrages and artemisia – grow in the high-mountain meadows and amid the rocks and rubble at the foot of the peaks.

The forests are populated by numerous roe-deer and deer, as well as by badgers, foxes, martens, squirrels and several native species of birds (*crociere, nocciolaia,* etc.). It is also possible to spot royal eagles, grouse, owls, marmots, chamois, white partridges, ermine, crows and the alpine finch. Invertebrates include some beautiful butterflies.

The nearest town is **Brunico** (Bruneck) the city of Bruno, a 13th-century bishop of Bressanone who is traditionally credited with founding it. Set amid a broad circle of wooded hills topped with castles, it stands at the mouth of the Valle di Tures. The main Via di Città is lined with pretty alpine houses with bay windows and fanciful gables; many of the shops have old (or old-fashioned) wrought-iron signs. The castle, on a hill, was built in the 13th and 14th

Interior of the Abbazia di Novacella, Bressanone

centuries and altered in the 15th and 16th centuries. In the courtyard are frescoed coats of arms. In the suburb of Teodone (Dietenheim), on the Mair am Hof farm, is an interesting museum of local agricultural methods and folk customs, the Museo Provinciale degli Usi e Costumi.

Walk: Cascate di Riva

Departure point: Winkel (860m), near Campo Tures. Time: 1½–2½ hours (round trip). Difficulty: easy.

Near the bridge at Winkel signs mark the beginning of the trail to the waterfall, a mule track that enters the forest toward the east. After about 200m, a sign indicates on the left the turning for the first, spectacular cascade on the **Torrente di Riva**. From here you climb through the forest to rejoin the mule track, which you follow uphill as far as a rock on the left in the woods. Here you leave it again, following the signs for the second and third cascade. After passing a dizzying viewpoint on the second cascade, the path climbs again and, after skirting the edge of the ravine, reaches the third waterfall, which ends in a narrow gorge crossed by a small iron bridge. Beyond the bridge you clamber up steep steps through the woods to a fork where, on the left, you can climb in five minutes to the Ristorante Toblhof and the paved road, or on the right, you can follow a brook and a steep climb to the ruins of the 12th-century **Castello di Tobl**. From here you can return to Winkel by the same route or reach the road and return to Campo Tures by bus.

The Fanes-Sennes-Braies Nature Reserve

Established in 1980, the **Parco Naturale Fanes-Sennes-Braies** covers 25,680 hectares. Situated between the Val Pusteria on the north and the Val Badia on the west, the park extends eastwards to the Val di Landro and the Parco delle Dolomiti di Sesto, whereas on the south it joins with the Parco Regionale delle Dolomiti d'Ampezzo.

The three parks form an immense reserve that is unique in the world. The central nucleus of the protected area is formed by the limestone plateaux of Fanes and Sennes, separated by the deep furrow of the Val dai Tàmersc and dominated on the north by the Dolomiti di Braies with the **Croda Rossa** (3148m, the highest peak of the park), the **Picco di Vallandro** (2839m) and the **Croda del Becco** (2810m), at the foot of which lies the marvellous **Lago di Braies**.

Imposing stratifications of sedimentary dolomite constitute the geological underpinnings of these mountains. Over these lie deposits of Jurassic limestone (Piccola and Grande Alpe di Fanes, Alpe di Sennes, Croda del Becco, Croda Rosso), often marked by dolinas, furrows, etc., caused by water erosion of the porous stone. Here surface waters vanish rapidly in the subsoil, leaving on the plateaux especially those of Sennes and Fosses, a fairly arid environment where streams flow only during summer storms and spring thaw.

This fact determines a marked contrast between the high central areas, with scarse plant cover, and the lower regions, on the mountainsides and in the valleys, where the waters re-emerge: these are covered by dense forests of red fir, alternating, at the higher altitudes, with larch and cembra pine. Further up, beyond the low growths of scrub pine, rhododendron, and whortleberry, the alpine meadows, rocks and rubble are populated by a rich alpine flora that includes the *papavero retico, linaiola alpina,* certain saxifrages, *androsace, raponzolo chiomoso, semprevivo delle Dolomiti,* edelweiss, *orecchia d'orso,* and many other species.

The park's fauna includes roe-deer, chamois and small colonies of ibex in the area of the Croda del Becco, where they were introduced in the 1960s. There are also the classic alpine mammals (marmots, hare, ermine, weasel), amphibians (*rana temporaria, tritone alpino*) and a wide variety of birds (royal eagle, kestrel, owls, crows, grouse, white partridge, red woodpecker, *picchio muraiolo, crociere,* alpine finches, *spioncello, fiorancino, cinca dal ciuffo,* etc.).

Walk: Via della Pace to Monte Vallon Bianco (2687m)

Departure point: Rifugio Pederù (1545m), reached from San Vigilio di Marebbe via the long Valle di Tamores. Time: 8–9hrs. Difficulty: moderate.

From the Rifugio Pederù you climb by a dirt track (Trail 7) that ascends the Valle di Rudo below by way of the steep walls of the Furcia dai Fers on the right, and of the Croda Ciamin on the left. In about two hours you reach the Malga Fanes Piccola and the shelters of **La Varella** (2042m, tel. 0474 501 092) and **Fanes** (2060m, tel. 501 097). If you want to shorten the walk you can take one of the jeeps that ferry visitors back and forth from the Rifugio Pederù. From the Rifugio Fanes you climb in a southeasterly direction by a mule track (Trails 10, 11, and 17), which leads to the **Passo di Limo** (2172m) and to the little lake of the same name, overlooking the broad basin of the Alpe di Fanes Grande. From here you descend to the **Malga di Fanes Grande** (2104m), then continue southwards (Trail 17) to the fork where Via della Pace begins on the left. This is an Austrian military trail from World War I, recently restored, which, passing beneath the Cime di Furcia Rossa, climbs with a last steep tract to the crest of the Furcia Rossa, near the **Bivacco Baccon-Baborka** (2665m), overlooking the deep Val Travenanzes and the Tofane massif. From here, on the ridge top, you reach the panoramic peak of **Monte Vallon Bianco** (2687m). The return follows the same course.

The Dolomiti di Sesto Nature Reserve

The **Parco Naturale Delle Dolomiti di Sesto** was established in 1981 and extends over 11,650 hectares. Seen from the Val Pusteria, the landscape of the here is indescribably dramatic. In the foreground are the subgroups of the Baranci and the Tre Scarperi, among which open two parallel valleys (Val di

Dentro and Val Fiscalina) closed at their upper ends by the spectacular vertical walls of the **Tre Cime di Lavaredo** (2999m), the **Paterno** (2744m), and **Cima Dodici** (3094m).

The oldest rocks of this last northeastern bastion of the Dolomites are conglomerates of porphyry and sandstone, buried beneath layers of black limestone, dolomite and grey marl. Werfen layers reach altitudes of nearly 2000m; but they are largely concealed by dense forests. The spectacular dolomitic peaks were formed in the Middle and Upper Triassic periods, 65 million to 1.8 million years ago. During the Ice Age the region was almost completely buried beneath a gigantic glacier, which has left clear signs of its presence – particularly in the Valle del Rio Alto Fiscalina, where you can see moraines and streaked and round-backed rocks formed by the retreating ice. Today the glaciers have practically disappeared.

The forests here (which reach a maximum altitude of 1900m), are composed mainly of red fir mixed with larch and a few, rare white firs and cembra pines. Sylvan pine grows in groups in the Val di Landro on the more arid slopes. Above the tree line scrub pine and rhododendron abound. Interesting semi-natural environments are the *prati a larice* ('larch meadows') of the Val Fiscalina and Val Campo di Dentro. The flora includes several species of gentians (for example, *G. punctata* and *G. asclepiadea*), saxifrages (*S. squarrosa, S. oppositifolia, S. caesia*), edelweiss and alpine poppies, just to mention a few.

There is quite a variety of fauna, too, including chamois, roe-deer, deer, marmots, hares, foxes, badgers, martens, weasels and ermines. Other mammals include the alpine bat (*Hypsugo savii*), which is found in the forests and even above the tree line. Among the numerous species of birds are royal eagles, sparrowhawks, goshawks, falcons, owls, grouse, white partridge, the black woodpecker, and some 70 songbirds.

The Dolimiti di Sesto take their name from the village of **Sesto** (Sexten), a small summer and winter resort with a Baroque parish church (San Vito), frescoed houses, and a small museum with works by local painter Rudolf Stolz (1874–1960). Of greater interest, however, is **San Candido** (Innichen), where the **Collegiata**, perhaps the most beautiful Romanesque church in the Dolomites, was consecrated in 1284. It stands on the site of an 8th-century Benedictine monastery and preserves its Lombard Romanesque appearance despite 15th-century alterations. **Dobbiaco** (Toblach) was the summer retreat of the Austrian composer Gustav Mahler. The parish church of San Giovanni Battista dates from 1769; the castle, from the 16th century. At the southern extreme of the park is **Cortina d'Ampezzo,** once frequented by the best society and now definitely *démodé*. It has a parish church with a wooden tabernacle carved by Andrea Brustolon and an altarpiece painted by Antonio Zanchi; a small Geological Museum; and a picture gallery containing works by modern Italian masters.

Walk: Rigugio Zsigmondy-Comici to Rifugio Locatell

Departure point: Hotel Dolomitenhof (1454m) in Val Fiscalina, near Sesto Pusteria. Time: 6½–7½ hours. Difficulty: moderate.

From the car park of the Hotel Dolomitenhof you set out along the valley floor through meadows and pine woods, reaching in roughly half an hour the Rifugio Fondovalle (*Talschlusshütte*, 1526m). From here you continue along Trail 102-103 in the Valle di Sasso Vecchio (Altsteiner Tal) to a fork where you take the trail on the left (No. 103) which, passing beneath the rocks of **Cima Uno** (2698m) climbs to the **Rifugio Zsigmondy-Comici** (2224m, tel. 0474 70358). From the shelter you follow Trail 101, in a westerly direction, climbing steeply to the Passo Fiscalino and then climbing more gently to the **Rifugio Pian di Cengia** (*Büllele Joch Hütte*, 2528m, tel. 0474 70258), among clear signs of World War I. From the shelter, again on Trail 101, you descend to the slopes of **Monte Paterno** (2744m) and then, after a short climb, reach the **Rifugio Locatelli** (*Drei Zinnen Hütte*, 2405m, tel. 0474 72002), from which you have a spectacular view over the **Tre Cime di Lavaredo** (2999m). From the shelter, Trail 102 descends to Val di Sasso Vecchio, by way of the Laghi dei Piani, and returns to the Val Fiscalina.

Practical Information

Getting There

The international **airports** nearest to Trento, Bolzano and Bressanone are at Verona in Italy, and Innsbruck in Austria.

By **road** the area is reached from Verona or Innsbruck by Autostrada A22 and State Highway 12. A long but scenic road (State Highway 38) connects Lombardy with Bolzano via the Stelvio Pass, and a series of beautiful but tiring mountain roads link Trieste, Venice, Padua and Vicenza with Trento and Bressanone.

Trento, Bolzano and Bressanone are on the main **rail** line from Verona to Innsbruck (with direct through service to Munich, Munster, Dortmund, Berlin and Vienna; or in the other direction, to Florence, Rome and Naples). A secondary **rail-and-bus** line runs from Padua to Cortina d'Ampezzo via Castelfranco, Feltre and Belluno, with connections for the Val Pusteria, Bressanone and Bolzano; and there are frequent bus services between Trento and Bolzano and all points in the Dolomites.

To reach the northern area of the **Parco Naturale Paneveggio-Pale di San Martino** take Autostrada A22 north from Verona or south from Innsbruck to the Egna-Ora exit, then State Highway 48 to Predazzo and State Highway 50 to Paneveggio. To reach the southern area, take Highway 47 from Bassano del Grappa to Primolano, then Highway 50 to San Martino di Castrozza. By train, take the branch line from Padua to Feltre and proceed to San Martino by bus. Maps: Kompass 1:25,000, Parco Naturale Paneveggio-Pale di San Martino.

To reach the **Parco Naturale dello Sciliar** take Autostrada A22 north from Verona or south from Innsbruck, exiting for Tires, Siusi or the Val Gardena (northern region). By train, take the Brennero line to Bolzano or Ponte Gardena, from which country buses run to the principal centres in and around the park. **Maps**: Tabacco 1:50,000, sheet 02 Val Gardena-Alpe di Siusi-Marmolada; Kompass 1:50,000, sheet 59 Gruppo Sella e Marmolada; Tabacco 1:25,000, sheet 05.

To reach the **Parco Naturale delle Vedrette di Ries** take Autostrada A22 north from Verona or south from Brennero, exiting at Bressanone for the Val Pusteria and Brunico. From Brunico follow the Valle di Tures to Riva di Tures, in the centre of the park. By train, take the Verona–Brennero line and change at Fortezza for Brunico, from where country buses reach the towns of the Valli di Tures and Anterselva. **Maps**: Kompass 1:35,000, sheet 082 Monti di Valle Aurina; Freytag & Berndt, 1:50,000, sheet S3 Pustertal-Bruneck-Drei Zinnen.

To reach the **Parco Naturale Fanes-Sennes-Braies** take Autostrada A22 north from Verona or south from Brennero, exiting at Bressanone for the Val Pusteria (State Highway 49), which you follow to the turning for Val Badia (western area, Fanes and Sennes), Lago di Braies (northern area) or Val di Landro (eastern area). From the Veneto take State Highway 51 to the Val di Landro and Val Pusteria via Cortina d'Ampezzo; or turn west at Cortina to enter the Val Badia via the Passo di Falzarego and Passo di Valparola. From the Friuli the Val Pusteria is entered via the Passo di Monte Croce Comelico. By train, take the Verona–Brennero line and change at Fortezza for Brunico or Dobbiaco. From Brunico there are frequent country buses to the centres of the Val Pusteria, Val Badia, and Val di Landro. **Maps**: Freytag & Berndt, 1:50,000, sheets S3 Pustertal-Bruneck-Drei Zinnen (Sennes and Braies areas) and S5 Cortina d'Ampezzo-Marmolada-Ortisei (Fanes area); Kompass 1:50,000, sheets 57 Brunico-Dobbiaco and 55 Cortina d'Ampezzo; Tabacco 1:25,000 sheets 07, 03 and 010.

To reach the **Parco Naturale delle Dolomiti di Sesto** take Autostrada A22 north from Verona or south from Brennero, exiting at Bressanone and following the Val Pusteria (State Highway 49) to Dobbiaco (Val di Landro) or to San Candido (Val di Sesto). From Venice take State Highway 51 to Dobbiaco via Cortina d'Ampezzo. From the Friùli take Highway 52 to the Val di Sesto via the Passo di Monte Croce Comelico. By train, take the Verona–Brennero line, changing at Fortezza for Dobbiaco or San Candido. There are bus connections from these towns to the centres of the Landro, Sesto and Fiscalina valleys. **Maps**: Freytag & Berndt, 1:50,000, sheet S3, Pustertal-Bruneck-Drei Zinnen; Kompass 1:50,000, sheet 58, Dolomiti di Sesto; Tabacco, 1:25,000, sheet 010.

Tourist Information

TRENTO 132 Corso III Novembre (tel. 0461 98000, fax 231 597); 4 Via Alfieri (tel. 983 880, fax 984 508).

BOLZANO 8 Piazza Walther (tel. 0471 970 660, fax 980 300).

BRESSANONE 9 Viale Stazione (tel. 0472 836401, fax 36067).

PARKS **Parco Naturale Paneveggio-Pale di San Martino**, Sede (park offices), 19 Via Roma, 38054 Tonadico (tel. 0439 64854, fax 762 419); Centri Visitatori (Visitors Centres), Paneveggio-Predazzo (tel. 0462 576 283); San Martino di Castrozza (tel. 0439 768 859); Azienda Promozione Turistica di San Martino di Castrozza e Primiro, 165 Via Passo Rolle, 38058 San Martino di Castrozza (tel. 0439 68352, fax 768 814). **Parchi Naturali dello Sciliar, Dolomiti di Sesto, Fanes-Sennes-Braies, Vedrette di Ries**, Ufficio Parchi, Provincia Autonoma di Bolzano, 21 Via Cesare Batisti (tel. 0471 994 300); Ufficio Provinciale per il Turismo dell'Alto Adige, Servizio Informazioni Alpine, 8 Walther Platz, 39100 Bolzano (tel. 0471 993 809, fax 993 899).

Hotels

BOLZANO

Here you are likely to find a great many visitors from Austria and Germany, as well as a wide range of hotels to accommodate them. Undoubtedly the finest in town, the **Park Hotel Laurin**, 4 Via Laurin (tel. 0471 311 000, fax 311 148), is named after the mythical dwarf–king of the Dolomites. It is a great historic hotel in a lovely park a stone's-throw from the train station and from Piazza Walther.

The **Alpi**, 35 Via Alto Adige (tel. 0471 970 535, fax 400 156), is a modern place conveniently located near the train station; the **Grifone-Greif**, 7 Piazza Walther (tel. 0471 977 056, fax 980 613), established in the 16th century and managed by the same family since the early 19th century, is located across the square from the cathedral. A pleasant garden where meals can be taken in summer and a traditional *Stube* for colder weather make the less centrally located **Luna-Mondschein**, 15 Via Piave (tel. 0471 975 642, fax 975 577) a nice place to stay. All the above are moderately priced.

The most attractive of the inexpensive hotels are the **Scala-Stiegl**, 11 Via Brennero (tel./fax 0471 976 222), a fully renovated turn–of–the–century house with spacious rooms and garden restaurant; and the **Magdalenerhof**, 48a Via Rencio (tel. 0471 978 267, fax 981 076), a carefully appointed place with Tyrolean ambience, set amid vineyards on the outskirts of town. On the Renon hill above Bolzano, the **Kemten**, at Caminata (tel. 0471 356 356, fax 356 363; closed mid-Nov–mid-Dec and mid-Jan–early Feb), is a particularly tranquil place in a lovely park with great views of the Dolomites and a very good restaurant. The **Lichtenstern**, at Costalovara/Wolfsgruben (tel./fax 0471 345 147), is set in an immense park with walking paths and a playground. Both of these are also inexpensive.

BRESSANONE

This is the best place to stay if you wish to explore Bolzano and Trento as well as the Sciliar, Dolomiti di Sesto, Fanes–Sennes–Braies, and/or Vedrette di Ries parks without changing hotels. The **Elefante**, 4 Via Rio Bianco (tel. 0472 832 750, fax 836 579; closed mid-Nov–Christmas and 7 Jan–March), is a 16th–century building with antique furniture, a large garden, and a fine restaurant. It takes its name from an illustrious guest of the former coach–stop, an elephant en route to the court of Archduke Maximilian of Austria. The **Dominik**, 13 Via Terzo di Sotto (tel. 0472)830 144, fax 836 554; closed Dec–Easter), is an extremely refined, comfortable place in a quiet, secluded position amid trees and lawns yet within walking distance of the cathedral; it has an excellent restaurant, with table service under an arbour in warm weather. The **Grüner Baum**, 11 Via Stufles (tel. 0472 832 732, fax 832 607; closed late Nov–early Dec), offers a cordial, homey atmosphere in an elegant old house on the left bank of the Isarco, near the Dominik. All are moderately priced.

The **Gasser**, 19 Via Giardini (tel. 0472)832 732, fax 832 697; closed late Nov–early Dec), is particularly good value. It is situated in the oldest part of town, near the Parco Rapp, and guests use the pool and other facilities of the Grüner Baum, which is under the same management. At Cleran (Klerant), 5km (3 miles) south, is another attractive place, the **Fischer** (tel. 0472 852 075, fax 852 060; closed Nov), in a magnificent position overlooking Bressanone and the Valle d'Isarco; inexpensive.

PARCO NATURALE DELLO SCILIAR

Moderately priced hotels in the area include **Emmy**, at Fie' allo Sciliar (tel. 0471 725 006, fax 725 484; closed Nov–Mar), in a fine position surrounded by meadows, with views of the forests and mountains; the **Schlosshotel Mirabell**, 1km (half a mile) north of Siusi (tel. 0471 706 134, fax 706249; closed mid-Apr–May and mid-Oct–mid-Dec), in a tastefully renovated villa; the **Sporthotel Floralpina**, 50 Saltria, Alpe di Siusi (tel. 0471 727 907, fax 727 803; closed mid-Apr–mid-Jun, and mid-Oct–Dec), in a picturesque location with views of the mountains and forests; the **Steger Dellai** (tel. 0471 727 964, fax 727 848; closed Oct–Nov and May), with swimming in a nearby lake; and the **Cavallino d'Oro-Goldenes Rössl**, on the main square of Castelrotto/Kastelruth (tel. 0471 706 337, fax 707 172; closed Nov–Dec), dating back to the 14th century and offering the most distinctive Tyrolean atmosphere, including two fine Stuben. Simpler and less expensive is the **Waldrast**, 25 Via Hauenstein, Siusi (tel. 0471 706 117, fax 707 062; closed Oct–Dec and late Apr–early May).

PARCO NATURALE DOLOMITI DI SESTO

Near the park are the **Park Hotel Sole Paradiso-Sonnenparadies** at San Candido/Innichen (tel. 0474 73120, fax 73193; closed Apr–May and Oct–Nov), offering warm atmosphere, good location, and a great restaurant; the **Sport e Kurhotel Bad Moos** at Moso/Moos (tel. 0474 70365, fax 70509), a modern establishment incorporating 15th- and 16th-century Stuben, in a fine location; and the **Dolomiti–Dolomitenhof**, at Campo Fiscalino/Fischleinboden), 4km (2½ miles) south of Sesto/Sexten (tel. 0474 70364, fax 70131), starting point for most excursions in the Val Fiscalino and Tre Cime areas of the park as well as a marvellous place to stay. All three hotels are moderately priced. If you're looking for an inexpensive place, try the **Alpino Monte Rota-Alpen Ratsberg**, at Monte Rota (Radsberg, 1650m), 5km (3 miles) northwest of Dobbiaco/Toblach (tel. 0474 72213, fax 72916; chair lift; closed mid-Apr–May and Nov–mid-Dec). Fresh air, magnificent surroundings, and a view you won't soon forget more than compensate for the trouble of getting here.

PARCO NATURALE FANES-SENNES-BRAIES

The hotels and restaurants of the lower Val Pusteria are equally convenient for this park and the **PARCO NATURALE VEDRETTE DI RIES**. On the Riscone highland, 3km (1¾ miles) southeast of Brunico (Bruneck) is the **Rudolf**, (tel. 0474 570570, fax 550806) in truly splendid surroundings. At San Vigilio di Marebbe is the **Hotel Monte Stella** (tel. 0474 501034, fax 501714; closed mid-Apr–mid-May and mid-Oct–mid-Dec), a delightful villa in *Jugendstil*, built for the Austrian aristocracy at the turn of the century and tastefully renovated. An eminently charming place. At Valdàora/Olang) the **Posta-Post**, 6 Vicolo della Chiesa, Valdàora di Sopra/Oberolang (tel. 0474 46127, fax 48019; closed mid-Apr–mid-May and mid-Oct–mid-Dec), offers a beautiful position, comfortable rooms and horses on request. Both are moderately priced. The **Messnerwirt**, 7 Vicolo della Chiesa, Valdàora di Sopra/Oberoland (tel. 0474 46178, fax 48087; closed Nov–Dec), cosy and distinctive; the **Berghotel Zirm**, at Sorafurcia (1360m; tel. 0474 592 054, fax 592 051; closed mid-Apr–May and Nov–mid-Dec), a warm, friendly place in a truly magnificent position; and the **Chalet Olympia** (tel. 0474 944 079, fax 944 650; closed May, Jun and Nov), and **Alpenhof** (tel. 0474 944 212, fax 994 775; closed mid-Apr–mid-May and mid-Oct–mid-Dec), at Monguelfo/Welsberg, are inexpensive and perfectly comfortable.

PARCO NATURALE PANEVEGGIO-PALE DI SAN MARTINO

Physically in the centre of the area, but outside the park boundaries is **SAN MARTINO DI CASTROZZA**, with several fine hotels. **Des Alpes**, 118 Via Passo Rolle (tel. 0439 769 069, fax 769068; closed Mar–Jun, mid-Sep–Christmas); the **Colfosco**, 8 Via Passo Rolle (tel. 0439 68319, fax 68427; closed mid-Apr–mid-Jun and mid-Sep–mid-Dec); the **Cristallo**, 51 Via Passo Rolle (tel./fax 0439 68134; closed mid-Apr–mid-Jun and mid-Sep–mid-Dec); the **Letizia**, 8 Via Colbricon (tel. 0439 768 615, fax 762 386; closed mid-Sep–Dec and Easter–Jun); the **Regina**, 154 Via Passo Rolle (tel./fax 0439 68017; closed April–mid-Jun and mid-Sep–Dec); the **San Martino**, 277 Via Passo Rolle (tel. 0439 68011, fax 68841; closed mid-Apr–Jun and mid-Sep–Christmas); and the **Stalon**, 21 Via Pez Gaiard (tel. 0439 68126, fax 768 738; closed Apr–May and Oct–Nov), are all warm, comfortable, and moderately priced places enjoying views of the forests and mountains.

TRENTO
Because it is not a resort (notwithstanding its many natural and cultural assets) Trento is somewhat short on good hotels. Two comfortable, moderately priced places are the **Buonconsiglio**, 16–18 Via Romagnosi (tel. 0461 980 089, fax 980 038; closed for a few days in Aug), situated between the train station and the castle; and the **America**, 50 Via Torre Verde (tel. 0461 983 010, fax 230 603), between the castle and the cathedral.

Restaurants

BOLZANO
The large, comfortable bar at the Hotel Laurin is frescoed with the legend of King Laurin, and is a good place to spend an evening with friends (summer seating on the open veranda) even if you don't stay there. The **Belle Epoque** restaurant (tel. and fax as the hotel), one of the finest in the city, serves traditional local dishes prepared with great care – *tagliolini con asparagi e gamberi, saltimbocca di rana pescatrice, bavarese al caffè* – with a wide selection of regional, Italian and imported wines. Its prices are surprisingly moderate, given the setting, and you get excellent value. Elegantly decorated interiors and summer garden service go hand in hand with skilfuly prepared traditional dishes to make **Da Abramo**, 16 Piazza Gries (tel. 0471 280 141, fax 288 214; closed Sun and a few days in Aug), one of the favourite restaurants of Bolzanini. Here, too, you'll find an interesting wine list and moderate prices.

Inexpensive places include **Amadè**, 8 Vicolo Cà dè Bezzi (tel./fax 0471 971 278; closed Sun and a few days in Aug), offering traditional cuisine with a personal twist – specialities include *paté di fagiano, sfogliatina di asparagi, filetto di cavallo in crosta d'aglio, capriolo con castagne, tortino di ricotta* and *mousse di cannella*; **Rastbichler**, 1 Via Cadorna (tel./fax 0471 261 131; closed Sat morning and Sun, and a few days in Jan and Jul), a well-known place with a nice garden for the warmer months, offering periodic 'gourmet weeks'; and **Da Cesare**, 15 Via Perathoner (tel. 0471 976 638, fax 972 792; closed Mon), a friendly, centrally located establishment where fresh pasta and grilled meats are specialities.

BRESSANONE
If you prefer something simpler than the fancier restaurants mentioned in the Hotels section, above, try one or both of Bressanone's inexpensive eating places. **Oste Scuro-Finsterwirt**, 3 Vicolo del Duomo (tel. 0472 835 343, fax 835 624; closed Sun evening, Mon, and a few days in Jan and Jun), is a characteristic Tyrolean restaurant established in 1879, with a lovely garden for the warm months. An innovative twist on traditional recipes gives rise to specialities such as *fagottini di rocotta con ripieno di spinaci, filetto di manzo con mantello di speck, testina di vitello marinata con insalata di verdura*, and *soufflé di ricotta in mela al forno*, and there is a good selection of regional and Italian wines. **Fink**, 4 Via Portici Minori (tel. 0472 834 883, fax 835 268;

closed Tue evening, except Jul–Oct, Wed and two weeks in Jul), is a homey place established in 1896, serving local specialities. Try the *frittelle di patate e di grano saraceno, zuppa di vino, cervo* and *montone al forno,* local cheeses (Zieger, Graukaese, Lista), strudel and *semifreddo ai mirtilli.*

PARKS

After a brisk walk in the **PARCO NATURALE PANEVEGGIO-PALE DI SAN MARTINO**, stop in at Malga Ces, at Ces, 3km (1¾ miles) west of San Martino (tel. 0439 68145, fax 68223; closed May–Jun and Oct–Nov), an elegant and inexpensive restaurant in a magnificent position, serving traditional Tyrolean fare with regional and Italian wines – specialities include *paté di selvaggina, risotto alle erbe, zuppa montanara, crespelle alle noci, tagliata alle erbe fini, capriolo al firno, piatto Ces (polenta gialla, salsiccia alla brace, funghi trifolati e Tosella), sella di vitello al tartufo,* apple strudel and cheesecake – or at the slightly more expensive **Tressane**, 30 Via Roma, Tonacico (tel. 0439 62415, fax 762 204), another traditional restaurant in splendid ni, atural surroundings, specialising in *bocconcini di capriolo su insalatina, torte agli ortaggi, faraona alla creta, carne salada e fasoi, crostata alla crema di lamponi, fragole flambées con gelato,* and offering a good selection of local cheeses (Tosella, Monte, Asiago).

If you go to the **PARCO NATURALE DELLO SCILIAR**, try **Heubad** (with rooms), 13 Via Sciliar, Fie' (tel. 0471 725 020, fax 725 425), a family-run restaurant in a historic building, now a hotel with pool and garden, in a good position – specialities include *terrina di selvaggina, crema d'orzo, agnello al forno, braciola di manzo con cipolle, semifreddo alla menta, krapfen* and grappe – or **Tschafon** (tel./fax 0471 725 024; closed Mon and a few days in Jan and Nov), a small, cosy restaurant (with rooms), offering refined, creative interpretations of regional and French cuisine. Both are inexpensive.

Near the **PARCO NATURALE DOLOMITI DI SESTO** your best bets are **Gratschwirt** (with rooms), 1km (half a mile) southwest of Dobbiaco/Toblach (tel. 0474 72293, fax 72915; closed Tue, Easter–May and mid-Oct–mid-Dec), offering regional specialities prepared with care; and **Kupferdachl**, at San Candido/Innichen (tel. 0474 913711; closed Thu, late Jun and two weeks in Nov), with friendly ambience and excellent regional cuisine that appeals to locals as well as to travellers. Both are inexpensive. Near Cortina d'Ampezzo are the moderately priced **Tivoli**, 2km (1¼ miles) northwest of the town (Località Lacedel; tel. 0474 866 400, fax 3413; closed mid-Apr–mid-Jul and Oct–Nov), a good restaurant that is even better in summer, when you can eat outside on the terrace – specialities include *fegato grasso d'anatra affumicato con confettura di fichi, tagliatelle al ragù bianco e porcini, germano reale in coccio con cipolle glassate* – and the inexpensive **Al Duca d'Aosta-Alle Tofane** (tel. 0436 2780; closed Oct–mid-Dec), serving local specialities in an Alpine shelter with a memorable view (try the *torta di polenta con formaggio condito, knödel di spinacci, stinco di maiale, capriolo,* apple strudel and *kaiserschmorm*).

In the area of the **PARCO NATURALE FANES-SENNES-BRAIES** and

PARCO NATURALE VEDRETTE DI RIES, the moderately priced **Pichler**, at Rio di Pusteria (tel. 0472 849 458; closed Mon, Tue morning and Jul), is known for its creative interpretations of traditional Tyrolean specialities, as well as for its ambience and service, and regional and Italian wines. Try the *antipasto di pesce al vapore, gnocchi di formaggio di capra*, and *fegato d'agnello con mele croccanti.*

TRENTO

The **Osteria a Le Due Spade**, 11 Via Don Rizzi (tel. 0461 234 343; closed Sun, Mon morning and a few days in Aug), was established in 1545. Situated one block west of the cathedral, it offers creative interpretations of traditional recipes and regional, Italian and imported wines, at moderate prices. Specialities include *punte d'asparagi al vapore con foglie di senape fresche, gnocchetti di tarasacco e aglio selvatico, pappardelle rustiche al rosmarino con crema di lepre e vèzzena piccante, tagliata di Angus alla griglia con salsa alle erbe aromatiche, sfogliatina calda di mele in salsa di frutta* and *semifreddo al formaggio magro.*

There are several inexpensive places to eat in and around Trento. The **Trattoria Piedicastello**, Piazza Piedicastello 11 (tel. 0461 232 914; closed Sun and Aug), is a traditional trattoria, with outside seating in summer. Try the *speck della Val di Non, reginette al Tonco de fasoi*, grilled meat and vegetables, local cheeses and apple strudel. Regional wines only. **Villa Madruzzo** (with rooms), Ponte Alto 26 (tel. 0461 986 220, fax 986 361; closed Sun), is a fine hotel and restaurant in a tranquil 19th-century villa with park, situated in a panoramic position above the city. Here you'll find traditional recipes, freely interpreted – *tortino di funghi, zuppa d'orzo, salmerino con salsa di crescione con cestino di verdure, stufato di manzo con uvetta e pinoli, budino di pane allo zabajone* and appel strudel – and regional and Italian wines. At Pergine Valsugana, 12km (7½ miles)east, **Al Castello** (tel./fax 0461 531 158; closed some Mons and mid-Oct–May), is an excellent restaurant and small hotel in a 10th–century castle enjoying marvellous views over the surrounding countryside.

Special Events

TRENTO

Mostra dei Vini del Trentino (regional wine fair, Apr); **Festival Internazionale del Film della Montagna, dell'Esplorazione e dell'Avventura** (International Festival of Mountain, Exploration, and Adventure Films, Apr–May); **Feste Vigiliane**, with the **Palio dell'Oca** (popular feast and pageant, Jun); **Mostra Micologica** (mushroom fair, Sep); **Autunno Trentino** (classical music, Sep–Oct).

Museums and Monuments

BOLZANO
Museo Provinciale di Scienze Naturali.
San Giovanni in Villa: by request (tel. 0471 978 145).
Museo Civico: Tue–Sat 9.00–12.00, 14.30–17.30, Sun 10.00–13.00.
Museion–Museum für Moderne Kunst: Tue–Sun 10.00–12.00, 15.00–19.00; closed Mon and hols.
Parish Church: mid-Mar to late Oct 10.30–12.00, 14.30–16.00; closed Sat, Sun and hols.
Castel Ròncolo (Schloss Runkelstein): by request, Mar–Nov 10.00–16.00; closed Sun and Mon.

BRESSANONE
Museo Diocesano: 15 Mar–31 Oct, Mon–Sat 10.00–17.00; closed the rest of the year; the *presepi* are on view also 15 Dec–10 Feb, daily 14.00–17.00 except 24 and 25 Dec.
Abbazia di Novacella (Neustift), 3km (1¾ miles) north: guided tours Mon–Sat, May–Oct 9.30, 10.00, 10.30, 11.00 ,14.00, 14.30, 15.00, 15.30, 16.00, 16.30; Nov–Apr 10.00, 11.00, 14.00, 15.00, 16.00; closed Sat afternoon and Sun; for reservations tel. 0472 36189.
Castello di Velturno (Schloss Ziernberg): guided tours Tue–Sun, March–Nov 10.00, 11.00, 14.30, 15.30.

TRENTO
Duomo, Archaeological area: Tue–Sat 10.00–12.00, 14.30–18.00.
Museo Diocesano Tridentino: Mon–Sat 9.30–12.30, 14.30–18.00.
Palazzo Geremia: Mon–Thu 9.00–12.00, 15.00–19.00, Fri 9.00–13.00.
Palazzo Pedrotti: Sat 10.00–12.00, 15.00–17.00.
Museo del Castello del Buonconsiglio: Tue–Sun, Oct–Mar 9.00–12.00, 14.00–17.00; Apr–Sep 9.00–12.00, 14.00–17.30.
Museo Civico del Risorgimento e della Lotta per la Libertà: as Museo del Castello.
Palazzo delle Albere: Tue–Sat 9.00–12.00, 14.30–18.00.
Museo d'Arte Moderna e Contemporanea di Trento e Rovereto: Tue–Sun, 16 Sep–15 Jun 9.00–12.30, 14.30–18.15; 16 Jun–15 Sep 10.00–12.30, 14.30–19.00.
Museo Storico delle Truppe Alpine: Tue–Sun, Apr–Sep 9.30–12.00, 14.00–17.30,; Oct–Mar 9.00–12.00, 14.00–16.30.
Giardino Botanico Alpino: Jun and Sep 9.00–12.00 and 14.30–17.00; Jul–Aug 9.00–12.00, 14.30–18.00.
Museo Aeronautico Gianni Caproni: Tue–Sun 9.00–13.00, 14.00–18.00.

GLOSSARY

AEDICULE, a small edifice or room.

AENEOLITHIC, a transitional period between the Neolithic and Bronze ages.

AMBO (pl. *ambones*), pulpit in a Christian basilica; two pulpits on opposite sides of a church from which the gospel and epistle were read.

AMBULATORY, a sheltered walkway (as in a church or cloister).

ANCONA, a painted altarpiece.

ARCH, a typically curved structural member spanning an opening and serving as a support for the wall above. Among the forms of arch common in Northeastern Italy are the round, the pointed (also called lancet or ogival), the trefoil (three-part) and the quatrefoil (four-part).

ATLAS (pl. *atlantes*), a male figure used as a supporting column.

BAROQUE STYLE, a style of artistic expression prevalent especially in the 17th century, calculated to over-whelm the emotions of the spectator through the use of dramatic form, colour and movement.

BASILICA, originally a Roman building used for public administration; in Christian architecture, an aisled church with an apse and no transepts.

BAS-RELIEF, a sculptural relief in which the projection from the surrounding surface is slight.

BIEDERMEIERSTIL, a clear, simple style of furniture and decoration that developed in Germany in the first half of the 19th century.

BIOTOPE, an area of uniform environment, flora and fauna.

BRONZE AGE, the period of human culture characterised by use of bronze tools; in Northeastern Italy, c 1700-800BC.

BUCRANIC, from *bucrania*, a common form of metope decoration – heads of oxen garlanded with flowers.

CAMPANILE, a bell-tower, often detached from the building to which it belongs.

CANTORIA, a choir loft, often richly decorated.

CAPITAL, the top of a column.

CAVEA, the part of a theatre or amphitheatre occupied by the rows of seats.

CHALICE, a drinking vessel with a foot and stem, such as the eucharistic cup.

CHIAROSCURO, distribution of light and shade, apart from colour in a painting; also, a painting using light and shade as the primary means of defining form.

CIBORIUM, a casket or tabernacle containing the host.

CIRQUE, a deep, steep-walled basin shaped like half a bowl, formed by glacial erosion.

CLASSICAL STYLE, the style embodied in the literature, art or architecture of ancient Greece and Rome.

CORINTHIAN, belonging to or resembling the Corinthian order of Greek architecture, distinguished especially by elaborate, bell-shaped capitals adorned with acanthuses.

CORNICE, a molded and projecting horizontal member in architecture.

CROSIER, a staff carried by bishops

and abbots as a symbol of office.
CROSS, in Christian religious art, an
emblem recalling the Crucifixion
and invoking the blessing of Christ;
common forms include the Greek
cross, in which the four linear
members are equal in length, and
the Latin cross, in which one of the
members is longer than the others.
DOLINA, a steep-walled oval or
circular depression caused by water
erosion.
DOLOMITE, a mineral (calcium
magnesium carbonate) found in
crystals and in extensive beds as a
compact limestone.
DORIC, belonging to or resembling
the Doric order of Greek architecture, distinguished especially by
simple, cushion-shaped capitals.
EDELWEISS, *Leontopodium
alpinum*, a small perennial
composite herb that grows high in
the Alps and has a woolly white
flower.
EXEDRA, a semicircular recess in
architecture.
FRESCO, a mural painting executed
on moist plaster with pigments
suspended in a water medium.
FRIEZE, a horizontal member in
architecture, often sculpted or ornamented.
GENTIAN, a family of herbs
(*Gentianaceae*) having opposite
smooth leaves and usually blue
flowers.
GNEISS, a laminated or foliated
metamorphic rock corresponding in
composition to granite.
GOTHIC STYLE, a style of artistic
expression developed in Europe
from the 12th century to the 16th
century, marked in architecture
especially by the converging of
weights and strains at isolated

points and by an emphasis on verticality, and in painting and sculpture
by graceful, elongated forms.
HELLENISTIC, the period of Greek
history, culture and art falling after
the death of Alexander the Great
(323 BC) and before the Roman
conquest of Egypt (30 BC).
HEXASTYLE, having six columns.
ICE AGE, the Pleistocene glacial
epoch.
ICON, an image; especially, a
conventional religious image
painted on a small wooden panel
and venerated by Eastern Christians.
ICONOSTASIS, a screen or parti-
tion, usually adorned with icons,
that divides the public part of a
church from that reserved for the
clergy
IONIC, belonging to or resembling
the Ionic order of Greek architecture, distinguished especially by
capitals in the form of spiral volutes.
JUGENDSTIL, the German variation
of *art nouveau*, a style based on a
naturalistic conception of plants
rather than on formalised decoration
and current in Europe and America
around the turn of the 19th century.
JURASSIC, the period of geological
history ranging from 195 million to
140 million years ago.
KESTREL, a small European falcon
(*Falco tinnunculus*), bluish gray
above in the male and reddish
brown in the female, known for its
habit of hovering in the air against a
wind.
LOGGIA, a covered gallery or
balcony, usually preceding a larger
building.
LOMBARDESQUE STYLE, a
Renaissance architectural style
developed by the Venetian sculptor
and architect Pietro Lombardo and

his family and characterised by a strong sense of classicism.

LUNETTE, a semicircular space in a vault or ceiling, often decorated with a painting or relief.

MALGA, a pasture for cattle usually located above the tree line and equipped with a rudimentary dairy.

MESOZOIC, the era of geological history between the Palaeozoic and the Tertiary, c 270-65 million years ago.

METAMORPHIC ROCK, a rock whose constitution has been effected by pressure, heat, and water, giving rise to a more compact and more highly crystalline condition.

METOPE, a decorative panel on the frieze of a Doric temple.

MORAINE, an accumulation of earth and stones deposited by a glacier.

MOUFLON, a wild sheep (*Ovis musimon*) of the mountains of Sardinia and Corsica with large curling horns in the male.

MULLION, a slender vertical pier between lights of a window or door.

NEOCLASSICAL STYLE, the revival of the Classical style, especially in architecture, which swept Europe in the 18th and 19th centuries.

NEOLITHIC, the latest period of the Stone Age (in Northeastern Italy, c 5000-1700 BC), characterised by polished stone implements.

OROGRAPHIC, of or relating to mountains; the right orographic side of a valley is the side adjoining the right bank of the principal water course; the left orographic side, that adjoining the left bank.

PALAEOZOIC, the era of Geological history that extends from the beginning of the Cambrian to the close of the Permian, c 550-280 million years ago.

PANTOKRATOR, the Almighty.

PEDIMENT, the gable above the portico of a Classical building, or a similar form used as a decoration.

PENDENTIVE, one of the sections of vaulting that spring from the corners of a structure having a rectangular ground plan.

PIANO NOBILE, the most elaborate floor of a secular building, usually the first above street level.

PIETÀ, a representation of the Virgin Mary mourning over the dead body of Christ.

PLATEA, the area of a theatre facing the stage and holding the spectators.

PLEISTOCENE, the earlier part of the Quarternary period (c 1.8 million years ago) or the corresponding system of rocks.

PLIOCENE, the latest epoch of the Tertiary (c 3 million years ago) or the corresponding system of rocks.

PLUTEUS, a low wall that encloses the space between column bases in a row of columns, or a decorative structure resembling such a wall.

POLYPTYCH, a painting or tablet in more than three sections.

PORPHYRY, a rock consisting of crystals embedded in a compact dark red or purple groundmass.

PREDELLA, a small painting attached below a large altarpiece.

RATIONALIST STYLE, an early Modern architectural style in which form follows function.

RELIQUARY, a container for religious relics.

RENAISSANCE, the transitional movement in Europe between medieval and modern times, beginning in the 14th century in Italy, lasting into the 16th century, and marked in the arts especially by a revival of Classical influence.

ROADSTEAD, an area less sheltered than a harbour where ships may ride at anchor.

ROE-DEER, a small European and Asiatic deer (*Capreolus capreolus*) that has large, flat antlers forked at the summit, and is reddish brown with white spots in summer and grayish in winter.

ROMANESQUE STYLE, a style of architecture developed in western Europe between the 10th and 12th centuries and distinguished in Northeastern Italy especially by the use of the round arch and vault.

RUSTICATE, to bevel or blunt the edges of stone blocks to make the joints conspicuous.

SCHIST, a metamorphic crystalline rock having a closely foliated structure.

SHIP'S-KEEL ROOF, a roof shaped like the hull of a ship and culminating in a longitudinal timber like that of a keel.

SPLAY, a slope or bevel especially of the sides of a door or window.

SQUINCH, a support (such as an arch) carried across a corner of a room.

TABERNACLE, a receptacle for the consecrated elements of the eurcharist; also, a small shelter for a religious image.

TERTIARY, the era of geological history ranging from 65 million to 1.8 million years ago.

TRABEATION, a design of horizontal lines or lintels in architecture.

TRACERY, architectural ornamental work with branching lines, especially decorative openwork in the head of a Gothic window.

TRANSENNA, an open grille or screen, usually of marble, in an early Christian church separating nave and chancel.

TRANSEPT, the part of a cruciform church that crosses at right angles to the nave and the apse or choir.

TRIASSIC, the earliest period of the Mesozoic era or the corresponding system of rocks.

TRIBUNE, a dais or platform from which an assembly is addressed.

TRIPTYCH, a painting in three sections.

TYMPANUM, the face of a pediment within the frame made by the upper and lower cornices; also, the space within an arch and above a lintel or subordinate arch.

VAULT, an arched structure of masonry usually forming a ceiling or roof. Forms common in Northeastern Italy are the barrel vault, built along a single axis, and the cross vault, built along two perpendicular axes.

INDEX